2013 Vol. 69, No. 1

The Aftermath of Genocide: Psychological Perspectives

Issue Editors: Johanna Ray Vollhardt and Michal Bilewicz

Journal of Social Issues, Vol. 69, No. 1, 2013, pp. 1–15

After the Genocide: Psychological Perspectives on Victim, Bystander, and Perpetrator Groups

Johanna Ray Vollhardt*
Clark University

Michal Bilewicz
University of Warsaw

Interest in the aftermath of genocide and mass violence has increased in the last few years, and some researchers in various subdisciplines of psychology have begun to address this urgent social issue. Genocide and mass violence continue to influence intergroup relations, conflicts, and policy attitudes. Nevertheless, these topics are still understudied. We introduce this issue by providing a brief overview of the scarce psychological research on the aftermath of genocide among members of former victim, perpetrator, and bystander groups. Although this distinction is too simplistic to explain individual behavior during genocide and its aftermath, we hold on to it as a framework for organizing existing scholarship, and because of the ongoing relevance of these social representations in discourse on this topic. The introduction concludes with an overview of the issue and its organization, including a brief summary of each article.

More than 60 years ago, the United Nations defined genocide as a crime with the intention to destroy, in whole or in part, a national, ethnic, racial, or religious group. Since then, social scientists and historians have contributed significantly to our understanding of genocide: by explaining its roots, describing its dynamics, and discussing its consequences (Fein, 2002; Newman & Erber, 2002; Staub, 1989). The UN Convention on the Prevention and Punishment of the Crime of Genocide created important tools for punishing perpetrators of genocidal crimes; however, it failed to prevent genocide in the decades thereafter. This is why researchers studying genocide are confronted not only with historical cases such

---

*Correspondence concerning this article should be addressed to Johanna Ray Vollhardt, Department of Psychology, Clark University, 950 Main Street, Worcester, MA 01610 [e-mail: JVollhardt@clarku.edu].

1

as the Armenian genocide (1915–1917) and the Holocaust during World War II, but also with more recent events such as genocides in Cambodia in the 1970s, Bosnia in 1992–1995, Rwanda in 1994, Darfur, and others.

These recent cases are not the only reason why genocide affects present-day politics and intergroup relations. Historical genocide continues to deeply impact relations between nations and between ethnic groups. For example, the Armenian Genocide Resolution, recently passed by the U.S. House Committee on Foreign Affairs, has led to tensions in American–Turkish relations (McKinnon & Champion, 2010); and the Katyn Forrest massacre remains the greatest obstacle in Polish–Russian relations, for example, shaping Polish reactions to the recent air disaster in Smolensk (Hunter, 2010). These are only two of many cases in which collective memories of genocide and cultural trauma in general (Alexander, Eyerman, Giesen, Sztompka, & Smelser, 2004) shape collective identities and political responses of ethnic groups and nations, such as in Israel (Zertal, 2005), Germany (Fulbrook, 1999), or Armenia (Miller, 1999). National identities are built around symbolic commemorations of the past and the narratives of victims as well as of perpetrators. Motivated denial of these memories sometimes serves to restore moral self-image among national groups that were once involved in a genocide as bystanders or perpetrators. Accordingly, such denial was used as a strategy to build national identities in Poland (Steinlauf, 1997), Ukraine (Bartov, 2007), Rwanda (Lemarchand, 2009), and several other countries. At the same time, postgenocidal guilt and forgiveness are equally important for understanding current relations between Germans, Poles, and Jews in Europe; Turks, Armenians, and Azeris in the Caucasus region; Tutsis and Hutus in East Africa; as well as many other groups around the world (Branscombe & Doosje, 2004). In sum, the impact of historical genocide and mass violence on current social and political issues cannot be underestimated, and it is heavily influenced by psychological reactions among members of former victim, bystander, and perpetrator groups. The aim of this issue is to highlight the role that psychology has to play in explaining intergroup relations, policies, and other social issues shaped by genocidal pasts.

Psychological Research on Genocide

Genocide as a significant social issue has been tackled by some psychologists. Books such as "The roots of evil: The origins of genocide and other group violence" by Ervin Staub (1989), "The Nazi doctors: Medical killing and the psychology of genocide" by Robert J. Lifton (1986), "Man's search for meaning" by Viktor Frankl (1984), and "The altruistic personality" by Samuel and Pearl Oliner (1988) became key readings in the field of genocide studies, inspiring researchers from several disciplines. The history of genocides, and particularly of the Holocaust, has also stimulated basic social psychological scholarship. In addition to research on obedience (Milgram, 1974), the atrocities committed during World War II have also influenced research on intergroup discrimination (Tajfel & Turner, 1979), dehumanization (Bandura, 1999; Kelman, 1973), delegitimization (Bar-Tal, 1990), moral exclusion (Opotow, 1990), and role-based aggression (Zimbardo, 2007). In several social psychology textbooks, the Holocaust is presented as a result of basic psychological processes of stereotyping, prejudice, conformity, and social identity (e.g., Aronson, Wilson, & Akert, 2006; Hogg & Vaughan, 2004; Smith & Mackie, 2007). Nevertheless, within the field of psychology, genocide in and of itself remains a rather marginal and understudied issue. This is due, at least in part, to the methodological and practical challenges of studying this topic, which does not lend itself easily to experimental research or even to survey research, and which requires integrating historical sources and other materials and methods that are less commonly used in current (mainstream) psychological research.

The Perpetrator—Victim—Bystander Triangle in Research on Genocide

Most scholars distinguish three major social roles in genocide: perpetrators, bystanders, and victims (Hilberg, 1993). However important these social categories are, they do not provide sufficient information about individual behavior and the multiplicity of roles in times of genocide. These roles are indeed complex and often not as clear-cut as the literature suggests. For example, some members of perpetrator groups perceive themselves as victims (Čehajić & Brown, 2010), while many victims retaliated against perpetrators in armed struggle (Robins & Jones, 2009), and many bystanders were also victims (Steinlauf, 1997) while others were violent co-perpetrators (Gross, 2001). In addition, some individuals even occupied all three roles during the same genocide (Bauman, 2000; Perechodnik, 1996). Acknowledging these contradictions and complexities, we continue to use the bystander—perpetrator—victim triangle because most psychological research on genocide and its aftermath addresses these distinct social roles (e.g., Shnabel, Nadler, Ullrich, Dovidio, & Carmi, 2009; Staub, 1989; Wohl & Branscombe, 2005), and this framework can be used to organize existing research on this topic. However, it is important to view these distinctions merely as social representations of positions in genocide, and not as explanations for individual behavior of those to whom these roles are ascribed. Several contributions in this issue discuss the fluidity of these roles that needs to be kept in mind when using these seemingly entitative (see Lickel et al., 2000) terms.

Psychological Research on the Aftermath of Genocide

While some seminal work by psychologists and other social scientists has addressed how genocide evolves (see Newman & Erber, 2002), in recent years there has been an increasing interest in the aftermath of genocide and mass violence. This has been stimulated by attempts to redress historical injustices and human rights abuses, for example, through international war crime tribunals or truth and reconciliation commissions (Barkan, 2000). Psychology can contribute a lot to these discussions, which have practical implications for reconciliation and the prevention of violence. Nevertheless, research in this area is still scarce.

Psychological research on the aftermath of genocide can also be organized along the social roles of previous victim, perpetrator, and bystander groups. This research is located in various subdisciplines of psychology such as social, clinical, and community psychology. In the following, we provide a brief overview of topics that have been studied in this underresearched field, and point to unexplored areas that are addressed in this issue.

Psychological Research among Perpetrator Groups in the Aftermath of Genocide

Recent research on psychological consequences of genocide among perpetrator groups has focused on positive and negative appraisals of historical victim groups. Descendants of perpetrator groups tend to exonerate their ancestors' misdeeds. When explaining historical crimes, descendants of perpetrator groups often use biased attributions. They perceive historical crimes as caused by situational factors and as unstable, and the perpetrator groups as highly variable (Doosje & Branscombe, 2003). This bias in explaining historical genocide fits to the pattern of ethnocentric explanations of intergroup behavior, known as the ultimate attribution error (Pettigrew, 1979). Another exonerating strategy among descendants of perpetrator groups is to blame historical victims for their fate (Lerner, 1980). In a similar vein, Imhoff and Banse (2009) showed that reminders of ongoing Jewish suffering after the Holocaust elicit implicit anti-Semitic resentment among contemporary Germans. Thus, prejudice may serve as a strategy to distance oneself from ingroup responsibility for historical genocides. Other distancing strategies are even more direct. For example, Germans who read about atrocities committed by their nation during the Holocaust perceived this period as more remote— and this temporal distancing reduced feelings of collective guilt (Peetz, Gunn, & Wilson, 2010).

Descendents of perpetrator groups, however, do not always seek to exonerate the crimes committed by their group during genocide. On the individual level, children and grandchildren of Nazi perpetrators have participated in dialogue groups with descendents of Holocaust survivors (Bar-On & Kassem, 2004), and on the institutional level several German institutions oppose historical denial through educational efforts and exhibitions (Opotow, 2011). Historical gestures by politicians such as the German Chancellor Willy Brandt kneeling in front of the Warsaw Ghetto Memorial in 1970, Polish President Aleksander Kwaśniewski apologizing on behalf of the Polish people in 2001 for the Jedwabne massacre, or British prime minister Tony Blair's statement in 1997 about the Irish Potato Famine are some visible examples of public apologies and expressions of guilt for historical harm doing. Although not all apologies are perceived as sincere (Blatz & Philpot, 2010), they often become milestones in reconciliation after genocide. They are also an important strategy to restore the group's positive self-image as moral (Shnabel et al., 2009)—an image that is severely threatened by a genocidal past.

Positive appraisals of historical victim groups often result from aversive emotions felt by members of the perpetrator group (however, see Imhoff & Banse, 2009, for backlash effects). Emotions such as collective guilt, shame, remorse, or regret were found in several studies in response to reminders of crimes committed by ingroup members—sometimes even historically very distant ingroup members (e.g., Brown & Čehajić, 2008; Doosje, Branscombe, Spears & Manstead, 1998). Both negative and positive appraisals of victim groups are caused by essentialist ingroup perceptions. Those who believe that they share the same essence with historically distant perpetrators of genocide should feel obliged to compensate for injustice; however, the same essentialist perception also leads to denial of ingroup responsibility. This paradoxical impact of essentialism on collective guilt sheds some light on the psychological limitations of post-genocidal reconciliation (Zagefka, Pehrson, Mole, & Chan, 2010).

After years of research on perpetrator groups' emotional response to the past (see Wohl, Branscombe, & Klar, 2006) it is still unclear how common moral reactions to historical atrocities are, and it is still difficult to predict societal reactions to information about historical misdeeds of one's ancestors. The focus on antecedents and consequences of collective guilt constrained researchers' interest in the content of representations of past atrocities. What is still missing in the literature is a detailed analysis of how specific depictions of past crimes among perpetrator groups are linked to emotions and behavioral intentions toward historical victim groups.

Psychological Research among Victim Groups in the Aftermath of Genocide

Research among victim groups in the aftermath of genocide includes studies with immediate survivors, with descendants of survivors (second or third generation), and with members of the victim group who are at least one generation removed from the events.

Immediate survivors have been studied primarily in clinical psychology. Most of this research has focused on the consequences of trauma. This includes negative outcomes such as posttraumatic stress disorder and revenge (e.g., Field & Chhim, 2008; for a meta-analysis of studies among Holocaust survivors see Barel, Van IJzendoorn, Sagi-Schwartz, & Bakermans-Kranenburg, 2010), but also (though less frequently) positive phenomena such as resilience, meaning-making, coping, and posttraumatic growth, which includes altruism (Gasparre, Bosco, & Bellelli, 2010; Suedfeld, 2000; Vollhardt, 2009). While a lot of this research has been conducted among Holocaust survivors in Israel and in the United States, some scarce research also exists on survivors of the Armenian genocide (Kalayjian & Shahinian, 1998; Kalayjian, Shahinian, Gergerian, & Saraydarian, 1996), the Cambodian genocide (Field & Chhim, 2008), and the Guatamalan genocide (Gasparre et al., 2010). As for more recent genocides, there are a number of studies on survivors of the Rwandan genocide (e.g., Kanyangara, Rimé, Philippot, & Yzerbyt, 2007), and some research among Bosnian survivors (Witmer & Culver, 2001). Notably, a lot of the existing research is published in psychiatric journals and takes a rather medical than social-constructivist approach to exploring these phenomena.

Clinical research on the aftermath of genocide also includes work on transgenerational trauma and the question whether trauma symptoms are passed down to descendants of survivors. While qualitative and psychoanalytic research has found some evidence to support this idea (e.g., Gruenberg & Rosental, 2007), meta-analyses of quantitative studies among the second and third generations conclude that there is not sufficient evidence of widespread transmission of trauma symptoms (Sagi-Schwartz, van Ijzendoorn, & Bakermans-Kranenburg, 2008; van Ijzendoorn, Bakermans-Kranenburg, & Sagi-Schwartz, 2003).

The scarce social psychological research on the aftermath of genocide and mass violence among victim groups has focused on forgiveness and reconciliation (e.g., Shnabel et al., 2009; Staub, Pearlman, Hagengimana, & Gubin, 2005) as well as on attributions and construals of the events (Doosje & Branscombe, 2003; Wohl & Branscombe, 2005). For example, some research has examined how a more inclusive categorization of the Holocaust (i.e., as a crime against humanity) reduces the level of guilt that is assigned to the perpetrator group and increases willingness for forgiveness among members of the victim group (Wohl & Branscombe, 2005). Other research has focused on emotional needs among members of the victim group, showing that fulfilling the need for empowerment may increase the willingness for reconciliation among members of victim groups (Shnabel et al., 2009). In addition, several studies illustrate how collective memories and reminders of ingroup victimization through genocide can strengthen ingroup-serving behaviors (Wohl, Branscombe, & Reysen, 2010) and affect current conflicts by legitimizing what is perceived as defensive violence (Bar-Tal & Antebi, 1992; Wohl & Branscombe, 2008). In a way, these phenomena can be viewed as the transmission of trauma and societal trauma symptoms on the collective level (see also Alexander et al., 2004; Volkan, 2001).

Some research has examined interventions that may gradually bring about reconciliation with members of the perpetrator group. These interventions focus on social modeling and understanding of the influences that contribute to mass violence (Paluck, 2009; Staub et al., 2005) and, above all, on contact and dialogue (Albeck, Adwan, & Bar-On, 2002; Maoz & Bar-On, 2002). However, these studies also show that these encounters are faced with many challenges, and that backlash is common (e.g., Bar-On & Kassem, 2004; Bilewicz, 2007).

In sum, there is only scarce social psychological research among descendants of victim groups in the aftermath of genocide, and most of the existing research in social and in clinical psychology has focused on trauma and destructive consequences. Therefore, more research is needed on positive phenomena after genocide and mass violence, such as altruism and solidarity with other victim groups that may be facilitated through inclusive perceptions of similarity and shared fate (Vollhardt, 2009; see also Suedfeld, 2000).

Psychological Research among Bystander Groups in the Aftermath of Genocide

Even less research addresses the problem of bystander groups in genocide, their construals of the past, and emotions in response to the events. It is well known that during genocide, bystanders' behaviors allow and even encourage perpetrators to commit atrocities, and that perpetrators' actions significantly affect bystanders' attitudes toward victims (Monroe, 2008; Staub, 1989). Bystanders include not only those who are physically present during genocide, but also distant spectators who did not intervene early enough and thereby allowed genocidal acts to occur (Staub, 2002) – such as Americans during the Holocaust or the international community during the genocide in Darfur. The responsibility of bystanders of genocide, broadly discussed in social sciences (Vetlesen, 2000), has not been extensively studied by social psychologists.

One of the rare studies focusing on bystander descendents who live where the atrocities occurred found that they expressed great interest in the history of genocide in their hometown (Wójcik, Bilewicz, & Lewicka, 2010). Collective memory of Polish people living in the area of the former Warsaw ghetto focused mainly on the Jewish Holocaust, although the Jewish population and their material heritage had disappeared from the city landscape. The extent to which bystanders' descendents experience collective guilt for their ancestors' passivity depends on the extent to which they are able to take the perspective of historical victims and perpetrators—but this does not affect people who strongly identify with their in-group (Zebel, Doosje, & Spears, 2004). Thus, reconciliation between descendants of bystanders and victims of genocide is difficult. Focusing on the past makes the historical bystander role salient (Bilewicz, 2007) and likely threatens the bystander group's moral image (Shnabel et al., 2009).

Overview of this Issue

This issue aims to fill some of the gaps in this scarce area of research and to bring together perspectives from various subdisciplines in psychology (primarily social and clinical) to better understand the consequences of genocide for current communities and for intergroup relations in different parts of the world. The articles cover a wide range of methods, theoretical approaches, as well as geographical and sociopolitical contexts. Drawing on the established historical distinction of social roles during genocide (Hilberg, 1993), this issue is divided into sections on (1) psychological processes among perpetrator groups and (2) psychological processes among victim groups in the aftermath of genocide. The last section deals with (3) interventions and reconciliation between groups that have experienced genocide—processes that include victim, bystander, and perpetrator perspectives.

Destructive and Constructive Psychological Processes among Perpetrator Groups

Different forms of moral disengagement and denial of responsibility are dominant reactions to the ingroup's involvement in inhumane actions (Bandura, 1999). In the first section of this issue, two papers explore such destructive processes. Rezarta Bilali (2013) presents social psychological strategies used by Turks to defend their social identity in the aftermath of the Armenian genocide. Bilali (2013) also finds that the level of perceived ingroup responsibility and support for reparations is low. This corroborates analyses presented by Leach, Zeinnedine, and Čehajić-Clancy (2013). In their review of research on collective emotions after genocide and mass violence in the context of colonialism in Africa, Asia, Australia, and the Americas, they find that self-critical reactions to ingroup atrocities are scarce. Feelings of responsibility do not seem to be a dominant reaction among perpetrator groups.

Two other contributions give insight into conditions under which perpetrator groups might come to terms with their burden of historical responsibility, and engage in more constructive responses that contribute to redress and positive intergroup relations. In the context of pogroms committed by Poles during WWII, Kofta and Sławuta (2013) show that focusing on cultural similarities between victims and perpetrators might elicit collective guilt among groups accused of historical crimes. Imhoff, Wohl, and Erb (2013) provide evidence for another guilt-inducing process. In the context of two genocides committed by Germans in the past (of Herero in Namibia and Jews during the Holocaust), they show that awareness of the victims' continuous suffering elicits moral emotions among members of the perpetrator group. These emotions are more pronounced and lead to greater willingness for reparations when the perpetrators' actions are perceived as intentional.

Processes among Victim Groups: Clinical and Social Psychological Perspectives

While the section on processes among perpetrator groups addresses primarily the social psychological perspective, the second section in this special issue, on victim groups, also includes two contributions from a clinical perspective. These articles deal with the more immediate aftermath of genocide, specifically with trauma symptoms and healing among survivors. Kaplan (2013) presents a qualitative analysis of interviews with orphans after the Rwandan genocide. From a psychodynamic perspective, she explores their affect regulation as well as factors in their environment that shape their responses and recovery process. Pearlman (2013) argues that in most postgenocide contexts, healing must occur not only on the individual level, but primarily through community-based interventions. She reviews models of community healing after genocide in Bosnia, Rwanda, and other contexts of mass violence and focuses on interventions that provide respect, information, connection, and hope (RICH), all of which are expected to contribute to healing from the massive trauma of genocide.

The two articles that deal with consequences of historical genocide among the victim groups address this issue from a social psychological perspective. Two contributions examine how collective memories of the Holocaust among Israeli and American Jews affect present-day intergroup relations and policy attitudes. Rather than merely focusing on the destructive outcomes of historical trauma, the authors also demonstrate constructive responses that promote peaceful intergroup relations. Klar, Schori-Eyal, and Klar (2013) discuss four lessons that can be drawn from the Holocaust. They show that two of these ("never be a passive victim" and "never forsake your brothers") have fed into the Israel–Palestinian conflict, while two alternative lessons ("never be a passive bystander" and "never be a perpetrator") have motivated humanitarian aid and peace activism in Israel. In an experimental study among Jewish Americans, Vollhardt (2013) shows that inclusive construals of the Holocaust give rise to prosocial attitudes and behavior toward other victims of genocide if both the ingroup's and outgroup's distinct victimization are acknowledged.

Interventions and Policy Implications

The third section of this issue addresses implications for interventions and policies in the aftermath of genocide and in the service of genocide prevention. Staub (2013) describes how awareness of cultural and psychological precursors of genocide can serve as a starting point for reconciliation between past perpetrators, victims, and bystanders. He reviews a reconciliation radio program in Rwanda, Burundi, and DRC, as well as other interventions to show how experiential understanding facilitates the emergence of peaceful societies after genocide. He argues that this process needs to be strengthened by institutions and positive socialization. Staub's call for active bystandership resonates with a similar call for civil courage expressed by other psychologists writing about genocide prevention (Zimbardo, 2007), who depict heroic helpers as role models for future generations. Bilewicz and Jaworska (2013) show that exposure to heroic helpers can also change relations between grandchildren of bystanders and of victims of genocide. Extending the needs-based model of reconciliation (Shnabel et al., 2009) to bystander groups,

Bilewicz and Jaworska (2013) discuss how heroic helpers' narratives can restore the group's moral image in encounters between Polish and Israeli students, and how perceived acceptance improves attitudes between these groups.

Overall, these contributions show that the processes of reconciliation between groups affected by historical genocide and prevention of future genocides must be viewed as interconnected. Without reconciliation, victimized groups may choose violent retaliatory actions instead of peaceful solutions to current conflicts, and perpetrator groups may further derogate victim groups and prevent redress. This explains, at least in part, attitudes in recent conflicts in Nagorno Karabakh, DRC, or the Middle East. Thus, understanding psychological processes in the aftermath of genocide can also help us resolve and prevent current political violence and add to our knowledge about these issues (see previous JSI issues edited by Alexander & Levin, 1998; de Rivera & Paez, 2007; Finchilescu & Tredoux, 2010; Muldoon, 2004).

Summary and Conclusion

In sum, this issue brings together novel research and theorizing on the psychological processes that influence individual and collective healing, reconciliation, and intergroup relations in the aftermath of genocide and other forms of mass violence. The issue showcases the potential psychology has — in conjunction with and informed by other disciplines such as history, political science, sociology, and social work — to contribute to our understanding of these processes, and to shape interventions and policies in the aftermath of mass violence. The issue also shows the unique perspective that psychology can contribute to the interdisciplinary and increasingly popular field of collective memory studies (Olick, Vinitzky-Seroussi, & Levy, 2011).

This issue aims to integrate a broad range of perspectives on this area of study in terms of the subdisciplines, theoretical frameworks, and geographical and historical contexts involved. This multiplicity of perspectives is necessary in order to even begin to address the complexity of the subject matter. Accordingly, this issue includes social psychological and clinical perspectives and touches on community psychology and developmental issues. The authors draw on a variety of psychological theories and constructs that can be applied to the aftermath of genocide, such as attribution, intergroup emotions, social categorization, contact theory, and trauma theories, and build on existing findings while also contributing severely understudied perspectives such as on bystander groups or on constructive processes in the aftermath of genocide. The methods range from interviews and grounded theory to surveys, experiments, and intervention research. The contexts explored in this issue include the Holocaust, the Rwandan genocide, the Armenian genocide, the Herero genocide, and genocidal violence during colonization in the Americas, Asia, Australia, and Africa. Researchers located in Bosnia and Herzegovina, Canada, Germany, Israel, Poland, Sweden, and the United States present studies with samples from Israel, Germany, Poland, Rwanda, Turkey, and the United States and discuss findings from several other contexts.

Even so, this spectrum is still limited, in part due to accessibility of samples. Likewise, authors from Armenia, Cambodia, Rwanda, and other societies that grapple with the experience of genocide and mass violence are missing in this issue. Our hope is nevertheless to document the state of the art in research on the psychological aftermath of genocide and suggest new directions to demonstrate the potential psychology has to contribute to debates and policies around these issues, and to stimulate further debate and research in a variety of contexts.

References

Albeck, J. H., Adwan, S., & Bar-On, D. (2002). Dialogue groups: TRT's guidelines for working through intractable conflicts by personal storytelling in encounter groups. *Peace and Conflict: Journal of Peace Psychology, 8,* 301–322.

Alexander, J. C., Eyerman, R., Giesen, B., Smelser, N. J., & Sztompka, P. (2004). *Cultural trauma and collective identity.* Berkeley, CA: University of California Press.

Alexander, M., & Levin, S. (Eds.). (1998). Understanding and resolving national and international group conflict [Special issue]. *Journal of Social Issues, 54*(4).

Aronson, E., Wilson, T., & Akert, R. M. (2006). *Social psychology.* Harlow: Prentice Hall.

Bandura, A. (1999). Moral disengagement in the perpetration of inhumanities. *Personality and Social Psychology Review, 3,* 193–209.

Barel, E., Van IJzendoorn, M. H., Sagi-Schwartz, A., & Bakermans-Kranenburg, M. J. (2010). Surviving the Holocaust: A meta-analysis of the long-term sequelae of a genocide. *Psychological Bulletin, 136,* 677–698.

Barkan, E. (2000). *The guilt of nations: Restitution and negotiating historical injustices.* Baltimore, MD: John Hopkins University Press.

Bar-On, D., & Kassem, F. (2004). Storytelling as a way to work through intractable conflicts: The German–Jewish experience and its relevance to the Palestinian-Israeli context. *Journal of Social Issues, 60,* 289–306.

Bar-Tal, D. (1990). Causes and consequences of delegitimization: Models of conflict and ethnocentrism. *Journal of Social Issues, 46,* 65–81.

Bar-Tal, D., & Antebi, D. (1992). Siege mentality in Israel. *International Journal of Intercultural Relations, 16,* 251–275.

Bartov, O. (2007). *Erased: Vanishing traces of Jewish Galicia in present-day Ukraine.* Princeton, NJ: Princeton University Press.

Bauman, Z. (2000). *Modernity and the Holocaust.* Ithaca, NY: Cornell University Press.

Bilali, R. (2013). National narrative and social psychological influences in the Turkish denial of the Armenian Genocide. *Journal of Social Issues, 69,* 16–33.

Bilewicz, M. (2007). History as an obstacle: Impact of temporal-based social categorizations on Polish–Jewish intergroup contact. *Group Processes & Intergroup Relations, 10,* 551–563.

Bilewicz, M., & Jaworska, M. (2013). Reconciliation through the righteous: The narratives of heroic helpers as a fulfillment of emotional needs in Polish–Jewish intergroup contact. *Journal of Social Issues, 69,* 162–179.

Blatz, C. W., & Philpot, C. (2010). On the outcomes of intergroup apologies. *Social and Personality Psychology Compass, 4,* 995–1007.

Branscombe, N., & Doosje, B. (Eds.). (2004). *Collective guilt. International perspectives.* Cambridge: Cambridge University Press.

Brown, R., & Čehajić, S. (2008). Dealing with the past and facing the future: mediators of the effects of collective guilt and shame in Bosnia Herzegovina. *European Journal of Social Psychology, 38*, 669–684.

Čehajić, S., & Brown, R. (2010). Silencing the past: Effects of intergroup contact on acknowledgment of ingroup responsibility. *Social Psychological and Personality Science, 1*, 190–196.

de Rivera, J., & Paez, D. (Eds.). (2007). Emotional climate, human security, and culture of peace [Special issue]. *Journal of Social Issues, 63*(2).

Doosje, B., & Branscombe, N. R. (2003). Attributions for the negative historical actions of a group. *European Journal of Social Psychology, 33*, 235–248.

Doosje, B., Branscombe, N. R., Spears, R., & Manstead, A. S. R. (1998). Guilty by association: When one's group has a negative history. *Journal of Personality and Social Psychology, 75*, 872–886.

Fein, H. (2002). Genocide: A sociological perspective. In A. L. Hinton (Ed.), *Genocide: An anthropological reader* (pp. 74–90). Oxford: Blackwell.

Field, N. P., & Chhim, S. (2008). Desire for revenge and attitudes toward the Khmer Rouge tribunal among Cambodians. *Journal of Loss and Trauma, 13*, 352–372.

Finchilescu, G., & Tredoux, C. (Eds.). (2010). Intergroup relations in post Apartheid South Africa: Change, and obstacles to change. *Journal of Social Issues, 66*(2).

Frankl, V. (1984). *Man's search for meaning.* New York: Pocket/Simon and Shuster.

Fulbrook, M. (1999). *German national identity after the Holocaust.* Cambridge: Polity Press.

Gasparre, A., Bosco, S., & Bellelli, G. (2010). Cognitive and social consequences of participation in social rites: Collective coping, social support, and post-traumatic growth in the victims of Guatemala genocide. *Revista de Psicología Social, 25*, 35–46.

Gross, J. T. (2001). *Neighbors: The destruction of the Jewish community in Jedwabne, Poland.* Princeton, NJ: Princeton University Press.

Gruenberg, K., & Rosental, N. (2007). Contaminated generativity: Holocaust survivors and their children in Germany. *The American Journal of Psychoanalysis, 67*, 82–96.

Hilberg, R. (1993). *Perpetrators victims bystanders: Jewish catastrophe 1933–1945.* New York, NY: Harper Perennial.

Hogg, M., & Vaughan, G. (2004). *Social psychology.* Harlow: Prentice Hall.

Hunter, R. J. (2010). Katyn: Old issues threaten Polish–Russian economic and political relations. *European Journal of Social Sciences, 17*, 288–297.

Imhoff, R., & Banse, R. (2009). Ongoing victim suffering increases prejudice: The case of secondary antisemitism. *Psychological Science, 20*, 1443–1447.

Imhoff, R., Wohl, M. J. A., & Erb, H.-P. (2013). When the past is far from dead: How ongoing consequences of genocides committed by the ingroup impact collective guilt. *Journal of Social Issues, 69*, 74–91.

Kalayjian, A., & Shahinian, S. P. (1998). Recollections of aged Armenian survivors of the Ottoman Turkish Genocide: Resilience through endurance, coping, and life accomplishments. *Psychoanalytic Review, 85*, 489–516.

Kalayjian, A. S., Shahinian, S. P., Gergerian, E. L., & Saraydarian, L. (1996). Coping with Ottoman Turkish genocide: An exploration of the experience of Armenian survivors. *Journal of Traumatic Stress, 9*, 87–97.

Kanyangara, P., Rimé, B., Philippot, P., & Yzerbyt, V. (2007). Collective rituals, emotional climate, and intergroup perception: Participation in "Gacaca" tribunals and assimilation of the Rwandan genocide. *Journal of Social Issues, 63*, 387–403.

Kaplan, S. (2013). Child survivors of the 1994 Rwandan Genocide and trauma-related affects. *Journal of Social Issues, 69*, 92–110.

Kelman, H. (1973). Violence without moral restraint: reflections on the dehumanization. *Journal of Social Issues, 29*, 25–61.

Klar, Y., Shori-Eyal, N., & Klar, Y. (2013). The "Never Again" state of Israel: The emergence of the Holocaust as a core feature of Israeli identity and its four incongruent voices. *Journal of Social Issues, 69*, 125–143.

Kofta, M., & Sławuta, P. (2013). Thou shall not kill... your brother: Victim-perpetrator cultural closeness and moral disapproval of Polish atrocities against Jews after the Holocaust. *Journal of Social Issues, 69*, 54–73.

Leach, C. W., Bou Zeinnedine, F., & Čehajić-Clancy, S. (2013). Moral immemorial: The rarity of self-criticism for previous generation's genocide or mass violence. *Journal of Social Issues, 69*, 34–53.

Lemarchand, R. (2009). *The dynamics of violence in central Africa*. Philadelphia, PA: University of Pennsylvania Press.

Lerner, M. (1980). *The belief in a just world. A fundamental delusion*. New York, NY: Plenum Press.

Lickel, B., Hamilton, D., Wieczorkowska, G., Lewis, A., Sherman, S. J., & Uhles, A. N. (2000). Varieties of groups and the perception of group entitativity. *Journal of Personality and Social Psychology, 78*, 223–246.

Lifton, R. J. (1986). *The Nazi doctors: Medical killing and the psychology of genocide*. New York, NY: Basic Books.

Maoz, I., & Bar-On, D. (2002). From working through the Holocaust to current ethnic conflicts: Evaluating the TRT group workshop in Hamburg. *Group, 26*, 29–48

McKinnon, J. D., & Champion, M. (2010, March 4). Genocide vote riles Turkey. *Wall Street Journal*. Retrieved from http://online.wsj.com/article/SB10001424052748704187204575101981018521028.html

Miller, D. E. (1999). The role of historical memory in interpreting events in the Republic of Armenia. In R. G. Hovannisian (Ed.), *Remembrance and denial* (pp. 187–200). Detroit, MI: Wayne State University Press.

Milgram, S. (1974). *Obedience to authority*. New York, NY: Harper & Row Publishers.

Monroe, K. R. (2008). Cracking the code of genocide: the moral psychology of rescuers, bystanders and Nazis during the Holocaust. *Political Psychology, 29*, 699–673.

Muldoon, O. (Ed.). (2004). The cost of conflict: Children and the Northern Irish Troubles. *Journal of Social Issues, 60*(3).

Newman, L. S., & Erber, R. (2002). *Understanding genocide: The social psychology of the Holocaust*. New York, NY: Oxford University Press.

Olick, J., Vinitzky-Seroussi, V., & Levy, D. (Eds.). (2011). *The collective memory reader*. New York, NY: Oxford University Press.

Oliner, S. P., & Oliner, P. M. (1988). *The altruistic personality: Rescuers of Jews in Nazi Europe*. New York, NY: Free Press.

Opotow, S. (1990). Moral exclusion and injustice: an introduction. *Journal of Social Issues, 46*, 1–20.

Opotow, S. (2011). How this was possible: Interpreting the Holocaust. *Journal of Social Issues, 67*, 205–224.

Paluck, E. L. (2009). Reducing intergroup prejudice and conflict using the media: A field experiment in Rwanda. *Journal of Personality and Social Psychology, 96*, 574–587.

Pearlman, L. A. (2013). Restoring self in community: Collective approaches to psychological trauma after genocide. *Journal of Social Issues, 69*, 111–124.

Peetz, J., Gunn, G., & Wilson, A. E. (2010). Crimes of the past: Defensive temporal distancing in the face of past in-group wrongdoing. *Personality and Social Psychology Bulletin, 36*, 598–611.

Perechodnik, C. (1996). *Am I a murderer? Testament of a Jewish Ghetto policeman*. Boulder, CO: Westview Press.

Pettigrew, T. F. (1979). The ultimate attribution error: Extending Allport's cognitive analysis of prejudice. *Personality and Social Psychology Bulletin, 5*, 461–476.

Robins, N. A., & Jones, A. (Eds.). (2009). *Genocides by the oppressed: subaltern genocide in theory and practice*. Bloomington, IN: Indiana University Press.

Sagi-Schwartz, A., van Ijzendoorn, M. H., & Bakermans-Kranenburg, M. J. (2008). Does intergenerational transmission of trauma skip a generation? No meta-analytic evidence for tertiary traumatization with third generation of holocaust survivors. *Attachment & Human Development, 10*, 105–121

Shnabel, N., Nadler, A., Ullrich, J., Dovidio, J. F., & Carmi, D. (2009). Promoting reconciliation through the satisfaction of the emotional needs of victimized and perpetrating group members: The needs-based model of reconciliation. *Personality and Social Psychology Bulletin, 4*, 1021–1030

Smith, E. R., & Mackie, D. M. (2007). *Social psychology* (3rd ed.). Philadelphia, PA: Psychology Press.

Staub, E. (1989). *The roots of evil: The origins of genocide and other group violence.* New York, NY: Cambridge University Press.

Staub, E. (2002). The psychology of bystanders, perpetrators, and heroic helpers. In L. Newman & R. Erber (Eds.), *Understanding genocide: The social psychology of the Holocaust* (pp. 11–42). New York: Oxford University Press.

Staub, E., Pearlman, L. A., Gubin, A., & Hagengimana, A. (2005). Healing, forgiveness, and reconciliation in Rwanda: Intervention and experimental evaluation. *Journal of Social and Clinical Psychology, 24,* 297–334.

Staub, E. (2013). A world without genocide: Prevention, reconciliation, and the creation of peaceful societies. *Journal of Social Issues, 69,* 180–199.

Steinlauf, M. C. (1997). *Bondage to the dead.* Syracuse, NY: Syracuse University Press.

Suedfeld, P. (2000). Reverberations of the Holocaust fifty years later: Psychology's contributions to understanding persecution and genocide. *Canadian Psychology, 41,* 1–9.

Tajfel, H., & Turner, J. (1979). An integrative theory of intergroup conflict. In W. Austin & S. Worchel (Eds.), *The social psychology of intergroup relations.* Monterey, CA: Brooks-Cole.

van Ijzendoorn, M. H., Bakermans-Kranenburg, M. J., & Sagi-Schwartz, A. (2003). Are children of Holocaust survivors less well-adapted? A meta-analytic investigation of secondary traumatization. *Journal of Traumatic Stress, 16,* 459–469.

Vetlesen, A. J. (2000). Genocide: A case of the responsibility of the bystander. *Journal of Peace Research, 37,* 519–532.

Volkan, V. D. (2001). Transgenerational transmissions and chosen traumas: An aspect of large-group identity. *Group Analysis, 34,* 79–97.

Vollhardt, J. R. (2009). Altruism born of suffering and prosocial behavior following adverse life events: A review and conceptualization. *Social Justice Research, 22,* 53–97.

Vollhardt, J. R. (2013). "Crime against humanity" or "crime against Jews"? The importance of acknowledgment in construals of the Holocaust for intergroup relations. *Journal of Social Issues, 69,* 144–161.

Witmer, T., & Culver, S. M. (2001). Trauma and resilience among Bosnian refugee families: A critical review of the literature. *Journal of Social Work Research and Evaluation, 2,* 173–187.

Wohl, M. J. A., & Branscombe, N. R. (2005). Forgiveness and collective guilt assignment to historical perpetrator groups depend on level of social category inclusiveness. *Journal of Personality and Social Psychology, 88,* 288–303.

Wohl, M. J. A., & Branscombe, N. R. (2008). Remembering historical victimization: Collective guilt for current ingroup transgressions. *Journal of Personality and Social Psychology, 94,* 988–1006.

Wohl, M. J. A., Branscombe, N. R., & Klar, Y. (2006). Collective guilt: Justice-based emotional reactions when one's group has done wrong or been wronged. *European Review of Social Psychology, 17,* 1–37.

Wohl, M. J. A., Branscombe, N. R., & Reysen, S. (2010). Perceiving your group's future to be in jeopardy: Extinction threat induces collective angst and the desire to strengthen the ingroup. *Personality and Social Psychology Bulletin, 36,* 898–910.

Wojcik, A., Bilewicz, M., & Lewicka, M. (2010). Living on the ashes: Collective representations of Polish–Jewish history among people living in the former Warsaw Ghetto area. *Cities, 27,* 195–203.

Zagefka, H., Pehrson, S., Mole, R., & Chan, E. (2010). The effect of essentialism in settings of historic intergroup atrocities. *European Journal of Social Psychology, 40,* 718–732.

Zebel, S., Doosje, B., & Spears, R. (2004). It depends on your point of view: Implications of perspective-taking and national identification for Dutch collective guilt. In N. R. Branscombe & B. Doosje (Eds.), *Collective guilt: International perspectives.* New York, NY: Cambridge University Press.

Zertal, I. (2005). *Israel's Holocaust and the politics of nationhood.* Cambridge: Cambridge University Press.

Zimbardo, P. G. (2007). *The Lucifer Effect: Understanding how good people turn evil.* New York, NY: Random House.

JOHANNA RAY VOLLHARDT is currently Assistant Professor of Psychology at Clark University and affiliated with the Strassler Center for Holocaust and Genocide Studies. She received her Ph.D. in Social Psychology from the University of Massachusetts Amherst, with a concentration in the Psychology of Peace and Violence. For her dissertation work she has received the Best Dissertation Award of the International Society of Political Psychology and the Gert Sommer Award for Peace Psychology. Her research focuses on inclusive victim consciousness, prosocial behavior, and intergroup relations in the aftermath of collective violence.

MICHAL BILEWICZ (M.A. 2003, Ph.D. 2007, University of Warsaw) is an Assistant Professor at the Faculty of Psychology, University of Warsaw. He serves as the Director of the Center for Research on Prejudice at the University of Warsaw. He was Fulbright Junior Visiting Researcher at the New School for Social Research in New York and DAAD Post-Doctoral Researcher at Friedrich Schiller University of Jena in Germany. His key research interests are reconciliation processes, linguistic forms of prejudice, anti-Semitism, history-related moral emotions, and dehumanization.

Journal of Social Issues, Vol. 69, No. 1, 2013, pp. 16–33

National Narrative and Social Psychological Influences in Turks' Denial of the Mass Killings of Armenians as Genocide

Rezarta Bilali[*]

University of Massachusetts, Boston

This article sheds light on the nature of the Turkish denial of Armenian mass killings. A survey study investigates Turkish students' construals (i.e., attributions of responsibility and perceived severity of harm) of Turkish massacres of Armenians at the beginning of the 20th century. The results demonstrated a high correspondence between participants' individual construals and the Turkish official narrative of the events. Structural equation modeling indicated that in-group glorification, perceived in-group threat, and positive attitudes toward war predicted less acknowledgment of in-group responsibility, which in turn predicted less support for reparations of the harm inflicted on Armenians. The study highlights the influence of government-sponsored national self-images in the production and endorsement of legitimizing narratives of the in-group's violence. The findings call for research that examines the combined influence of psychological and societal mechanisms on people's beliefs about in-group actions.

Genocide is the most serious crime against humanity. Accordingly, allegations of genocide have significant legal and moral consequences for perpetrator groups,

---

[*]Correspondence concerning this article should be addressed to Rezarta Bilali, Department of Conflict Resolution, Human Security, and Global Governance, University of Massachusetts, 100 Morrissey Blvd, Wheatley Hall, 4th floor, Boston, MA 02125 [e-mail: Rezarta.Bilali@umb.edu].

This research was supported by a Harry Frank Guggenheim dissertation fellowship and grants from the International Peace Research Association Foundation and the Society for Psychological Study of Social Issues. The author thanks Linda Tropp, Nilanjana Dasgupta, David Matz and the issue editors for their comments in earlier drafts of this article.

which vehemently resist and oppose the charges. Probably, the best-known case of denial is the Turkish refutation that the mass killings of Armenians at the beginning of the 20th century amount to genocide.

The late 19th and early 20th century marked the disintegration of the Ottoman Empire and the establishment of Young Turks' regime, which sought to modernize and to "turkify" the Ottoman state into a modern Turkish nation (Hovannissian, 1997; Jorgensen, 2003). Ottoman Armenians were considered a minority group like other non-Muslim populations in the Ottoman Empire. During this period, the Ottoman and the Young Turk regimes targeted Ottoman Armenians in acts of mass violence culminating in the atrocities of 1915. Scholars of Armenian origin (e.g., Dadrian, 2003; Hovannisian, 1997), most international scholars (Bloxham, 2005; Melson, 1992; Nazer, 1968), and a few Turkish historians (e.g., Akçam, 2006) claim that about a million Armenians (estimates vary between 600,000 and 2,000,000, see Jorgensen, 2003) perished as a result of direct and unprovoked massacres by the Turkish military which intended to exterminate the Armenians of the Ottoman empire. Armenians and most international sources refer to the massacres in 1915 as the first genocide of the century, whereas Turks refer to the same events as inter-communal warfare (Lewy, 2005). Turkish governments since 1923 have firmly denied a genocide of Armenians by Turks (Jorgensen, 2003). The long-term effects of these events—both psychological and political—are highly visible today, a century after the massacres. Turkey and Armenia have never had diplomatic relations, and the border between the two countries is currently closed. The Turkish denial of the atrocities elicits rage, hatred, and resentment among Armenians (Kalayjian & Shahinian, 1998; for a review on psychological effects of genocide see Pearlman, 2013).

Acknowledgment of responsibility and reparative actions by perpetrator groups are essential elements of reconciliation in the aftermath of mass violence (Staub, 2006, 2013; Vollhardt, 2013). In contrast, legitimizing narratives of in-group's perpetuated violence serve to deny in-group responsibility (e.g., Sibley, Wilson, & Robertson, 2007) and reduce support for reparations for harm, thus undermining intergroup reconciliation. Understanding the processes that produce and maintain legitimizing narratives is imperative in order to find ways to address those narratives. Guided by this goal, the current study provides insights into Turks' construals of the mass killings of Armenians at the beginning of 20th century (see also Bilali, Tropp, & Dasgupta, 2012). The study examines the nature of denial embedded in the Turkish official narrative and the extent to which group members endorse this narrative. Then, the article investigates the influence of social psychological factors (in-group glorification, in-group threat, and attitudes toward violence in war) that perpetuate legitimizing narratives, as well as the role of these narratives in reducing support for reparations of harm.

The Role of Moral Disengagement in Legitimizing Narratives: Individual and Collective Processes

Bandura (1999, 2002) identified a variety of mechanisms by which people accept and legitimize violence and inhumane conduct done to others. These mechanisms, known as moral disengagement, include: (1) moral justification of the act, (2) denial, displacement, or diffusion of responsibility, (3) disregarding or minimizing the negative consequences of the violent acts, and (4) attribution of blame to the victim or circumstances. Moral disengagement strategies vary along at least two dimensions of construals of violence: attributions of responsibility for the harm inflicted (e.g., blaming the victim or the circumstances) and perceived severity of harm (e.g., minimization of the negative consequences of the harm done by the in-group). Originally developed to describe processes at the individual level, these mechanisms are also applicable to group members' judgments about their groups' conduct in war (Cohrs, Maes, Moschner, & Kielman, 2003), or reactions to in-groups' historical harm doing (Leidner, Castano, Zaiser, & Giner-Sorolla, 2010).

Moral disengagement mechanisms are a product of the interplay of psychological processes and social influences (Bandura, 1999). Psychologically, the in-group's misdeeds threaten group members' morality and self-worth. Striving to maintain a positive social identity (Tajfel & Turner, 1986), group members distort current and historical events in ways that portray the in-group in a favorable light (Baumeister & Hastings, 1997; Doosje & Branscombe, 2003). When confronted with reminders of in-group's misdeeds, to protect in-group's positive image and avoid feelings of guilt (Branscombe & Doosje, 2004), group members often legitimize the in-group's actions by either minimizing the consequences (Roccas, Klar, & Liviatan, 2006), denying in-group's responsibility (Iyer, Leach, & Crosby, 2003), or dehumanizing the victims (Castano & Giner-Sorolla, 2006; Kofta & Slawuta, 2013).

These mechanisms do not only operate at the individual level, but also at the collective level. Bandura (1999) noted that moral disengagement mechanisms are rooted in social structures and shaped by societal institutions. Political elites, institutions, and societal conditions determine what historical memories citizens are faced with (Olick & Robbins, 1998). Each nation's history highlights events that preserve a positive image of the nation while downplaying or "silencing" negative episodes in the nation's history (e.g., Liu et al., 2009; Liu & Hilton, 2005; Reicher & Hopkins, 2001). These historical memories produced by the elites are disseminated to all group members through the educational system, media, museums, hymns, rituals, as well as reinforced in the images that citizens are encountered with in their everyday lives, including public monuments, street names, coins and banknotes. Thus, the legitimization of past misdeeds must be understood not only as a psychologically driven process, but also as collectively driven.

Moral Disengagement in the Turkish Narrative of the Mass Killings of Armenians

Until recently, the discussion of the Armenian issue has been a taboo in Turkey (Akçam, 2006). Successive Turkish governments since the beginning of the Turkish Republic have produced an official narrative about the events of 1915 as well as a national consensus on the issue (Necef, 2003). National education in Turkey is highly centralized and viewed as a state affair (Kaplan, 2006); since 1924, the Ministry of Education approves all school textbooks in Turkey (Ulgen, 2010). Through these textbooks, the schools expose millions of Turkish youth to the same version of history. To assess how Turkish citizens learn about these events, I examined the narrative of Armenian massacres in Turkish primary education (8th grade) and high school (11th grade) history books, 'History of the Turkish Revolution and Ataturkism' (*T.C. Inkilâp Tarihi ve Atatürkçülük*).

Each history book devotes only one to three pages to the events of 1915. These sections emphasize the expulsion of the Armenians from their lands (i.e., the law of deportation), while denying the atrocities committed against them. According to these textbooks, Armenians, encouraged by external governments (particularly Britain and Russia), rebelled against the Ottoman Empire; they fought on the side of the enemy (i.e., Russia), and attacked the Muslim population in Anatolia. In fact, the textbooks state that it was Armenians who carried out massacres against the Turkish people in Anatolia, which in turn led the Young Turk government to take extreme measures to deport the Armenian population in order to protect Ottoman territories and the Muslim population (see also Uras, 1988). Furthermore, these texts note that despite the government's precautions to ensure the safety of Armenians during the deportations, many Armenians died due to the difficult conditions of World War I (e.g., starvation or attacks by armed groups). When officials committed abuses against Armenians, those officials were brought to trial. (For a detailed analysis of the representation of Armenians in Turkish history textbooks since the beginning of the Turkish Republic see Ulgen, 2010.)

The interpretations of this period of history in Turkish textbooks include accounts that may be interpreted as psychological justifications or excuses to deflect responsibility (see also Türközü, 1986): (a) blaming Armenians for treason or for attacking Turkish–Muslim populations; (b) claiming that violent acts were in self-defense (protection from territorial loss and/or protection of the Turkish population that was being targeted by Armenian banditry); (c) shifting responsibility to external factors and third parties (claiming that Armenian deaths were a result of hardship); (d) claiming benevolent motivations behind the deportations (stopping the inter-communal warfare). These interpretations exemplify how moral disengagement mechanisms operate at the level of collective narratives. Three targets of attribution can be readily identified: the in-group (i.e., denial of responsibility), the out-group (i.e., blaming the victim), and situational factors (i.e., blaming third parties or circumstances). The next section assesses the social psychological processes that produce and maintain this narrative, as well as the role of this narrative in legitimizing opposition to reparations of harm.

Historical Memory and a Nation's Self-Image

A nation's conception of itself (i.e., its self-image or national narrative) is grounded in its historical memory. Historical memory is essential for the formation of communities such as ethnicities and nations, which can exist as imagined communities only through selective remembering and forgetting of past events (Anderson, 1991). Nations remember their triumphs and heroes, but their crimes and atrocities not as well (Bilali & Ross, 2012). Historical memory is produced and disseminated in narrative forms through societal institutions, such as the educational system, public symbols, media, etc. (Liu & László, 2007). Historical narratives are central to the formation of national self-images. National self-images are self-perpetuating as they drive schema-consistent interpretations of past and current events (Hirshberg, 1993), which in turn in turn keep self-images alive.

The current study examines how social psychological factors (in-group glorification, national threat, and attitudes toward war) that reflect different aspects of a nation's narrative drive construals of historical events.

In-group glorification. In-group glorification is a central dimension of nationalistic attachment (Kosterman & Feshbach, 1989), and drives the silencing or moral justification of historical misdeeds. Recent studies (Leidner et al., 2010; Roccas et al., 2006) suggest that in-group glorification, rather than group attachment, elicit the typical negative effects of in-group identification (e.g., out-group derogation, legitimization of the in-group's wrong doing). In-group glorification refers to the endorsement of glorified national images. Glorified self-images position the in-group as superior to others, a notion that undergirds nationalistic ideologies. Such glorified images serve to establish a positive national identity. For instance, at the birth of Turkey, glorified national images helped overcome Western biases of Turks as a "barbaric people" and replaced these images of barbarism with those of civilization and modernity (Zarakol, 2010). Denials of the mass killings of Armenians are entangled with the foundational myths of modern Turkish identity (Ulgen, 2010). Admitting to the Armenian genocide undermines Turkey's foundational narrative as a civilized and modern nation (Ulgen, 2010; Zarakol, 2010).

I hypothesize that the more Turks glorify their nation, the more they will endorse in-group favoring constructions of the Armenian massacres (in line with the official narrative of the events), which in turn will predict less support for reparations of the harm against Armenians.

In-group threat.   Historical memories serve to identify one's current foes and allies, as well as identify and anticipate future threats (Liu & Hilton, 2005). Historical experiences elicit sensitivity to various threats. Sometimes a threat becomes central to a group's narrative and self-concept. Bar-Tal and Antebi (1992) proposed a new construct, siege mentality, to refer to the "mental state in which members of a group hold a central belief that the rest of the world has highly negative behavioral intentions toward them" (p. 633). Siege mentality implies chronic perception of threat toward the in-group; it is embedded in the group's image of itself and the world, and it is grounded in historical experiences (Bar-Tal & Antebi, 1992). Exemplifying a siege mentality, Turkish social science and history textbooks portray internal and external threats to the country's terri- torial integrity (Çayir, 2009). Such sensitivity to threat is known as the "Sèvres Syndrome," named after the Treaty of Sèvres, through which the territories of the former Ottoman Empire were almost divided among the Allied Powers at the end of WWI. Although the Treaty of Sèvres was never ratified, Turks have seen various pre- and post-treaty struggles through the siege mentality lens, which has also shaped Turkey's policies today (Aydin, 2004). A National Public Opinion Survey conducted in 2006 in Turkey revealed that 78% of Turks believed that the West wants to 'break up Turkey like they broke up the Ottoman Empire' (as cited in Göcek, 2011, p. 98). The Sèvres Syndrome fuels Turkey's self-image as the "oppressed nation" (*mazlum millet*; Ulgen, 2010), and reaffirms the belief that it faces territorial threats. For instance, Turks perceive current Western interests in minority rights as attempts to undermine Turkish sovereignty (Zarakol, 2010). Similarly, Turks portray the events of 1915 as an issue of territorial sovereignty rather than one of minority rights (Ulgen, 2010).

The literature on intergroup threat demonstrates that perceived threats toward the in-group are associated with prejudice and negative attitudes toward out-groups (e.g., Bizman & Yinon, 2001; Stephan & Stephan, 1996). Perceived national threats also predict public support for aggressive foreign policy and domestic security policies (e.g., Herrmann, Tetlock, & Visser 1999; Huddy, Feldman, & Weber, 2007). However, the above discussion suggests that perceived national threats might not only influence the attitudes toward ongoing conflicts, but also toward past conflicts. I hypothesize that the more Turks perceive their country to be threatened by internal and external groups, the more they will endorse legitimizing construals of Armenian massacres, which in turn will reduce support for reparation of harm.

Attitudes toward war.   Warfare occupies a central place in people's repre- sentations of history (Liu et al., 2009). Nations not only justify wars they fight, but sometimes they also view them as desirable (just war theory: see Walzer, 1992). Each nation links its greatness to war—countries remember and glorify wars of independence, which citizens associate with ideas of honor and sacrifice and judge to be central to their country's existence (Hedges, 2002). Embedded in national symbols (e.g., national heroes and anthems), war becomes part of the national culture. Glorification of war is particularly common in militaristic societies such as Turkey. Historical and cultural processes have led to the internalization of militarism in Turkish society through the creation of societal narratives that draw connections between masculinity and military service, as evident in the common expression that "every (male) Turk is born a soldier" (Altinay, 2004). When war is morally justified, specific instances of war and violence and their negative consequences for the enemy are more likely to be deemed acceptable and justifiable. I predict that Turks' positive attitudes toward war will be related to increased legitimization of Armenian massacres and to less support for reparations of the harm committed.

Overview of the Current Study

The current study investigated Turks' construals of Armenian massacres by assessing perceived severity of harm and legitimizing narratives along three dimensions of attributions of responsibility (in-group vs. out-group vs. external). First, the study examined whether Turkish participants perceive the events as in-group perpetration (as compared to intercommunal warfare or even in-group victimization); in addition, it assessed the extent of perceived harm inflicted on each group as well as the endorsement of the legitimizing narrative along dimensions of attributions of responsibility. Then, the study investigated social psychological influences (in-group glorification, in-group threat, and attitudes toward war) on these construals. Lastly, using structural equation modeling, the mediating role of legitimizing attributions between social psychological factors and support for reparation of harm inflicted on Armenians was examined. I hypothezied that higher in-group glorification, more positive attitudes toward violence in war, and heightened perceived threat toward the in-group would lead to increased endorsement of legitimizing narratives (i.e., less in-group responsibility, more out-group and external responsibility), which in turn would decrease willingness to repair the harm inflicted on Armenians.

Methods

Participants

Participants were 93 Turkish students studying in the United States (41 women, 49 men, 3 participants did not report their gender). The data was collected as part of a broader survey research on this topic (e.g., see Bilali et al., 2012, Study 1); here, I have included only data from participants who completed all scales used in this study. All participants were Turkish citizens recruited from the Turkish foreign student population at various universities in the United States. Participants were contacted via Turkish student associations. Participants' age ranged from 22 to 49 years ($M = 29.2$, $SD = 4.93$). Overall, respondents had lived for the most part in Turkey (years in Turkey: $M = 22.89$, $SD = 5.43$), and in recent years lived in the United States (years in the United States: $M = 5.10$, $SD = 4.49$).

All participants completed a survey online in Turkish. The study was introduced as investigating views of historical events involving intergroup violence. Participants were told that they would be asked questions about a period of violence in their group's history, particularly the violent conflict with Armenians between the 1880s and 1920s. The word *genocide* was purposely not used in order to avoid reactive responses or drop outs.

Measures

In-group's role in violence: perpetrator or victim? To assess how participants construe the violent events, a 3-point multiple-choice item asked participants to identify the victim and the harm doer. The three choices included: (a) Armenians were the victims, Turks were the harm doers; (b) Turks were the victims, Armenians were the harm doers; and (c) Both groups harmed each other equally.

Perceived severity of harm. Additionally, to assess whether participants view the in-group as a perpetrator or a victim, several items measured the perceived severity of harm inflicted on each group. In two open-ended questions, participants were asked to provide an estimate of the number of Armenian [Turkish] casualties inflicted by Turks [Armenians] during the violence between the 1880s and 1920s. In addition, four close-ended items were used to assess perceived severity of harm inflicted on the in-group versus out-group in 1915: perceived severity of harm caused by the in-group was assessed with two items asking participants to estimate (1) the number of Armenians killed by Turks in 1915, and (2) the number of Armenians forcefully displaced from their villages by Turks in 1915. The perceived severity of harm caused by the out-group was assessed in a similar way by asking participants to estimate (1) the number of Turks killed by Armenians in 1915, and (2) the number of Turks forcefully displaced from their villages by Armenians in 1915. Participants rated the severity of harm using 6-point scales consisting of the following estimate ranges (the ranges were chosen so that Turkish official estimates fall in the middle of the scale): (1) less than 100,000 people killed; (2) 100,001 to 300,000; (3) 300,001 to 500,000; (4) 500,001 to 700,000; (5) 700,001 to 900,000; (6) more than 900,000.

Attributions of responsibility. A series of close-ended questions assessed participants' construals of the massacres of 1915 along dimensions of attributions of responsibility. The items were constructed using statements reflecting the Turkish official narrative of the events of 1915. The statements were chosen to vary along three targets of attributions: (a) placing the responsibility on the out-group (3 items), (b) placing responsibility on external factors (i.e., situational factors and third parties; 5 items), and (c) placing responsibility on the in-group (i.e., acknowledgment vs. denial of responsibility; 3 acknowledgment and 3 denial items). All items were assessed on 6-point scales (1 = *strongly disagree*; 6 = *strongly agree*). A sample item that places responsibility on Armenians is: "The Turkish decision to evacuate Armenians in 1915 was a reaction to Armenian revolt and territorial loss." A sample item that places responsibility on third parties is: "Most Armenian casualties in 1915 were due to unfortunate circumstances such as epidemics and starvation." A sample item that places responsibility for the massacres on Turkish government is: "The Turkish evacuation of Armenians was an act premeditated to achieve the destruction of the Armenian people."

In-group glorification. Three items adopted from Roccas et al. (2006) assessed the degree to which participants glorified their in-group. These items included: "The Turkish nation is better than other nations in almost all respects," "Relative to other nations, we are a very moral nation," and "It is disloyal for Turks to criticize Turkey" ($\alpha = .83$, $M = 2.32$, $SD = 1.21$). These items, and the rest of the items presented below, were measured on six-point scales ranging from 1 (*strongly disagree*) to 6 (*strongly agree*).

In-group threat. Two items were constructed to assess perceived divisive threats toward Turkey (as embedded in the national narrative). These items were: "Many countries and groups have hostile intentions toward Turkey" and "There are many groups, inside and outside Turkey, that aim to make Turkey disintegrate" ($\alpha = .97$, $M = 4.39$, $SD = 1.40$).

Attitudes toward war. To assess attitudes toward war, six items were adopted from the violence in war subscale of the Revised Attitudes towards Violence Scale (Anderson, Benjamin, Wood, & Bonacci, 2006). These items included: "War can be just," "Any nation should be ready with a strong military at all times," "Violence against the enemy should be part of every nation's defense," "Killing of civilians should be accepted as an unavoidable part of the war," "Our country has the right to protect its borders forcefully," and "A violent revolution can be perfectly right." The last item was dropped due to low item-scale reliability. The 5 items were averaged to form a scale that had very good reliability ($\alpha = .85$, $M = 3.5$, $SD = 1.27$).

Support for reparation. Two items assessed support for reparation for the atrocities of 1915. The items were: "Turkey should make reparations for the killings of Armenians in 1915" and "I believe that I should take part to help repair the damage done to Armenians" ($\alpha = .68$, $M = 2.47$, $SD = 1.49$). The latter item was adopted from Doosje, Branscombe, Spears, and Manstead's (1998) collective guilt scale.

Results

Turks' Construals of Armenian Massacres: Perpetrator or Victim?

In line with the official framing of the events as an inter-communal warfare, the majority of the sample (65%) believed that both groups have harmed each other equally. Twenty-three participants (25% of the sample) believed that Armenians were the victims and Turks the harm doers; and nine participants (10% of the sample) believed that Turks were the victims while Armenians were the harm doers.

To assess the relative harm perceived to be inflicted on Armenians by Turks, as compared to the harm inflicted on Turks by Armenians, paired samples t-tests were conducted with each indicator of harm as the dependent variable (i.e., number of casualties and people displaced). In both open and close-ended items, participants estimated a higher number of Armenian casualties (open-ended measure: $M = 425{,}035$, $SD = 349{,}154$; close-ended measure: $M = 2.26$, $SD = 1.41$) and displaced Armenians ($M = 3.36$, $SD = 1.57$) compared to the number of the Turkish casualties (open-ended measure: $M = 202$, 124, $SD = 260.770$, $t(56) = -5.85$, $p < .001$; close-ended measure: $M = 1.80$, $SD = 1.19$, $t(75) = 2.48$, $p = .015$) and of the displaced Turks ($M = 1.57$, $SD = 1.11$), $t(73) = 7.46$, $p < .001$. Overall, the Armenian casualty estimates in this sample matched Turkish official statistics of "slightly less than 600,000" (Republic of Turkey Ministry of Foreign Affairs, n.d.).

To examine whether in-group glorification, attitudes toward war, and perceived in-group threat explain individual differences in construals of harm, multivariate regression analyses were conducted with these factors as continuous predictors of perceived severity of harm measures. Due to the difference in the number of participants that reported estimates in different question formats (in open-ended format, $n = 57$; in closed-ended items, $n = 75$), two separate multivariate analyses were conducted for each measure type. The two analyses revealed similar results.

For the open-ended measures, in-group glorification was the only predictor of the number of Armenian casualties, such that higher in-group glorification predicted a lower number of casualties inflicted by Turks on Armenians, $F(1, 53) = 5.59$, $p = .02$, $\eta^2 = .10$. Higher in-group threat was associated with a larger number of Turkish casualties inflicted by Armenians, $F(1, 53) = 3.76$, $p = .058$, $\eta^2 = .07$. None of the other effects were significant (all $ps > .5$).

Similarly, for the close-ended measures, in-group glorification predicted more perceived harm inflicted on Armenians by Turks in 1915 ($F(1, 67) = 6.73$,

$p = .01$, $\eta^2 = .09$ for number of casualties, and $F(1, 67) = 4.24$, $p = .04$, $\eta^2 = .06$ for number of displaced people), whereas in-group threat predicted a higher number of Turkish casualties inflicted by Armenians, $F(1, 67) = 4.60$, $p = .04$, $\eta^2 = .06$. All other effects were nonsignificant (all $ps > .11$).

These results suggest that in-group glorification and perceived national threat influence different aspects of construals of harm. The first reduces perceptions of the in-group as a perpetrator by minimizing the harm inflicted by the in-group, whereas the latter amplifies the extent of in-group victimization by influencing the amount of perceived in-group harm.

The Structure of Legitimizing Mechanisms: Attributions of Responsibility

To assess the structure of the legitimizing narrative adopted from the Turkish official narrative of the 1915 events, I performed confirmatory factor analyses to compare a three-dimensional attribution structure where each target (i.e., in-group vs. out-group vs. external factors) served as a latent factor, with an alternative one-factor model in which all items loaded onto a common "legitimization" factor. The three-dimensional attribution structure revealed a better fit ($\chi^2 (62) = 103.54$, $p < .001$, RMSEA $= .08$, CFI $= .98$, SRMR $= .048$) than the alternative one-factor structure ($\chi^2 (65) = 132.46$, $p < .001$, RMSEA $= .10$, CFI $= .97$, SRMR $= .05$), $_{\text{diff}}\chi^2 (3) = 28.92$, $p < .001$. In the final three-factor model, only one item loaded below .50 on the respective factor; all other items' loadings exceeded .60. The correlations between the three latent factors were considerably high ($r > .80$).

Following the CFA analyses, three composite scales were constructed for each component by averaging the scores of the items loading on each factor. The three in-group responsibility items suggesting denial of in-group responsibility were reverse-coded. The 6-item in-group responsibility ($\alpha = .87$), 3-item out-group responsibility ($\alpha = .80$), and 5-item external responsibility ($\alpha = .86$) scales revealed very good reliabilities. To assess whether participants attributed different degrees of responsibility to different target groups, I conducted a repeated measures ANOVA with target of responsibility as the repeated measures factor and amount of responsibility as the dependent variable. The results indicated that Turkish participants placed most responsibility on Armenians ($M = 4.21$, $SD = 1.33$), followed by responsibility on external factors ($M = 3.89$, $SD = 1.13$), and the least responsibility on Turks ($M = 2.84$, $SD = 1.27$), $F(2, 184) = 23.72$, $p < .001$, $\eta^2 = .21$. All pair-wise differences were significant ($ps < .005$).

Path Analysis

Structural equation modeling with Lisrel was used to assess the hypothesized relationships. Bivariate correlations between the variables included in the path model are shown in Table 1. The model included paths from predictor variables

Table 1. Descriptive Statistics and Bivariate Correlations among Variables Included in the Structural Equation Model

	M	SD	1	2	3	4	5	6	7
1. In-group responsibility	2.84	1.27	1						
2. Out-group responsibility	4.21	1.33	−.79	1					
3. External responsibility	3.89	1.14	−.80	.76	1				
4. In-group threat	4.39	1.40	−.59	.52	.59	1			
5. In-group glorification	2.32	1.21	−.60	.56	.63	.62	1		
6. Attitudes toward war	3.50	1.27	−.56	.60	.60	.52	.58	1	
7. Support for reparation	2.47	1.49	.69	−.60	−.65	−.49	−.55	−.57	1

Note. All correlations are significant at $p < .001$. Scores on all scales ranged from 1 (strongly disagree) to 6 (strongly agree).

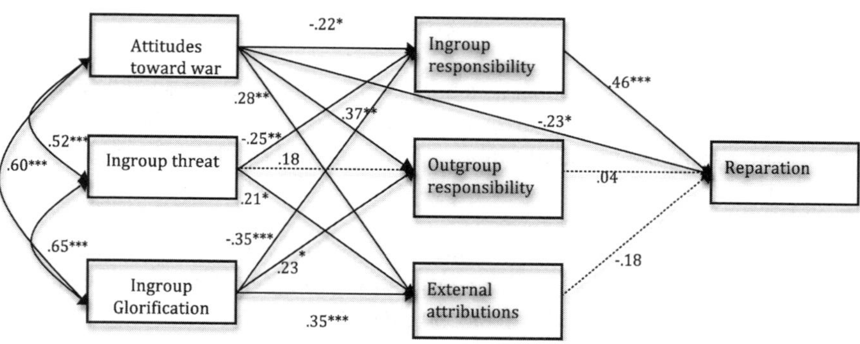

Fig. 1. Structural equation model predicting individual differences in Turkish students' support for reparations for the harm inflicted on Armenians in 1915. Dashed lines indicate nonsignificant paths. *$p < .05$, **$p < .01$, ***$p < .001$.

(in-group glorification, in-group threat, and attitudes toward war) to the mediator variables (legitimizing attributions: in-group, out-group, and external responsibility), and from the mediators to the criterion variable (support for reparation). Due to the limited sample size, the path model included composite scores rather than latent variables. The covariances among the predictors and among the mediator variables were set free. The results revealed an adequate fit of the model, $\chi^2 (3) =$ 6.45, $p = .09$, RMSEA $= .11$, CFI $= .99$, SRMR $= .03$. Post hoc modification indices, however, indicated a large negative residual for the link between attitudes toward war and reparations. The addition of a direct path from attitudes towards war to support for reparation improved the model significantly, $\chi^2 (2) = .35$, $p = .84$, RMSEA $= 0$, CFI $= 1$, SRMR $= .01$. The final revised model is shown in Figure 1. The nonsignificant paths are represented by dotted lines. Notably among attributions of responsibility, only in-group responsibility was associated with support for reparations. The model explained a substantial portion of the variance in support for reparation ($R^2 = .54$).

Alternative model.   Because the data is cross-sectional and nonexperimental, it is not possible to imply causal inference. Alternative models are also plausible. For instance, it is possible that construals of Armenian massacres along the lines of the official narrative might elicit higher in-group glorification, more perceived in-group threat, and more positive attitudes toward war, which would in turn lead to lower support for reparation of harm. A structural equation model was computed where attributions for the massacres were exogenous variables, whereas in-group threat, attitudes toward war, and in-group glorification served as mediators. The results showed that this alternate model did not fit the data well, $\chi^2 (4) = 16.64$, $p = .002$, RMSEA $= .18$, CFI $= .98$, SRMR $= .05$. Including direct paths from attributions to support for harm also did not improve the data fit.

Discussion

The current study demonstrates a correspondence between collective and individual construals of violence towards Armenians. In line with the Turkish narrative, participants minimized the in-group's responsibility while placing blame on Armenians and external factors (i.e., the third parties and the grave circumstances of WWI) (see also Bilali et al., 2012). At the same time, participants acknowledged some harm inflicted on Armenians, while also viewing Turks as victims of Armenian violence. Indeed, the majority of the sample (75%) did not construe the events as an instance of one-sided in-group perpetration. Rather, they either endorsed the "inter-communal warfare" interpretation promoted by the Turkish official narrative (65%), or they viewed Armenians as the perpetrators of violence (10% of the sample).

Interestingly, in-group glorification and perceived threat differentially predicted Turks' construals of harm inflicted during the mass violence. In-group glorification minimized perceived in-group perpetration (i.e., predicted less perceived harm inflicted by Turks), whereas in-group threat elevated the perceived in-group victimization. These results are in line with the idea that in-group glorification is driven by identity-enhancing motives (i.e., perceiving the in-group in a positive light via minimizing in-group perpetration). Additionally, national threat, especially when beliefs about such threat are embedded in the national narrative, might influence perceptions of past violence by enhancing perceived in-group victimization.

The justifications, excuses, and silences embedded in the collective narrative and disseminated by societal institutions constitute a "social reality" for Turkish citizens. However, these collective legitimizations correspond to psychological mechanisms of moral disengagement. At the individual level, higher in-group glorification, higher perceived national threat, and more positive attitudes toward war in general, predicted the endorsement of narratives that deny in-group responsibility and place blame on the out-group and on external factors for the mass killings of Armenians. Additionally, the endorsement of these legitimizing narratives mediated the relation between social-psychological factors and support for reparative action.

The current study replicated previous findings (Leidner et al., 2010; Roccas et al., 2006) of the role of in-group glorification on the endorsement of legitimizing narratives. In addition to identity enhancing and image-protective motives that drive the effects of in-group glorification, I suggest that in-group glorification reflects a glorified national image. Taking seriously the self-confirming nature of self-images (Hirshberg, 1993), the glorified image of the in-group should serve as a schema through which past and current events are interpreted (see also Kurtis, Adams, & Yellow Bird, 2010). The self-perpetuating nature of glorified images might protect group members from feeling guilt or shame, leading to denials of the past and to low levels of self-criticism among members of perpetrator groups (see Leach, Zeinnedine, & Čehajić-Clancy, 2013).

In the current study, national threat was used as a specific form of realistic threat. Different from previous literature on intergroup threat, the realistic threat used here had an additional characteristic—it was embedded in the national narrative. Turkish textbooks not only glorify the nation, but they also demand martyrdom to protect it from internal and external threats (Çayir, 2009). Kubali-Camoglu's (1996) warnings of the dangers of the post-cold war era for the Turkish nation best capture the prominence of the Sèvres Syndrome:

> More is being threatened by her internal as well as external enemies who are using the instability created in the global scene as a result of the demise of the bipolar world to re-establish goals as articulated in the Sèvres Treaty of 1919 (p. 305).

The belief in threats to the territorial integrity of the nation might serve to delegitimize genocide accusations as a conspiracy to destroy the nation. Turkey is not a unique case; often, existential threat is an important characteristic of national narratives of victimization (Bar-Tal & Antebi, 1992). Threat is functional for groups as it enhances perceptions of common fate (e.g., Rothgerber, 1997) and elicits moral self-images and delegitimization of one's adversaries (Bar-Tal, 2003). At the same time, it has the potential of escalating conflict and poses obstacles for conflict resolution, including conflicts in the aftermath of genocide and mass killings.

Positive attitudes toward violence in war legitimize violent actions toward groups perceived to undermine national security. The more war and violence are viewed as normative and acceptable solutions to a nation's problems, the more likely it is that great harm inflicted on "enemy" populations can be justified. "Doing what is necessary" to protect one's country implies use of any method, regardless of consequences. Interestingly, in the path analysis, attitudes toward war were the only precursor that had a direct (negative) effect on support for reparations. That is, independent of the interpretation of specific incidents (e.g.,

Armenian massacres), the more people view violence in war to be legitimate, the less they support reparatory actions.

The path model indicated that acknowledgment of in-group responsibility, more than the other aspects of attributions, elicited support for reparations of harm inflicted on Armenians. This result is in line with Cohrs et al.'s (2003) findings that denial of in-group responsibility was the most crucial aspect of moral disengagement mechanisms related to attitudes toward the United States' war in Afghanistan. However, it is important to note that in this study the three targets of responsibility were highly correlated; there was little unique variance left to account for relations between out-group and external responsibility and the dependent variable.

One important limitation of this study was that the sample included Turks living in the United States. Therefore, it is unclear how the findings of this research generalize to Turks living in Turkey. On one hand, Turks living in the United States are likely to encounter alternative narratives that might provide new perspectives beyond government-sponsored narratives of the events. On the other hand, such narratives might also be particularly threatening to Turks who live outside the country, away from the support of Turkish communities–thereby leading to increased endorsement of the official Turkish narrative.

In concluding, the current research considered the construction of Armenian massacres to be rooted in a broader "master narrative" (see Hammack, 2009) of the Turkish nation. In studying psychological reactions to genocide and mass killing, it is important to consider narratives that go beyond the specific violent acts. Each historical event is situated within a broader representation of a nation's history (i.e., its national narrative), therefore people's reactions to historical events should be understood within the context of that national narrative. Additionally, social psychological factors such as in-group glorification, attitudes toward war, and perceived national threat, in addition to their psychological significance, were considered to be markers of this national narrative. Thus, psychologists should go beyond explanations that use only internal psychological processes to also account for the influence of cultural frameworks on social psychological phenomena. This analysis suggests that interventions to address historical mass violence— for instance, to increase acknowledgment of harm and support for amends for the wrong done—might be most effective if they target historical and cultural narratives (Bilewicz & Jaworska, 2013), as well as by introducing new narratives and social norms (Paluck, 2009).

References

Akçam, T. (2006). *A shameful act: The Armenian genocide and the question of Turkish responsibility.* New York, NY: Metropolitan Books.

Altinay, A. G. (2004). The myth of the military-nation. *Militarism, gender, and education in Turkey.* New York, NY: Palgrave Macmillan.

Anderson, B. (1991). Imagined communities. *Reflections on the origin and spread of nationalism.* London, U.K.: Verso.

Anderson, C. A., Benjamin, A. J., Wood, P. K., & Bonacci, A. M. (2006). Development and testing of the Velicer Attitudes Toward Violence Scale: Evidence for a four-factor model. *Aggressive Behavior, 32,* 122–136. doi: 10.1002/ab.20112.

Aydin, M. (2004). Foucault's pendulum: Turkey in Central Asia and Caucasus. *Turkish Studies, 5,* 1–22.

Bandura, A. (1999). Moral disengagement in the perpetration of inhumanities. *Personality and Social Psychology Review, 3,* 193–209. doi: 10.1207/s15327957pspr0303_3.

Bandura, A. (2002). Selective moral disengagement in the exercise of moral agency. *Journal of Moral Education, 31,* 101–119. doi: 10.1080/0305724022014322.

Bar-Tal, D. (2003). Collective memory of physical violence: Its contribution to the culture of violence. In E. Cairns & M. D. Roe (Eds.), *The role of memory in ethnic conflict* (pp. 75–93). London, England: Palgrave Macmillan.

Bar-Tal, D., & Antebi, D. (1992). Beliefs about negative intentions of the world: A study of the Israeli siege mentality. *Political Psychology, 13,* 633–645.

Baumester, R. F., & Hastings, S. (1997). Distortions of collective memory. How groups flatter and deceive themselves. In J. W. Pennebaker, D. Paez, & B. Rime (Eds.), *Collective memory of political events: Social psychological perspectives* (pp. 277–293). Mahwah, NJ: Lawrence Erlbaum.

Bilali, R., & Ross, M. (2012). Remembering intergroup conflict. In Tropp, L. R. (Ed.), *The Oxford handbook of intergroup conflict* (pp. 123–135). New York: Oxford University Press.

Bilali, R., Tropp, L. R., & Dasgupta, N. (2012). Attributions of responsibility and perceived harm in the aftermath of mass violence. Peace & Conflict. *Journal of Peace Psychology, 18,* 21–39. doi: 10.1037/a0026671.

Bilewicz, M., & Jaworska, M. (2013). Reconciliation through the righteous: The narratives of heroic helpers as a fulfillment of emotional needs in Polish-Jewish intergroup contact. *Journal of Social Issues, 69,* 162–179.

Bizman, A., & Yinon, Y. (2001). Intergroup and interpersonal threats as determinants of prejudice: The moderating role of in-group identification. *Basic and Applied Social Psychology, 23,* 191–196. doi: 10.1207/153248301750433669.

Bloxham, D. (2005). *The great game of genocide: Imperialism, nationalism, and the destruction of the Ottoman Armenians.* New York, NY: Oxford University Press.

Branscombe, N. R., & Doosje, B. (2004). (Eds.) *Collective guilt: International perspectives.* New York, NY: Cambridge University Press.

Castano, E., & Giner-Sorolla, R. (2006). Not quite human: Infrahumanization in response to collective responsibility for intergroup killing. *Journal of Personality and Social Psychology, 90,* 805–818. doi: 10.1037/0022-3514.90.5.804.

Çayir, K. (2009). Preparing Turkey for the European Union: Nationalism, national identity, and 'otherness' in Turkey's new textbooks. *Journal of Intercultural Studies, 30,* 39–55.

Cohrs, C. J., Maes, J., Moschner, B., & Kielmann, S. O. (2003). Patterns of justification of the United States' 'war against terrorism' in Afghanistan. *Psicologia Politica, 27,* 105–117.

Dadrian, V. (Ed.). (2003). *Warrant for genocide: Key elements of Turko-Armenian conflict* (3rd ed.). New Brunswick, NJ: Transaction Publishers.

Doosje, B., & Branscombe, N. R. (2003). Attributions for the negative historical actions of a group. *European Journal of Social Psychology, 33,* 235–248. doi: 10.1002/ejsp.142.

Doosje, B., Branscombe, N. R., Spears, R., & Manstead, A. S. R. (1998). Guilty by association: When one's group has a negative history. *Journal of Personality and Social Psychology, 25,* 872–886. doi: 10.1037/0022-3514.75.4.872.

Göçek, F. M. (2011). *The transformation of Turkey: Redefining state and society from the Ottoman Empire to the modern era.* London, England: I. B. Tauris.

Hammack, P. L. (2009). Exploring the reproduction of conflict through narrative: Israeli youth motivated to participate in a coexistence program. *Peace and Conflict: Journal of Peace Psychology, 15,* 49–74. doi: 10.1080/10781910802589923.

Hedges, C. (2002). *War is a force that gives us meaning.* New York, NY: Anchor Books.

Herrmann, R. K., Tetlock, P. E., & Visser, P. S. (1999). Mass public decisions to go to war: A cognitive-interactionist framework. *American Political Science Review, 93*, 553–573.

Hovannisian, R. (Ed.). (1997). *The Armenian genocide in perspective.* New Brunswick, NJ: Transaction Press.

Hirshberg, M. (1993). The self-perpetuating national self-image: Cognitive biases in perceptions of international interventions. *Political Psychology, 14*, 77–93.

Huddy, L., Feldman, S., & Weber, C. (2007). The political consequences of perceived threat and felt insecurity. *The Annals of American Academy of Political and Social Science, 614*, 131–153. doi: 10.1177/0002716207305951.

Iyer, A., Leach, C. W., & Crosby, F. J. (2003). White guilt and racial compensation: The benefits and limits of self-focus. *Personality and Social Psychology Bulletin, 29*, 117–129. doi: 10.1177/0146167202238377.

Jorgensen, T. (2003). Turkey, the U.S. and the Armenian genocide. In S. L. B. Jensen (Ed.), *Genocide: Cases, comparisons, and contemporary debate* (pp. 193–224). Copenhagen, Denmark: Werks Offset.

Kalayjian, A., & Shahinian, S. P. (1998). Recollections of aged Armenian survivors of the Ottoman Turkish Genocide: Resilience through endurance, coping, and life accomplishments. *Psychoanalytic Review, 85*, 489–516.

Kaplan. S. (2006). *The pedagogical state: Education and the politics of national culture in the post-1980 Turkey.* Palo Alto, CA: Stanford University Press.

Kofta, M., & Slawuta, P. (2013). Thou shall not kill… Your brother: Victim-perpetrator cultural closeness and moral disapproval of Polish atrocities against Jews after the Holocaust. *Journal of Social Issues, 69*, 54–73.

Kosterman, R., & Feshbach, S. (1989). Toward a measure of patriotic and nationalistic attitudes. *Political Psychology, 10*, 257–274.

Kubali-Camoglu, I. (1996). Turkey in the eye of the storm: The indecisiveness of the West; Demise of NATO. *Journal of Muslim Minority Affairs, 16*, 305–307.

Kurtis, T., Adams, G., & Yellow Bird, M. (2010). Generosity or genocide? Identity implications of silence in American Thanksgiving commemorations. *Memory, 18*, 208–224. doi: 10.1080/09658210903176478.

Leach, C. W., Zeinnedine, F. B., & Čehajić-Clancy, S. (2013). Moral immemorial: The rarity of self-criticism for previous generation's genocide or mass violence. *Journal of Social Issues, 69*, 34–53.

Leidner, B., Castono, E., Zaiser, E., & Giner-Sorolla, R. (2010). In-group glorification, moral disengagement, and justice in the context of collective violence. *Personality and Social Psychology Bulletin, 36*, 1115–1139. doi: 10.1177/0146167210376391.

Lewy, G. (2005). The Armenian massacres in Ottoman Turkey. *A disputed genocide.* Salt Lake City, UT: The University of Utah Press.

Liu, J. H., & Hilton, D. J. (2005). How the past weights on the present: Social representations of history and their role in identity politics. *British Journal of Social Psychology, 44*, 537–556. doi: 10.1348/014466605×27162.

Liu, J. H., & László, J. (2007). A narrative theory of history and identity: Social identity, social representations, society and the individual. In G. Moloney, & I. Walker (Eds.), *Social representations and history: Content, process, and power* (pp. 85–107). New York, NY: Palgrave-Macmillan.

Liu, J. H., Paez, D., Slawuta, P., Cabecinhas, R., Techio, E., Kokdemir, D., Sen, R., Vincze, O., Muluk, H., Wang, F., & Zlobina, A. (2009). Representing world history in the 21st century: The impact of 9–11, the Iraq War, and the nation-state on the dynamics of collective remembering. *Journal of Cross-Cultural Psychology, 40*, 667–692. doi: 10.1177/0022022109335557.

Melson, R. (1992). *Revolution and genocide: On the origins of the Armenian Genocide and the Holocaust.* Chicago, IL: University of Chicago Press.

Nazer, J. (1968). *The first genocide of the twentieth century: The Armenian massacre.* New York, NY: T. and T. Publishing.

Necef, M. (2003). The Turkish media debate on the Armenian massacre. In S. L. B. Jensen (Ed.), *Genocide: Cases, comparisons, and contemporary debate* (pp. 225–262). Copenhagen, Denmark: Werks Offset.

Olick, J. K., & Robbins, J. (1998). Social memory studies: From "collective memories" to the historical sociology of mnemonic practices. *Annual Review of Sociology, 25,* 105–140.

Paluck, E. L. (2009). Reducing intergroup prejudice and conflict using the media: A field experiment in Rwanda. *Journal of Personality and Social Psychology, 96,* 574–587. doi: 10.1037/a0011989.

Pearlman, L. A. (2013). Restoring self in community: Collective approaches to psychological trauma after genocide. *Journal of Social Issues, 69,* 111–124.

Reicher, S., & Hopkins, N. (2001). *Self and nation: Categorization, contestation, and mobilization.* London, England: Sage.

Roccas, S., Klar, Y., & Liviatan, I. (2006). The paradox of group-based guilt: Modes of conflict identification, conflict vehemence, and reactions to the in-group's moral violations. *Journal of Personality and Social Psychology, 91,* 698–711. doi: 10.1037/0022-3514.91.4.698.

Rothgerber, H. (1997). External intergroup threat as an antecedent to perceptions of in-group and out-group homogeneity. *Journal of Personality and Social Psychology, 73,* 1206–1212.

Sibley, C. G., Wilson, M. S., & Robertson, A. (2007). Differentiating the motivations and justifications underlying individual differences in Pakeha opposition to bicultural policy. *New Zealand Journal of Psychology, 36,* 25–33.

Staub, E. (2006). Reconciliation after genocide, mass killing or intractable conflict: Understanding the roots of violence, psychological recovery and steps toward a general theory. *Political Psychology, 27,* 867–895. doi: 10.1111/j.1467-9221.2006.00541.x.

Staub, E. (2013). A world without genocide: Prevention, reconciliation and the creation of peaceful societies. *Journal of Social Issues, 69,* 180–199.

Stephan, W. G., & Stephan, C. W. (1996). Predicting prejudice. *International Journal of Intercultural Relations, 20,* 409–426. doi: 10.1016//0147-1767(96)00026-0.

Tajfel, H., & Turner, J. C. (1986). The social identity theory of intergroup behavior. In S. Worchel & W. G. Austin (Eds.), *Psychology of intergroup relations* (pp. 7–24). Chicago, IL: Nelson-Hall.

Republic of Turkey Ministry of Foreign Affairs. (n.d.). The Armenian allegation of genocide. The issue and the facts. Retrieved from http://www.mfa.gov.tr/the-armenian-allegation-of-genocide-the-issue-and-the-facts.en.mfa

Türközu, H. K. (1986). Armenian atrocity. *According to Ottoman and Russian documents.* Ankara, Turkey: Institute for the Study of Turkish Culture.

Ulgen, F. (2010). Sabiha Gokcen's 80-year-old secret. *Kemalist nation formation and the Ottoman Armenians (doctoral dissertation).* San Diego: University of California.

Uras, E. (1988). *The Armenians in history and the Armenian question.* Istanbul, Turkey: Documentary Publications.

Vollhardt, J. R. (2013). "Crime against humanity" or "Crime against Jews"? Acknowledgment in construals of the Holocaust and its importance for intergroup relations. *Journal of Social Issues, 69,* 144–161.

Walzer, M. (1992). *Just and unjust wars* (2nd ed.). New York, NY: Basic Books.

Zarakol, A. (2010). Ontological (in)security and state denial of historical crimes: Turkey and Japan. *International Relations, 24,* 3–23. doi: 10.1177/0047117809359040.

REZARTA BILALI is an Assistant Professor at the Department of Conflict Resolution, Human Security and Global Governance at the University of Massachusetts at Boston. She received her PhD in Social Psychology with a concentration in the Psychology of Peace and Violence from the University of Massachusetts at Amherst. Her current research focuses on topics related to intergroup conflict and violence, including historical memories, group identity, and denial/acknowledgment of responsibility for in-group's harm doing. She has studied these topics in a variety of national contexts including Albania, Burundi, Rwanda, Turkey, and the United States.

Journal of Social Issues, Vol. 69, No. 1, 2013, pp. 34–53

Moral Immemorial: The Rarity of Self-Criticism for Previous Generations' Genocide or Mass Violence

Colin Wayne Leach* and Fouad Bou Zeineddine
University of Connecticut

Sabina Čehajić-Clancy
Sarajevo School of Science and Technology

Partly in response to political leaders' public expressions of self-criticism for past generations' genocide or other mass violence, psychologists have suggested that individuals who are psychologically connected to perpetrators may view themselves as sharing some responsibility. Such broadened self-perception should enable self-criticism for past failures just as it enables self-congratulation for past triumphs. We review studies of self-criticism regarding European colonization (of Africa, the Americas, Australia, and Indonesia) and 20th century genocide (in Bosnia, Germany, Norway, and Rwanda). Self-criticism—feelings of guilt, shame, and responsibility; wanting reparation—tended to be low. Self-criticism appeared to be lowest among nonstudent samples, those allowed to explicitly disagree with self-criticism, and those asked about more recent violence. Theoretical and practical implications of these patterns are discussed.

Genocide is always an accusation. In the 60 years since the United Nations convention against it, no group has ever spontaneously pronounced themselves perpetrators of genocide (see Minow, 1998). Rwandan Prime Minister Jean Kambanda was the first, and only, head of state to confess to genocide. However, he did so only after being brought to the International Criminal Tribunal for Rwanda. And, he later tried to withdraw his plea.

In the immediate aftermath of the Holocaust, Germany did not admit to genocide. While actively pursuing the "Federal Law for the Compensation of

<hr>

*Correspondence concerning this article should be addressed to Colin Wayne Leach, Department of Psychology, University of Connecticut, Storrs, CT 06521-1020 [e-mail: colin.leach@uconn.edu].

We thank Laurent Licata, Michał Bilewicz, and two anonymous reviewers, for their helpful comments on a previous draft of this paper.

the Victims of National Socialist *Persecution* (italics added)," The FRG's first Chancellor avoided reference to genocide: "In our name, *unspeakable crimes* have been committed and demand compensation and restitution, both moral and material, for the persons and properties of the Jews who have been so seriously *harmed...*" (Konrad Adenauer, September 27, 1951, Brooks 1999, pp. 61–67, italics added). "Persecution," "harm," and "unspeakable crimes" are no substitute for the term genocide.

A fair number of highly publicized apologies and expressions of "remorse" and "regret" for mass violence have been recently offered by national representatives (Brooks, 1999; Minow, 1998). Most of these statements did not include direct acknowledgment that the in-group was a perpetrator of mass violence. For instance, several recent prime ministers have expressed remorse for the forced labor and prostitution practiced in Japan's mid-20th century colonization of Korea. In 1997, Prime Minister Tony Blair suggested that British government policy had some role in the one million deaths in the Irish Famine of 1845–1852. In 2009, the U.S. senate apologized for the enslavement of Africans and the systems of formal segregation that prevailed until the 1960s. As with the more extreme case of genocide, the perpetrators of mass violence rarely characterize themselves as such.

Perhaps as a result of politician's recent expressions of self-criticism, many psychologists argue that individuals may view themselves as morally implicated in past generations' mass violence. Indeed, group identity binds us just as strongly to our inglorious as to our glorious past. Where individuals view themselves as direct descendants of perpetrators, as sharing an identity with perpetrators, or as inheriting spoils, individuals may feel implicated in past generations' mass violence. This broadened self-perception is the putative basis for self-critical feelings based in membership in a perpetrator group, such as guilt and shame (for a review, see Iyer and Leach, 2008). And, these self-critical feelings are presumed to motivate support for compensation, apology, or other reparation (for reviews, see Branscombe & Doojse, 2004; Leach, Snider, & Iyer, 2002).

Somewhat surprisingly, recent research on self-criticism for past generations' mass violence ignores the fact that no group has ever spontaneously pronounced themselves perpetrators of genocide, crimes against humanity, or the like. As most research has focused on establishing that the notion of group-based self-criticism is possible, it has been unconcerned with the actual level of self-criticism that people express (for discussions, see Iyer & Leach, 2008; Leach, 2010a). Thus, we have little sense of how prevalent self-criticism is or how it varies across particular instances. For these reasons, we review recent quantitative research in social and political psychology of self-criticism regarding genocide and other mass violence. We focus on quantitative research because we can better compare levels of self-criticism across studies when participants use close-ended response scales.

To complement the present volume, we discuss less researched examples of 20th century genocide (in Australia, Bosnia, and Norway) and compare levels of self-criticism to that found among Germans and Rwandans. However, our main focus is the self-criticism expressed by present day Europeans about the 16th to 20th century colonization of Africa, the Americas, Australia, and Indonesia. European colonization is one of the most elaborate, long-lived, and far-reaching examples of concerted mass violence in human history. And, colonization quite often proceeded through genocidal violence (Dirks, 1992; Todorov, 1984; UNESCO, 1980). Thus, self-criticism of colonization seems important to an understanding of the aftermath of genocide.

In the first section below, we discuss studies of self-criticism among Europeans today regarding the 16th to 20th century colonization of Indonesia and Africa. In the second section, we review studies regarding the genocide and other mass violence committed against Indigenous peoples in Australia and the Americas in the 16th to 20th centuries. In the third section, we review studies of self-criticism regarding genocide in the 20th century in Norway and Bosnia-Herzegovina as well as in Germany and Rwanda. We close with a discussion of empirical trends and conceptual explanations and implications.

Examples of European Colonization

In many ways, genocide was part and parcel of 16th to 20th century European colonization of land and natural resources in Asia and Africa (see Dirks, 1992; UNESCO, 1980). The colonizers had the "intent to destroy, in whole, or in part" ethnic, "racial," and religious groups that complicated the colonial project. Fitting with the formal definition of genocide, this destructive intent was expressed in killing, physical and psychological harm, dangerous life conditions, sterilization and other means of preventing births, and forced removal of children. In the death throes of colonization, violence sometimes morphed into "politicide" as colonial powers sought to destroy the political groups fighting for independence.

Although the physical destruction of groups emphasized in the UN convention on genocide was present in many instances of colonization, sometimes this system of domination was more focused on physical and psychological subjugation. As such, it can be said that colonization also worked though "cultural genocide," as colonial authorities sought to destroy indigenous practices of religion, language, culture, and politics (see Dirks, 1992; Todorov, 1984; UNESCO, 1980). It is unclear if cultural genocide fits the "psychological harm" referred to in the UN convention on genocide. However, Ralph Lemkin (1944) seemed to include the prototypical practices of colonization in his original conceptualization of genocide:

> Generally speaking, genocide does not necessarily mean the immediate destruction of a nation, except when accomplished by mass killings of all members of a nation. It is intended rather to signify a coordinated plan of different actions aiming at the destruction

of essential foundations of the life of national groups, with the aim of annihilating the groups themselves. The objectives of such a plan would be disintegration of the political and social institutions, of culture, language, national feelings, religion, and the economic existence of national groups, and the destruction of the personal security, liberty, health, dignity, and even the lives of the individuals belonging to such groups (p. 79).

In his last sentence, Lemkin makes it clear that the physical annihilation of some or all of a group is not the only kind of annihilation sought in the perpetration of genocide. Later on the same page, Lemkin goes on to say,

Genocide has two phases: one, destruction of the national pattern of the oppressed group; the other, the imposition of the national pattern of the oppressor. This imposition, in turn, may be made upon the oppressed population which is allowed to remain or upon the territory alone, after removal of the population and the colonization by the oppressor's own nationals (p. 79).

Thus, we think that there is good reason to view colonization as a form of mass violence that was often genocidal in purpose and practice, even if it did not always focus on the physical annihilation of the colonized. However, little work in mainstream psychology has examined contemporary opinions or feelings about colonialism, either among perpetrators or victims. A 2010 special issue of the *International Journal of Conflict and Violence* edited by Volpato and Licata is a rare effort to highlight the psychological side of what present day Europeans make of the mass violence perpetrated by past generations in pursuit of colonization. We have relied heavily on this recent work in the section below.

The Dutch in Indonesia

The Netherlands was a major colonial empire, involved in the African slave trade until 1863. Indonesia, the most important colony, was ruled for over three centuries. Its independence was granted in 1949, after the failure of a four-year military intervention to prevent it (Dirks, 1992). In a pioneering paper, Doosje, Branscombe, Spears, and Manstead (1998, study 2) presented 135 Dutch university students with a summary of the 17th and 18th century Dutch colonization of Indonesia presumably written by respected historians. This history was portrayed positively, negatively, or ambivalently. Importantly, in the negative portrayal, the Dutch were said to have "(a) exploited Indonesian land, (b) abused Indonesian labor, and (c) killed a lot of Indonesians." This text was accompanied by images of emaciated Indonesian servants and laborers in rice paddies. Thus, the mass violence in Dutch colonization was made clear.

Doosje et al. (1998, study 2) asked participants to indicate their "feelings of guilt about the behavior of the Dutch during the colonial period" with a 1 *(strongly disagree)* to 7 *(strongly agree)* response scale. Participants expressed slightly more guilt when colonization was portrayed negatively ($M = 4.12$) rather

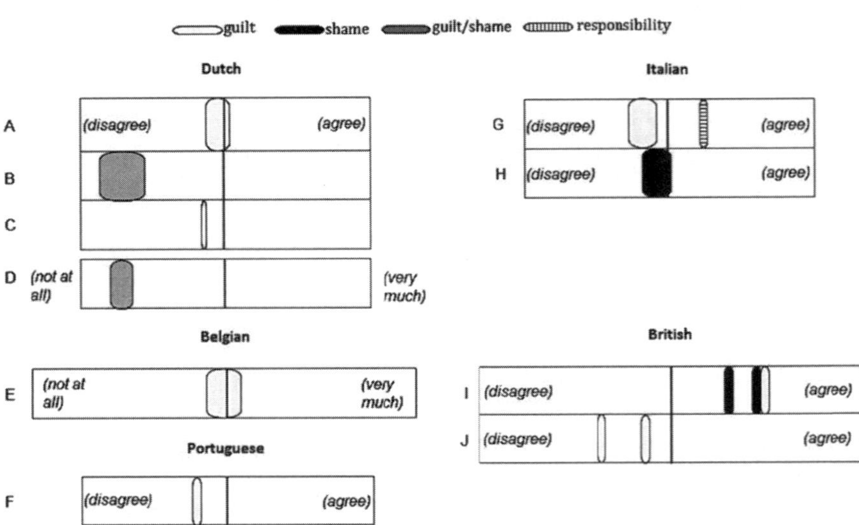

Fig. 1. Mean levels of self-criticism regarding past generations' mass violence. Each horizontal bar represents the range of the scale for a study. The dark vertical line in the middle of each bar represents the mid-point of the response scale. The width of the vertical marker within each bar represents the range of means obtained across conditions within a study.

than positively ($M = 3.60$) or ambivalently ($M = 3.76$). This range of responses is shown in case A of Figure 1. Thus, in all three experimental conditions, participants tended to *disagree* that they felt guilty. Participants also tended to disagree with the notion that they, or their country, should compensate Indonesians for colonization. Two subsequent studies with similar samples also showed the modal response to be disagreement with guilt about the colonization of Indonesia (Doosje et al., 2006).

In two studies with 141–150 Dutch university students each, Zebel et al. (2007) framed the colonization of Indonesia in a negative or positive light. Zebel et al. also provided participants with a suggestion that their ancestors were involved (or not) in colonization. Across all conditions in study 1, self-critical emotions tended to be very low (see case D of Figure 1). In fact, participants expressed much more pride and contentment than guilt and shame. In study 2, Zebel et al. (2007) manipulated family involvement more directly by presumably having a database match participant's family genealogy to historical records of those involved in colonialism. Across all conditions, participants tended to express fairly strong disagreement with feelings of guilt and shame (see case B in Figure 1). Although participants expressed the most self-criticism when their family was involved in colonization cast in a negative light, they still tended to disagree with guilt and shame in this experimental condition. In fact, participants expressed more positive feelings than guilt and shame, even when their family was involved in colonization cast in a negative light.

Figuereido, Doosje, Pires Valentim, and Zebel (2010, study 2) examined 157 Dutch students responses to the Netherlands' 1945–1949 military attempt to re-establish colonization after Indonesia declared its independence. Participants mildly disagreed that they felt guilty about Dutch violence and moderately disagreed that reparations should be made to Indonesia (see Figure 1, case C). Taken together, the studies of Dutch students' responses to their country's colonization of Indonesia offer little evidence of self-criticism or a willingness to make reparation. Portraying colonization negatively, or implicating people directly, did not increase self-criticism.

Europe in Africa

Belgium

In the 1885 conference of Berlin, King Leopold II of Belgium gained the Congo region of Africa as his personal property. He quickly indentured the native population and forced them to work for his profit. In 1908, after a global campaign against the killing, torture, and maiming, Leopold II gave the Congo to the Belgian government. The Congo gained independence in 1960.

Licata and Klein (2010) found that colonization of the Congo elicited very different views across three generations of (French-speaking) Belgians. Grandparents reported less guilt ($M = 3.70$) than parents ($M = 4.04$) or students ($M = 4.34$, see Figure 1, case E). However, the meaning of these moderate levels of guilt varied across generations. The grandparents' guilt was about leaving the Congo and "abandoning" the Congolese, who were seen as benefitting from colonial rule. In contrast, the students' guilt was about the exploitation of the Congo. This is consistent with Licata and Klein's (2010) argument that schools have recently moved to framing Belgian colonization in negative terms.

Portugal

Figuereido et al. (2010, study 1) asked 170 Portuguese university students about Portugal's colonization of Africa and its violent opposition to independence movements in Angola, Mozambique, and Guinea-Bissau in the 1960s and 1970s. Participants tended to slightly disagree that they felt guilty about colonization (see Figure 1, case F). Those who had negative stereotypes of Africans, or those who thought it important to remember the positive aspects of colonization, disagreed somewhat more with guilt. On average, participants expressed slight agreement that Portugal should compensate for colonization.

Cabecinhas and Feijó (2010) asked 118 Portuguese and 180 Mozambicans about the history of their country. For Mozambicans, Portuguese colonization and the fight for liberation were of moderate importance historically: 28% mentioned colonization and 36% mentioned the "war of liberation" as one of the five most important events in national history. When citing colonization as an important event, the Mozambicans made specific reference to some of its worst atrocities. For example, 11% remembered the slave trade and 8% remembered the Massacre of Mueda—where Mozambican protesters were murdered by order of a Portuguese administrator. Thus, colonization tended to be seen in quite negative terms by Mozambicans, whereas the fight for liberation was evaluated more positively.

The Portuguese offered a very different view of this shared history. Only 16% of the Portuguese mentioned colonialism, and only 10% mentioned the wars against colonial independence, as important events in the history of Portugal. None of the Portuguese mentioned the specific brutalities cited by the Mozambicans. A likely reason for the rarity of self-criticism among the Portuguese is their romantic view of the colonial period as marked by the "voyages of discovery." Indeed, 80% mentioned these "voyages" as one of the five most important events in national history. For the Portuguese, this aspect of colonization was marked by strong feelings of pride and admiration.

Italy

In Italy, content analyses of history textbooks by Leone and Mastrovito (2010) found little reference to the colonial past, particularly the atrocities committed in Ethiopia and Libya during the Fascist regime (e.g., the use of poison gas, civilian massacres, concentration camps). Given these representations of Italy's colonial period, it is not surprising that Mari, Andrighetto, Gabbiadini, Durante, and Volpato (2010) found little agreement with self-criticism in a study of 68 students and 84 people recruited through the internet (see Figure 1, case G, H). Despite general disagreement with guilt and shame, participants tended to acknowledge Italy's responsibility for the violence and other damage of colonization. The discrepancy between national responsibility and self-critical feelings suggests that participants did not see themselves as implicated in the acts of their forebears. Indeed, Mari et al. suggested that Italians attribute the colonization of Africa to the fascists rather than to Italy in general.

Britain

Britain had one of the most extensive colonial empires in the world. Its brutal resistance to independence movements, in India, southern Africa, Australia, and elsewhere is well documented. However, there are few published studies of contemporary British sentiment regarding the colonization of Africa. In a recent study, Allpress et al. (2010, study 2) queried 181 British university students about the deaths, "beatings, starvation, and torture" that the Kikuyu ethnic group was subjected to in British detention camps designed to end their involvement in the Mau Mau revolution in Kenya, 1952–1960. This information was presented as a factual report from a respected newspaper. Surprisingly, participants expressed near moderate agreement with guilt and shame (see Figure 1, case I). Agreement with compensation was slightly lower, but still on the agree side of the response scale. However, Morton and Postmes' (2010, study 1) study of 58 British university students produced mean *disagreement* with guilt about the British role in the African slave trade. A second study showed even stronger disagreement with such guilt (see Figure 1, case J). Both studies by Morton and Postmes (2010) presented participants with historical evidence of the damage done by slavery, but apparently made little reference to the quality or scale of the violence involved. Nevertheless, it is surprising that two different papers in Britain about mass violence in the colonization of Africa produced such different levels of self-critical feeling. Given findings regarding other examples of European colonization, it is the moderate *agreement* with guilt and shame in Allpress et al. (2010) that is unusual. This may have to do with the particular event that they examined.

Colonization of Indigenous Peoples in Australia and the Americas

In the colonization of Asia and Africa, the European powers sought to use some portion of the population for labor. In the 16th to 20th century colonization of Australia and the Americas, the Indigenous peoples were treated differently as the intent to destroy entire groups was explicit and aggressively pursued (see Broome, 2002; UNESCO, 1980). Todorov (1984) estimated that tens of millions of Indigenous Americans were killed by Spanish colonization.

The Americas

There are few studies of contemporary sentiment regarding the genocide of the indigenous population of the Americas. In one study, Kurtiş, Adams, and Yellow Bird (2010, study 3) exposed 173 university students to manipulations of the salience of Native Americans and their genocide in a speech. Across all conditions (see Figure 2, case A), participants tended to disagree with reparations to Native Americans (e.g., "The US should establish a National Day of Apology to memorialize and atone for suffering inflicted upon Native Americans"). Making reference to the genocide of Native Americans did not increase agreement with reparation. Castano and Giner-Sorolla (2006, Study 3) presented 92 European Americans recruited on the internet with more and less violent accounts of European colonization of Native American land. In the more violent account, population decline was attributed to either intentional killing or disease.

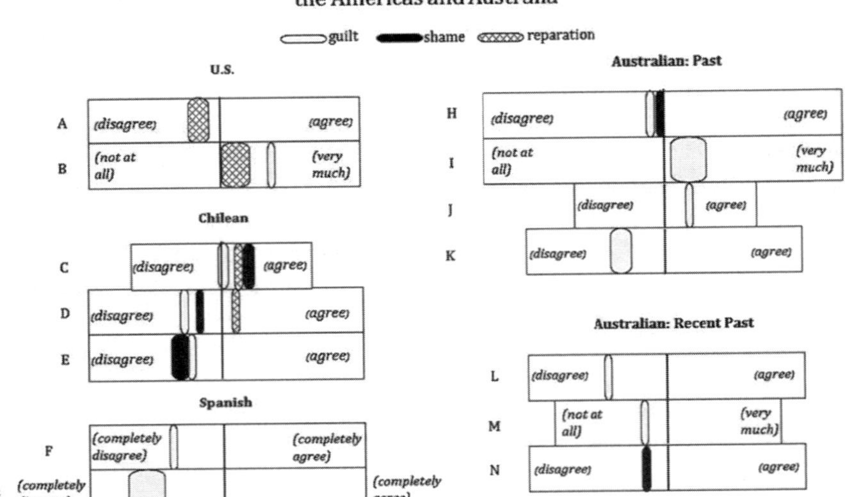

Fig. 2. Mean levels of self-criticism regarding past generations' mass violence. Each horizontal bar represents the range of the scale for a study. The dark vertical line in the middle of each bar represents the mid-point of the response scale. The width of the vertical marker within each bar represents the range of means obtained across conditions within a study.

Intentional killing led to high guilt, whereas death by disease or a less violent portrayal of colonization led to more moderate guilt. Support for material compensation to Native Americans was moderate (see Figure 2, case B). It is unclear why so much more guilt was expressed in Castano and Giner-Sorolla (2006) than in Kurtiş et al. (2010). However, it is worth noting that the only studies where we observed moderate self-criticism about the colonization of the Americas were those by Castano and Giner-Sorolla (2006), who did not allow participants to *disagree* that they felt guilt or shame. We return to this recurrent issue below.

Brown, Gonzalez, Zagefka, Manzi, and Čehajić (2008) asked samples of 124 (study 1) and 247 (study 2) nonindigenous secondary school students in Chile their views regarding past and present mistreatment of the Mapuche indigenous group. Guilt garnered neutral responses and there was slight agreement with shame in both samples (see Figure 2, case C). In a third study, 193 university students tended to disagree that they felt guilt or shame, but agreed with reparation (see Figure 2, case D). Manzi and Gonzalez (2007) produced similar results in another study in Chile (see Figure 2, case E).

In two studies, Fernández and Kurtiş (2012, unpublished data) presented university students in Spain with an ostensible newspaper article reporting that respected academics had concluded that Spain was responsible for "an important demographic catastrophe in which millions of natives died." Despite this near-genocidal framing, participants tended to disagree that they felt guilt (see Figure 2, case F and G). When the "demographic catastrophe" was not mentioned explicitly, participants disagreed even more strongly that they felt guilt about Spanish colonization of the Americas (see Figure 2, case G).

Australia

British colonization of Australia proceeded partly though declaring the land uninhabited because Indigenous people were classified as fauna. Aborigines and Torres Straits Islanders gained Australian citizenship only through referendum in 1967. In the more recent past, Indigenous peoples have suffered forced migration, forced sterilization, the removal of children from families, and multiple forms of "cultural genocide" (Broome, 2002). Some of these policies, only ended in the 1970s, were revived in 2007 in the Northern territory of Australia. To enact these policies the Australian government had to suspend its anti-discrimination law and the 1975 Racial Discrimination Act in the Northern territory. Thus, the past is very much present in the treatment of Indigenous people in Australia.

In 2008 Prime Minister Kevin Rudd offered the first federal apology for the national policy of removing Aboriginal children from their homes and placing them with white families or in institutions. Two days before, Allpress et al. (2010, study 1) asked 136 white Australian shoppers about the apology for the 1910–1970 policy. Agreement with the coming apology was moderate. However, participants slightly disagreed that they felt guilt or shame about their in-group's mistreatment of Aboriginal people (see Figure 2, case H). In Britain, Castano and Giner-Sorolla (2006, study 2) asked 57 university students about "what happened to the Aborigines as a consequence of British arrival on the Australian continent." In one condition "participants were told that the British were responsible for a dramatic decline in the number of Aborigines because of the diseases introduced by British settlers and their cattle and planned military campaigns they conducted against the Aborigines," whereas in the other condition colonization was presented more neutrally. Mentioning the features of genocide led to greater guilt about the past treatment of Aboriginals ($M = 5.65$, $SD = 1.02$) than the neutral description ($M = 5.05$, $SD = 1.41$). However, in both conditions, participants expressed only moderate guilt (see Figure 2, case I).

McGarty et al. (2005, study 2) presented 116 university students and older adults with a brief summary of the 19th century colonization of Australia: "it was considered acceptable for actions against Indigenous Australians that *would now be classified as genocide* to take place. Hostile treatment included the poisoning of waterholes and the active hunting of Indigenous Australians in many regions. Many of the actions that resulted in the deaths of Indigenous Australians throughout the 19th century followed directly from policies of the time" (emphasis added).

Participants somewhat agreed that they felt guilt and that they, and their country, should apologize (see Figure 2, case J). Participants tended to be neutral on the question of whether descendants should feel guilty about the acts of their ancestors. Importantly, those who most agreed that descendants are proxies for their ancestors reported the most guilt ($r = .63$) and agreement with apology ($r = .57$).

Several studies with nonstudent samples show less self-criticism among non-Indigenous Australians. For example, Pedersen, Beven, Walker, and Griffiths (2004) measured guilt about "past and present inequality" in two randomly selected samples in the city of Perth ($N = 122$ and 157). The average response in both samples was to somewhat disagree with feelings of guilt (see Figure 2, case K). In McGarty et al. (2005, Study 1) 163 Perth residents tended to somewhat disagree that they felt guilt about present and past treatment of Aboriginal people (see Figure 2, case L). Participants also tended to disagree with the notion of a federal apology to Aboriginal people. Leach, Iyer, and Pedersen (2006, Study 3) had local activists recruit 203 Perth residents concerned with social justice. Even this quite left-wing sample expressed modest feelings of guilt and responsibility (see Figure 2, case M). It is no surprise then that Leach et al. (2006, Study 1) found that 164 ordinary Perth residents tended to slightly disagree with the question, "I feel a sense of shame when I think of how non-Aborigines have treated Aborigines" (see Figure 2, case N).

20th Century Genocides

In addition to the mass violence of 20th century European colonization, a number of states pursued outright genocide against their own, or neighboring, ethnic, religious, and sexual minorities. The Nazi genocide is the best-known example, although we are not aware of many studies of contemporary German self-criticism comparable to those reviewed here. However, Dresler and Liu (2006) questioned 500 German university students about the Holocaust (see Figure 3, case A). Participants tended to slightly agree that they felt shame for "so many crimes against the Jews" and "what our grandparents did during the Third Reich." Thus, even in Germany, young people express little self-criticism about their country's genocide only fifty years after its end (see also Paez, Marques, Valencia, & Vincze, 2006).

The rapidity and scope of the killing in the 1994 genocide of Tutsis and moderate Hutus in Rwanda has been discussed in several contributions to this issue. In a remarkable study, Kanyangara, Rimé, Philippot, and Yzerbyt (2007) had fifty (mostly male) prisoners accused of genocide in Rwanda indicate their feelings about the trial 45 days before and after. The prisoners expressed moderate guilt and shame (see Figure 3, case B, C) and slightly higher sadness before their trial. Thus, even among those accused of perpetrating genocide, self-criticism is modest.

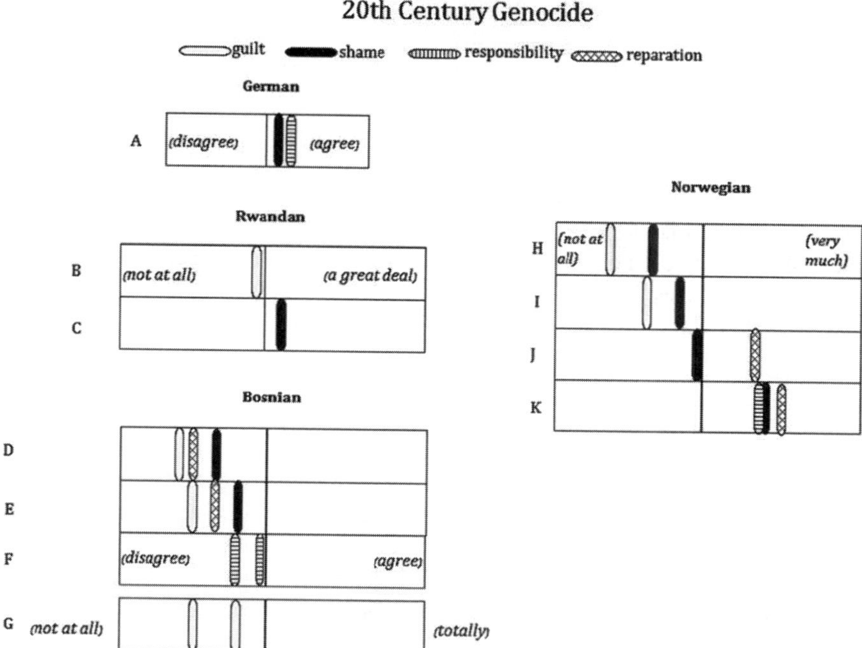

Fig. 3. Mean levels of self-criticism regarding past generations' mass violence. Each horizontal bar represents the range of the scale for a study. The dark vertical line in the middle of each bar represents the mid-point of the response scale. The width of the vertical marker within each bar represents the range of means obtained across conditions within a study.

Bosnia-Herzegovina

From 1992 to 1995, ethnic Serbs, Croats, and Bosniaks (Bosnian Muslims) fought for control of Bosnia-Herzegovina. The Serbs laid siege to the United Nations "safe havens" of Sarajevo and Srebrenica. In July 1995, Serbs massacred an estimated 8,000 Bosniak men and boys in Srebrenica. In February 2007, the International Court of Justice confirmed the Srebrenica massacre as genocide. Brown and Čehajić (2008, study 1) asked 173 Serb high school and university students about the 1992–1995 treatment of Bosniaks. They tended to strongly disagree that they felt guilt or shame about "past harmful actions," "human rights violations," and "how Serbs took away homes." They also tended to strongly disagree that Serbs should make reparations (see Figure 3, case D). In a second study, 247 Serb high school students also tended to disagree with self-criticism and reparation (see Figure 3, case E).

In a different approach, Čehajić, Brown, and Gonzalez (2009, study 2) asked 158 Serb high school students about Serbian responsibility for the "misdeeds" and "things that happened" from 1992 to 1995. In a control condition, participants tended to express mild disagreement with in-group responsibility (see Figure 3, case F). Those who read a brief interview of their peers discussing Serbs' responsibility for "atrocities" expressed slightly less disagreement with Serbian responsibility. In two studies in the Netherlands, Zebel et al. (2008) asked university students how much guilt they felt about the failure of Dutch peacekeepers to protect Bosniaks in Srebrenica. Guilt was low (the left most bar in Figure 3, case G). Even when this failure was presented in its most negative form, by portraying the Dutch as actively helping the Serbs's genocide, guilt remained fairly low (the right most bar in see Figure 3, case G).

Norway

Like many countries in northern Europe, Norway pursued eugenicist informed policies of genocide against its Romani (*Tater,* "gypsy") population well into the late 20th century. Indeed, official state mistreatment—forced sterilization, removal of children from families, forced labor, restricted movement—ended only in 1986. In 2001 and 2005 the Norwegian government admitted to these policies and to their purposeful destruction of all records, and offered monetary compensation to the victims (see Gausel, Leach, Vignoles, & Brown, 2012).

In a sample of 196 ethnic Norwegians in public places, Gausel and Brown (2012) found that those who were born after the state abuse ended (i.e., participants under 35) expressed little guilt and near moderate shame (see Figure 3, case H). Those over 35 expressed near moderate guilt and shame (see Figure 3, case I). In Gausel et al. (2012, study 1), 206 ethnic Norwegians were presented with an ostensible newspaper article describing the government's genocidal policies. In response, participants reported feeling moderate shame and somewhat stronger support for state restitution (see Figure 3, case J). Gausel et al. (2012, study 2) performed another study with 166 ethnic Norwegians. Here they presented the details of the genocide with a photo of a weeping Tater man recounting his forced sterilization. Participants reported somewhat strong shame, and blame of Norwegians, and slightly stronger support for state restitution (see Figure 3, case K). Thus, self-criticism for state genocide appeared to increase as the evidence for it became more detailed and more emotionally moving.

Discussion

Our review covered a wide range historically and geographically. In addition, studies varied a great deal on who was queried and how questions were asked. Despite this diversity, we can offer some general observations and interpretations. We must first note that explicit and strong self-criticism for past generations' genocide, or other mass violence, is a rarity in the studies we reviewed. In most cases, participants tended to *disagree* with self-critical sentiment when they were given the opportunity to do so. Some of the examples are surprising. Given the evidence, and its recency, one might expect more self-criticism about the Srebrenica massacre in Bosnia, Norway's genocidal policies against the Tatere, and the removal of Aboriginal children in Australia. Generally speaking, it seems most accurate to describe this literature as examining the *absence*, rather than the presence, of self-criticism for the in-group's mass violence (Leach, 2010a,b; see also Iyer & Leach, 2008; Leach et al., 2002). Although levels tended to be low, people expressed more self-criticism for their in-group's genocide or other mass violence when it (1) occurred in the more distant past, (2) was described more explicitly and movingly, and (3) was measured with a response scale whose lowest end-point was "0" and/or "not all" rather than some form of "disagree."

The More Distant Past

Surprisingly, people tended to express more self-criticism about older instances of genocide or mass violence (with the notable exception of Dutch colonization of Indonesia). Why should people feel worse about what their ancestors did centuries ago when the initial harm and on-going consequences of more recent violence should be more apparent? One possibility is that recent genocides are *too close* to the present day. The stronger temporal link to recent ancestors, perhaps even the generation of one's parents, may be enough to directly implicate those in the present day (see Gausel & Brown, 2012; Zebel et al., 2007). As such, people may have greater psychological, social, financial, and moral reasons to resist feeling connected to recent perpetrators. For example, those in the present day may fear that feeling connected to recent perpetrators will result in their own moral or financial responsibility to make reparation to victims (McGarty et al., 2005). More distant mass violence suggests less moral or financial cost in the present day.

Another possibility is that self-criticism about long past genocide may be more about individuals' association with their violent ancestors than their association with the violence itself. It is entirely possible that people in the present day feel bad and wish to make reparation because they believe that having genocidaires as ancestors taints their group's social image in the eyes of the world (see Allpress et al., 2010; Brown & Čehajić, 2008; Brown et al., 2008). Although people may use the term "shame" to express this concern for their group's social image, this is not genuine self-criticism. Thus, such reputation-oriented shame should do little to motivate effort for moral *self-improvement* (e.g., Allpress et al., 2010; Gausel et al., 2012; for a discussion, see Gausel & Leach, 2011).

Representing the Reprehensible

There is great variation in the form and style in which the mass violence was presented to participants in the studies reviewed. Most studies did not refer to the full set of acts that meet the technical definition of genocide. Some studies referred to mass killing and other violence directed at a national, ethnic, or religious group, whereas other studies referred to blocked fertility and physical displacement. Perhaps as a result, few studies referred to the term genocide in their communication with participants. Interestingly, those studies that presented participants with detailed and vivid information about actual genocides did appear to elicit more self-critical sentiment. This may be most readily observed in the set of studies conducted by Gausel and colleagues in Norway. Across four studies that used very similar materials, self-criticism appeared to increase as the description of the genocide was more detailed and vivid. The highest levels of self-criticism were obtained with a detailed description of the persecution of Tater that was accompanied by a photo of a man weeping as he recounted the story of his forced sterilization.

Although it makes sense that more moving materials are more moving, it is surprising how few studies accounted for this possibility (for discussions, see Iyer & Leach, 2008; Leach, 2010a). It is possible that the modest levels of self-criticism observed in many studies are due to pallid representations of the reprehensible. It is also possible that participants' modest self-criticism resulted from their pre-existing knowledge, beliefs, and feelings about the examples of genocide and mass violence examined. However vivid or moving a representation of the past may be, it is likely interpreted though an individual's pre-existing orientation to the issue. More studies must examine how pre-existing orientations guide individuals' responses to (little known or well known) examples of genocide and mass violence (for a discussion, see Leach, 2010a).

The Scale of Response

There was great variation in the response scales used to assess participants' degree of self-critical sentiment. Inspection of Figures 1 and 2 suggests that greater self-criticism was expressed when response scales began with an endpoint labeled as "none" or "not at all." Such response scales communicate to participants that some of the sentiment is expected by the researcher (for a review, see Schwarz, 1994). In contrast, response scales that range from "disagree" to "agree" communicate the researcher's expectation that participants may or may not have a particular opinion or feeling. Thus, disagree–agree scales more easily allow people to oppose the very idea that they should feel bad about what their group has done (for a discussion, see Leach, 2010a). When people were given the option to oppose the notion of moral self-criticism for their in-group's immorality they tended to do so. It seems likely then that studies that employ more restrictive response scales tend to exaggerate the degree of self-criticism reported. Future research would do well to take the communicative power of response scales into account, especially when examining a topic as morally loaded as mass violence.

Implications

Our main aim was to review *the degree* of self-critical sentiment about past generations' genocide and other mass violence. However, many studies examined possible explanations for the rarity of self-criticism that we observed. These explanations ran the gamut. Examples include the costs and rewards of colonization, the strength of national or other group identity, and the age of participants and their chronological link to events. However, of all of the explanations of the rarity of self-criticism, moral disengagement appears to be the most popular at present. Bandura (1999) identified a variety of strategies by which people disengage their behavior from the self-criticism that should typically follow from reprehensible acts such as genocide or other mass violence. These strategies work to either (1) frame actions as less unjust, (2) construe actions as causing little harm, or (3) frame victims as deserving of their treatment. Moral justification is a strategy of the first kind, as it provides a moral or practical reason for mistreatment. Dehumanization is a strategy of the third kind, as it renders victims deserving of mistreatment by portraying them as less human.

Many of the studies regarding colonization reviewed above provided evidence that participants engaged in moral justification and/or dehumanization. This is perhaps not surprising, given that the ideology and practice of colonization is based in part on both moral justification and dehumanization (Dirks, 1992; Todorov, 1984; UNESCO, 1980). As colonizers saw themselves as superior human beings, they had the "burden" of "taking care of" "inferior" subject populations. Thus, the death and destruction wrought by colonization could be justified by the "progress"—in infrastructure, education, medicine—it brought to an otherwise "backward" people. It is to this supposedly mixed legacy of colonization that many participants seemed to refer when asked to reflect on their country's colonization of others. By viewing colonization as a morally justified sacrifice of sub-humans to achieve progress, those in the present day can disengage past perpetration from present moral standards against genocide and mass violence.

There is little doubt that people sometimes use strategies of moral disengagement when facing past generations' genocide or other mass violence. However, the process of moral disengagement assumes that individuals view their ancestors' violence as morally reprehensible and thus disengage their moral standards to avoid the moral self-criticism that would otherwise follow (Leach, 2010b). This assumption seems questionable given that few people today actually view their ancestors as committing genocide or other morally reprehensible violence. Given the degree to which individuals are invested in viewing their in-groups as moral (Leach, Ellemers, & Barreto, 2007), individuals rarely consider the possibility that an in-group has acted immorally. Thus, rather than justifying past immorality to protect present self-image, people may not perceive an immorality in the first place. By projecting into the past the present image of the in-group as moral, individuals may prophylactically prevent moral self-criticism. If one's group is moral, then it is moral in the past, present, and future; it is moral immemorial. Leach (2010b) recently described this phenomenon as a "pre hoc" moral *mis-engagement* whereby evaluation of the in-group as moral in general guides the construal of particular group actions such that they are rarely viewed as immoral. He contrasted this pre hoc affirmation of the (individual and group) self to the post hoc defense proposed in the notion of moral disengagement.

There are few failures that threaten people's self-concept, as individuals or as group members, more than moral failures. And, there are few moral failures worse than genocide or other forms of mass violence. Thus, it is not surprising that so few people recognize past generations' mass violence or see themselves as implicated in it. It feels better to recognize, and share in, past generations' triumphs than tragedies. It feels better to be moral immemorial. Nevertheless, there are those who choose a more balanced view of the past and thereby choose to view their group's legacy critically. Where self-integrity is secure (e.g., Čehajić, Effron, Halperin, Liberman, & Ross, 2011), or where self-improvement is more important than self-defense (Gausel & Leach, 2011), individuals may *morally engage* in past generations' wrongdoing. Perhaps moral engagement of past perpetration serves as preparation for future prevention? This is an important question for future research.

References

Allpress, J. A., Barlow, F. K., Brown, R., & Louis, W. R. (2010). Atoning for colonial injustices: Group-based shame and guilt motivate support for reparation. *International Journal of Conflict and Violence, 4*, 75–88. Retrieved from www.ijcv.org.

Bandura, A. (1999). Moral disengagement in the perpetration of inhumanities. *Personality and Social Psychology Review, 3*, 193–209. doi: 10.1207/s15327957pspr0303.

Branscombe, N. R., & Doosje, B. E. J. (Eds.). (2004). *Collective guilt: International perspectives.* New York, NY: Cambridge University Press.

Brooks, R. (1999). *When sorry isn't enough: The controversy over apologies and reparations for human injustice.* New York, NY: New York University.

Broome, R. (2002). *Aboriginal Australians: Black responses to White dominance*, 1788–2001 (3rd ed.). Crows Nest, Australia: Allen & Unwin.

Brown, R., & Čehajić, S. (2008). Dealing with the past and facing the future: Mediators of the effects of collective guilt and shame in Bosnia and Herzegovina. *European Journal of Social Psychology, 38*, 669–684. doi: 10.1002/ejsp.466.

Brown, R., Gonzalez, R., Zagefka, H., Manzi, J., & Čehajić, S. (2008). Nuestra culpa: Collective guilt and shame as predictors of reparation for historical wrongdoing. *Journal of Personality and Social Psychology, 94*, 75–90. doi: 10.1037/0022-3514.94.1.75.

Cabecinhas, R., & Feijó, J. (2010). Collective memories of Portuguese colonial action in Africa: Representations of the colonial past among Mozambicans and Portuguese Youths. *International Journal of Conflict and Violence, 4*, 28–44. Retrieved from www.ijcv.org/.

Castano, E., & Giner-Sorolla, R. (2006). Not quite human: Infrahumanization in response to collective responsibility for intergroup killing. *Journal of Personality and Social Psychology, 90*, 804–818. doi: 10.1037/0022–3514.90.5.804.

Čehajić, S., Brown, R., & Gonzalez, R. (2009). What do I care? Perceived ingroup responsibility and dehumanization as predictors of empathy felt for the victim group. *Group Processes and Intergroup Relations, 12*, 715–729. doi: 10.1177/1368430209347727.

Čehajić, S., Effron, D., Halperin, E., Liberman, V., & Ross, L. (2011). Affirmation, acknowledgment of ingroup responsibility, group-based guilt, and support for reparative measures. *Journal of Personality and Social Psychology, 101*, 256–270. doi: 10.1037/a0023936.

Dirks, N. B. (Ed.). (1992). *Colonialism and culture.* Ann Arbor, MI: The University of Michigan.

Doosje, B. E. J., Branscombe, N. R., Spears, R., & Manstead, A. S. R. (1998). Guilty by association: When one's group has a negative history. *Journal of Personality and Social Psychology, 75*, 872–886. doi: 10.1037/0022–3514.75.4.872.

Doosje, B. E. J., Branscombe, N. R., Spears, R., & Manstead, A. S. R. (2006). Antecedents and consequences of group-based guilt: The effects of ingroup identification. *Group Processes and Intergroup Relations, 9*, 325–338. doi: 10.1177/1368430206064637.

Dresler-Hawke, E., & Liu, J. H. (2006). Collective shame and the positioning of German national identity. *Psicologia Politica, 32*, 131–153. Retrieved from www.uv.es/garzon/psicologia%20politica/N32–7.pdf.

Figueiredo, A., Doosje, B. E. J., Valentim, J. P., & Zebel, S. (2010). Dealing with past colonial conflicts: How perceived characteristics of the victimized outgroup can influence the experience of group-based guilt. *International Journal of Conflict and Violence, 4*, 89–105. Retrieved from http://www.ijcv.org/index.php/ijcv/article/view/64/189

Gausel, N., & Brown, R. J. (2012). Shame and guilt–Do they really differ in their focus of evaluation? Wanting to change the self and behavior in response to ingroup immorality. *The Journal of Social Psychology, 152*, 547–567. doi: 10.1080/00224545.2012.657265.

Gausel, N., & Leach, C. W. (2011). Concern for self-image and social-image in the management of moral failure: Rethinking shame. *European Journal of Social Psychology, 41*, 468–478. doi: 10.1002/ejsp.803.

Gausel, N., Leach, C. W., Vignoles, V. L., & Brown, R. J. (2012). Defend or repair? Explaining responses to in-group moral failure by disentangling feelings of shame, rejection, and inferiority. *Journal of Personality and Social Psychology, 102*, 941–960. doi: 10.1037/a0027233.

Iyer, A., & Leach, C. W. (2008). Emotion in inter-group relations. *European Review of Social Psychology, 19*, 86–125. doi: 10.1080/10463280802079738.

Kanyangara, P., Rimé, B., Philippot, P., & Yzerbyt, V. (2007). Collective rituals, emotional climate and intergroup perception: Participation in "Gacaca" tribunals and assimilation of the Rwandan genocide. *Journal of Social Issues, 63*, 387–403. doi: 10.1111/j.1540–4560.2007.00515.x.

Kurtis, T., Adams, G., & Yellow Bird, M. (2010). Generosity or genocide? Identity implications of silence in American Thanksgiving commemorations. *Memory, 18*, 208–224. doi: 10.1080/09658210903176478.

Leach, C. W. (2010a). The person in political emotion. *Journal of Personality, 78*, 1827–1859. doi: 10.1111/j.1467–6494.2010.00671.x.

Leach, C. W. (2010b). *Moral mis-engagement: How moral self-evaluation leads to injustice.* Paper presented at the Small Group Meeting: Forgotten Alternatives: Denaturalizing Conditions of Injustice and Exclusion, City University of New York Graduate Center, New York, NY.

Leach, C. W., Ellemers, N., & Barreto, M. (2007). Group virtue: The importance of morality (vs. competence and sociability) in the positive evaluation of in-groups. *Journal of Personality and Social Psychology, 93*, 234–249. doi: 10.1037/0022–3514.93.2.234

Leach, C. W., Iyer, A., & Pedersen, A. (2006). Anger and guilt about in-group advantage explain the willingness for political action. *Personality and Social Psychology Bulletin, 32*, 1232–1245. doi: 10.1177/0146167206289729

Leach, C. W., Snider, N., & Iyer, A. (2002). "Poisoning the consciences of the fortunate": The experience of relative advantage and support for social equality. In I. Walker & H. J. Smith (Eds.), *Relative deprivation: Specification, development, and integration* (pp. 136–163). New York, NY: Cambridge University Press.

Lemkin, R. (1944). *Axis rule in occupied Europe: Laws of occupation—analysis of government—proposals for redress*. Washington, DC: Carnegie Endowment for International Peace.

Leone, G., & Mastrovito, T. (2010). Learning about our shameful past: A socio-psychological analysis of present-day historical narratives of Italian colonial wars. *International Journal of Conflict and Violence, 4*, 11–27. Retrieved from ijcv.org/.

Licata, L., & Klein, O. (2010). Holocaust or benevolent paternalism? Intergenerational comparisons on collective memories and emotions about Belgium's colonial past. *International Journal of Conflict and Violence, 4*, 45–57. Retrieved from http://www.ijcv.org/index.php/ijcv/article/view/60/186.

McGarty, C., Pedersen, A., Leach, C. W., Mansell, T., Waller, J., & Bliuc, A. (2005). Group-based guilt as a predictor of commitment to apology. *British Journal of Social Psychology, 44*, 659–680. doi: 10.1348/014466604×18974.

Minow, M. (1998). *Between vengeance and forgiveness: Facing history after genocide and mass violence*. Boston, MA: Beacon Press.

Morton, T. A., & Postmes, T. (2010). Moral duty or moral defence? The effects of perceiving shared humanity with the victims of ingroup perpetrated harm. *European Journal of Social Psychology, 40*, 1–12. doi: 10.1002/ejsp.751.

Páez, D., Marques, J., Valencia, J., & Vincze, O. (2006). Dealing with collective shame and guilt. *Psicología Política, 32*, 59–78. Retrieved from http://www.europhd.eu/html/_onda02/07/PDF/12th_lab_scientificmaterial/valencia/collectiveshame.pdf.

Pedersen, A., Beven, J., Walker, I., & Griffiths, B. (2004). Attitudes toward indigenous Australians: The role of empathy and guilt. *Journal of Community and Applied Social Psychology, 14*, 233–249. doi: 10.1002/casp.77.

Todorov, T. (1984). *The conquest of America: The question of the other*. (R. Howard, Trans.). New York, NY: Harper Row.

United Nations Educational, Scientific, and Cultural Organization (Ed.). (1980). *Sociological Theories of Race and Colonialism*. Paris, France: UNESCO.

Zebel, S., Pennekamp, S. F., van Zomeren, M., Doosje, B. E. J., van Kleef, G. A., Vliek, M. L. W., & van der Schalk, J. (2007). Vessels with gold or guilt: Emotional reactions to family involvement associated with glorious or gloomy aspects of the colonial past. *Group Processes and Intergroup Relations, 10*, 71–86. doi: 10.1177/1368430207071342.

Zebel, S., Zimmermann, A., Viki, G. T., & Doosje, B. E. J. (2008). Dehumanization and guilt as distinct but related predictors of support for reparation policies. *Political Psychology, 29*, 193–219. doi: 10.1111/j.1467–9221.2008.00623.

COLIN WAYNE LEACH received BA in 1989, MA in 1991 from Boston University, and PhD in 1995 from University of Michigan. He is Professor of Psychology at the University of Connecticut. Colin's research examines status and morality in self-evaluation, emotion, and social relations.

FOUAD BOU ZEINEDDINE received BA in 2009, MA in 2010 from Clark University, also MA in 2012 from University of Connecticut. He is a graduate student in social psychology at the University of Connecticut. His research is mainly concerned with morality, power dynamics, and political engagement in international relations.

SABINA ČEHAJIĆ-CLANCY received BA in 2003 from University of Sarajevo; MSc in 2005, PhD in 2008 from University of Sussex. She is an assistant professor of political psychology at the Sarajevo School of Science and Technology. Her current research focus is on moral engagements with collective atrocities.

Journal of Social Issues, Vol. 69, No. 1, 2013, pp. 54–73

Thou Shall Not Kill . . . Your Brother: Victim−Perpetrator Cultural Closeness and Moral Disapproval of Polish Atrocities against Jews after the Holocaust

Miroslaw Kofta*
University of Warsaw

Patrycja Slawuta
New School for Social Research

This paper addresses the role of collective memory of post-Holocaust crimes in contemporary Polish−Jewish relations. We examined how reminding Polish participants of ingroup atrocities affects constructive as well as destructive attitudes and behavioral intentions toward the Jewish victim group. We address the question of how experimentally induced feelings of cultural closeness between the outgroup and the ingroup modify the effects of these reminders on intergroup relations. Our two experiments suggest that perceived sharing of culture is a crucial factor in dealing constructively with the "problematic past" in intergroup relations. In the baseline condition (where cultural closeness of Jews and Poles was not made salient), reminders of ingroup atrocities activated group-defensive strategies, resulting in more negative intergroup attitudes and dehumanization of Jews. In stark contrast, in the "culturally close" condition (where feelings of shared culture were induced), reminders of ingroup atrocities actually resulted in more positive intergroup attitudes and humanization of Jews.

Although the moral commandment "thou shall not kill" seems to be present in most major religions and civilizations, there are few ethnic, religious, or national

*Correspondence concerning this article should be addressed to Miroslaw Kofta, Faculty of Psychology, University of Warsaw, Stawki 5/7, 00-183 Warszawa, Poland [e-mail: kofta@psych.uw.edu.pl].

This research was supported by grants from the Polish Ministry of Science and Higher Education, N N106 0886 33 "Psychological Threat and Intergroup Relations," and Statutory Research Grant BST from the Psychology Faculty, University of Warsaw. PS would like to acknowledge linguistic help and support of her husband Edward Loh. Moreover, special thanks are due to two proofreaders of earlier versions of this paper, Agnieszka and Miroslaw Kowaluk.*

groups that have not committed injustices against another group. It seems easy to condemn members of other groups that inflicted unjustified harm; it becomes more uncomfortable as the responsibility for moral violations moves closer to home—when it is the ingroup that has killed.

Recognizing that members of one's own group engaged in unjust or cruel behavior can be painful, as it can tarnish the ingroup's positive image (Doosje, Brandscombe, Spears, & Manstead, 1998) and prompt efforts to defend the ingroup's integrity by derogating the victim group (Branscombe, Schmitt, & Schiffhauer, 2007). On the other hand, the disparity between perceived ingroup morality and actual immoral behaviors may evoke moral emotions motivating ingroup members to amend previous wrongs through apologies or reparations (Doosje et al., 1998; Powell, Branscombe, & Schmitt, 2005). However, acknowledgement of ingroup misdeeds occurs infrequently (see Leach, Bou Zeineddine, & Čehajić-Clancy, 2013). As Israeli psychoanalyst Zvi Rex insightfully noted, "The Germans will never forgive the Jews for Auschwitz." Reminders of ingroup atrocities may invoke defensive feelings that can contribute to negative attitudes toward the victims (Imhoff & Banse, 2009).

Therefore, collective responsibility for past wrongdoings has critical implications for postgenocidal societies (e.g., Turkey, former Yugoslavia, Rwanda) where memories of past atrocities are abiding and impede intergroup reconciliation. Psychological research has demonstrated that when people are reminded of ingroup inflicted harm, a number of negative reactions may occur. Those effects range from denial of the ingroup's negative behavior (Cohen, 2001), legitimization of the ingroup's actions (Dresler-Hawke, 2005; Wohl, Branscombe, & Klar, 2006) to dehumanization of the victims (Bandura, 1999; Castano & Giner-Sorolla, 2006). In this context, dehumanization is particularly dangerous as it may subsequently serve as an excuse for lesser justice for those who suffered (Leidner, Castano, Zaiser & Giner-Sorolla, 2010). All these findings reveal how difficult is the task of fostering reconciliation and building positive intergroup relations after a traumatic past.

Given the importance of reconciliation, in the present research we investigated how induced "cultural closeness" (understood as shared beliefs, norms, and values) influences responses to reminders of ingroup crime. The role of shared culture as a potentially critical precondition of positive intergroup relations has already been stressed by Milton Rokeach (1960) in his belief congruence theory. However, while some studies supported his predictions that high congruence of in- and outgroup beliefs should improve intergroup relations, in other studies high intergroup similarity resulted in more discrimination of the outgroup (e.g., Diehl, 1988). Our claim is, however, that perceptions of shared culture with the outgroup might substantially improve intergroup relations given that the moral context of ingroup behavior is invoked.

We hypothesize that when perceived cultural closeness of the victim group is high, reminders of the ingroup's moral transgressions will lead to moral disapproval of one's group, accompanied by positive changes in attitudes toward the victim group. This effect will be driven by the victims' inclusion into a moral community with the ingroup. However, when perceived cultural closeness of the victim group is low, reminders of the same transgressions—rather than promoting moral disapproval of the ingroup—will give rise to group-defensive processes. This will subsequently result in the inhibition of moral emotions and increased prejudice toward the victimized group. Under these circumstances, the victim group is likely to be excluded from the ingroup's moral community.

Several lines of research support our reasoning, albeit indirectly. For instance, including members of the perpetrator and victim groups into a shared category increases the perpetrator group's collective guilt and compensation efforts in response to reminders of the crime (Wohl & Branscombe, 2005). Presumably, an inclusive categorization makes members of the victim group more psychologically close and more human (e.g., Gaunt, 2009). In response, empathy and the desire to rectify previous group-based harms are likely to emerge. Additionally, including outgroup members into the self is associated with an increased perception of closeness between "us" and "them." This, in turn, improves general outgroup attitudes (e.g., increases empathy for outgroup problems: Aron & McLaughlin-Volpe, 2001).

However, the effects of perceived cultural closeness between "them" (victims) and "us" (perpetrators) cannot be reduced to recategorization (Gaertner et al., 2000) or self-expansion (Aron & McLaughlin-Volpe, 2001) processes alone. In the context of ingroup misdeeds, closeness to victims should lead to their inclusion into the moral community with the (perpetrating) ingroup, whereas low closeness should do the reverse. When belonging to a moral community (e.g., Opotow, 1990, 2008; Staub, 1990), people feel responsible for each other's fate, are empathetic, respond emotionally to unjust or otherwise immoral treatment, and are ready to engage in helping as well as compensation activities. They also expect reciprocity from others. The opposite occurs when one is excluded from the moral community—in which case moral rules of conduct and the scope of justice no longer apply to this group (Opotow, 1990; 2008; Staub, 1990).

Assuming that perceived cultural closeness between "us" (the perpetrators) and "them" (the victims) results in the inclusion of the victims into the moral community, we hypothesize that, under these circumstances, reminders of ingroup crimes will lead to acceptance of group responsibility and evoke strong moral disapproval of the ingroup's actions, accompanied by the motivation to compensate wrongs and improve relations with the victim group. However, when cultural closeness between "us" and "them" is perceived to be low, the victim group is likely to be excluded from the moral community. In these circumstances, reminders of ingroup crimes will arouse group-defensive strategies resulting in increased prejudice toward and dehumanization of the victim group.

One may argue that perception of low cultural closeness is the default when people are reminded of ingroup moral transgressions. As recent research shows, in such instances reminders of ingroup crimes stimulate group-protective mechanisms, including explicit dehumanization where the victim group is perceived as exhibiting a backward culture that lacks moral values (Leidner et al., 2010).

Similar to other moral disengagement strategies, dehumanization can both contribute to intergroup conflict and justify ongoing violence (Bandura, 1999; Castano & Giner-Sorolla, 2006; Castano & Kofta, 2009). This mechanism allows the perpetrator group to create a version of reality that is not morally reprehensible and thus does not lead to self-sanctions (Bandura, 1999). The role of dehumanization in the maintenance of the perpetrator group's moral integrity has received empirical support through a series of studies where people presented with atrocities committed by their group attributed less uniquely human emotions to the victims (Castano & Giner-Sorolla, 2006). Perceiving victims as "not fully human" is an important pillar of intergroup violence. However, since blatant outgroup dehumanization occurs rarely, in our studies we measured victim dehumanization with a more subtle measure that detects both dehumanization and humanization of the outgroup (Leyens et al., 2000).

Dehumanization may be manifested in infrahumanization, i.e., in a reduced tendency to ascribe specifically human traits (such as secondary emotions, sophisticated intellect, creativity) to outgroup members (e.g., Leyens et al., 2000), or in dementalization, i.e., denying inner life to outgroup members (questioning that they are able to experience mental states such as emotions, intentions, thoughts, imaginations, etc.; see Harris & Fiske, 2009; Kozak, Marsh, & Wegner, 2006). With respect to our research, even tangential inclusion of outgroup members into the moral community should lead to their humanization, whereas moral exclusion should be associated with their dehumanization. It remains to be tested which aspect of dehumanization would be more salient in this process: infrahumanization or dementalization.

The context for the present studies is Polish–Jewish relations after the Holocaust. Until World War II, Jews made up approximately 10% of the Polish population. Today, the number is only about 5,000. As in most multiethnic countries, the relationship between the two groups was turbulent at times, with periods of peace and prosperity punctuated by periods of fear and violence caused by anti-Jewish pogroms. With that said, there was a high level of cultural assimilation of Polish Jews. They permeated most of society, including the local and national governments (Krajewski, 2005). The Second World War and Nazi-led Holocaust brought an abrupt end to the population of three million Jews living in Poland. Few Jews survived the Holocaust and most of those who did either emigrated to the United States, Israel, or other countries, leaving behind abandoned synagogues and cemeteries.

In the present studies, our material is based on reports of Polish historians on one of the worst times in Polish—Jewish history. Just after World War II, some Polish Jews who survived the Holocaust attempted to return to their homes and frequently faced strong anti-Semitism and overt violence (pogroms), resulting in approximately 1,500 Jews being killed (Gross, 2001). These facts have created a nation-wide and still ongoing debate on the role of Poles in the Holocaust. The existence of "Anti-Semitism without Jews" in today's Poland, which manifests itself in a variety of conspiracy theories, may stem from the fact that the painful past has not yet been embraced (Krzeminski, 2004).

Overview of the Present Studies

We conducted two experiments to test how perceived cultural closeness between the perpetrator and the victim group affects reactions to reminders of ingroup atrocities. Both variables were experimentally manipulated. We measured the effects of these treatments on a number of measures that can be categorized as constructive (e.g., compensation) or destructive intergroup attitudes (e.g., dehumanization of the victim group). We expected that in the cultural closeness condition, the crime reminder would increase constructive outcomes toward the victim group and moral disapproval of the perpetrators. Opposite effects of the crime reminder were expected when cultural similarity was not made salient.

Study 1

Method

Sample.   The study was conducted among 71 female and 35 male students of Warsaw University (age: $M = 19.8$, range 19–25). The participants volunteered to take part in the research and were recruited at the beginning of their classes. Participants were students of sociology, law, European studies, and mathematics.

Design and procedure.   To prime Polish national identity, in all conditions participants were first asked if they agreed or not that, in general, the Polish nation is similar to other nations of the European Union. Participants were then randomly assigned to one of the three conditions: (1) baseline (no crime reminder), (2) reminder of Polish crimes against Jews, (3) crime reminder plus induced cultural closeness condition.

Participants in both experimental conditions were presented with an excerpt of an article published by the Polish Institute of National Memory, an accomplished historical research institute in Poland. The article described historical accounts of anti-Jewish atrocities in postwar Poland, including the Kielce pogrom in 1946 where 42 Jewish Holocaust survivors were killed by a Polish mob. The article ended by stating that such anti-Semitic acts led to a massive exodus of Jews from Poland.

After reading the article, participants in the crime plus cultural closeness condition read a paragraph about "new and surprising results" of survey studies on values and habits of people from the European Union and Israel. These fictitious studies described Poles and Israeli Jews as the two most similar nations (in terms of values, norms, and life style), indicating their high cultural closeness. Participants then completed the measures presented below, were asked for demographic information, thanked, and debriefed.

Measures

Manipulation check.　　A five-item scale ($\alpha = .91$) of perceived similarity between Poles and Jews (end of questionnaire) served as a manipulation check. Sample items, with answers ranging from 1 (*No, I don't*) to 7 (*Yes, I do*), included: "*In general, do you feel similar to Jews?*" and "*Do you think you have common interests with Jews?*"

Collective guilt.　　After reading the article, participants in both experimental conditions were asked to assess the intensity of any guilt, remorse, and regret they may have experienced while reading the account. This composite measure of three guilt-related emotions ($\alpha = .84$) was adapted from previously used similar scales (see Iyer, Schmader, & Lickel, 2007). The answer format ranged from *1* (*not at all*) to *7* (*very intensely*).

Attitudes toward Jews: Interest in Jewish tradition.　　Interest in Jewish culture and history was measured with five items ($\alpha = .91$), with answers ranging from 1 (I completely disagree) to 7 (I completely agree): "I would like to learn more about Jewish history in Poland," "I would like to learn more about Jewish traditions (e.g. religious)," "I would like to learn more about the history of the state of Israel," "I would like to learn more about the life of modern day Polish-Jews" and "I would like to learn more about the cultural heritage left behind by the Polish Jews."

Desire for contact.　　Participants were asked about their interest in interacting with young Jews who either belong to the Polish–Jewish community or came to Poland for March of the Living. Eight items ($\alpha = .89$) were used, with answers ranging from 1 (*I completely disagree*) to 7 (*I completely agree*): "*I would like to meet members of the Jewish community in Poland,*" "*I am curious how*

Jews spend their free time," "I would agree to be a guide for a Jewish person visiting Warsaw," "I wouldn't mind if Jews lived in my building," "I would like to do something together with Jewish people, e.g. go kayaking," "I would like to have a Jewish pen pal," "I would like to have the opportunity to meet with young Jews visiting Poland and chat with them about the issues young people face (such as finding an apartment)," and finally "I wouldn't mind if there were Jews in my university lab courses."

Financial compensation to the Jewish community. As part of a fictional program helping victims of the Second World War, participants were asked to distribute 100 million Euros, which the European Union had allegedly given Poland, among six ethnic groups (Poles, Ukrainians, Jews, Germans, Russians, and Lithuanians), keeping in mind that prewar Poland had several ethnic minorities. To evaluate *ingroup bias* in financial compensation, the difference between financial compensation to Poles and to Jews was calculated.

Belief in Jewish conspiracy. Participants indicated their agreement with six statements addressing a naïve conspiracy theory about Jews ($\alpha = .88$), including *"Members of this group aim to control the world economy"* and *"Members of this group achieve their collective goals by secret agreements"* (see Kofta & Sędek, 2005). All items were answered on a scale ranging from 1 (*I completely disagree*) to 5 (*I fully agree*).

(De)humanization measures: Attributing emotions to victims' families. Participants were presented with 12 negative emotion terms, based on earlier research among a Polish sample (Mirosławska & Kofta, 2007). Six were primary emotions common to humans and animals: terror, anger, fear, suffering, fury, irritation, and six were uniquely human secondary emotions: despair, shame, guilt, disappointment, melancholy, and quandary. Each item was answered on a 9-point rating scale in response to the question: *"To what extent do you think that the pogrom victims' family members felt this emotion when they were informed about the deaths?"*

Attributing emotions to Israeli Jews and to Poles. Participants were asked to ascribe the tendency to experience primary and secondary emotions among present-day Israeli Jews and Poles. Six primary emotions and six secondary emotions were assessed, half of which were positive (e.g., pleasure, admiration) and half negative (e.g., fear, melancholy). This procedure allows us to construct (a) a measure of a general emotional sensitivity of the group, expressed in the attribution of emotions regardless of their quality and positivity—negativity dimension (when low, an important aspect of dementalization could be diagnosed), and (b) a measure of preferential attribution of specifically human, secondary emotions (when higher among ingroup than outgroup members, it allows to infer infrahumanization).

Table 1. Study 1: Effects of Crime Reminder and Cultural Closeness on Attitudes Toward Jews

Condition	Interest in Jewish tradition M (SD)	Desire for contacting Jews M (SD)	Compensation to Jews M (SD)	Compensation to Poles minus to Jews M (SD)	Belief in Jewish conspiracy M (SD)
Baseline	5.00_a (1.24)	5.02_a (1.07)	26.5_a (12.1)	6.8_a (11.0)	2.86_a (.86)
Crime	4.72_a (1.37)	4.36_b (1.21)	20.5_b (10.0)	15.4_a (11.2)	3.70_b (.81)
Crime + high closeness	5.79_b (.87)	5.97_c (1.51)	25.7_a (11.1)	4.4_b (8.2)	2.93_a (.83)
F for the main effect	8.13^{***}	14.09^{***}	$2.97^{\#}$	$2.71^{\#}$	10.99^{***}
Partial η^2	.14	.21	.05	.05	.18

$^{a\#}p < .10;\ ^{***}p < .001.$

Note 1. For testing the significance of differences between means, the *post hoc* least-squares differences test was applied. Means in columns differing at $p < .05$ are signed with different letters.

Note 2. Compensation to Poles—compensation to Jews is an ingroup favoritism index (the higher the number, the greater the ingroup favoritism in financial compensation).

Results

Manipulation Check

Those exposed to the crime reminder and induced cultural closeness perceived Jews and Poles as more similar ($M = 4.08$, $SD = .55$) than those in the baseline condition ($M = 3.22$, SD $= .69$) did, F (1, 70) $= 34.07$, $p < .001$, partial $\eta^2 = .33$, or the condition exposed to the crime reminder alone ($M = 3.06$, $SD = .71$), F (1, 103) $= 43.16$, $p < .001$, partial $\eta^2 = .40$. This confirms the effectiveness of the manipulation.

Collective Guilt

Compared to the crime-only condition ($M = 2.88$, $SD = 1.10$), in the condition with crime and induced closeness collective guilt was much higher ($M = 5.02$, $SD = 1.19$), F (1, 69) $= 65.21$, $p < .001$, partial $\eta^2 = .49$. Contrasts with the baseline conditions were not computed because this group had not received a description of ingroup crimes.

Attitudes toward Jews.   A one-way MANOVA yielded a significant main effect of the experimental treatment on the attitudinal measures, Rao's R (10, 198) $= 5.03$, $p < .001$, partial $\eta^2 = .20$. Univariate analyses (see Table 1) revealed that reminders of ingroup crime alone significantly decreased the need for contact with Jews as well as the readiness to provide compensation to the Jewish community, while also increasing the acceptance of Jewish conspiracy beliefs. However, when the crime reminder was accompanied by induced cultural closeness, participants showed more willingness for contact with Jews, increased interest in Jewish tradition, and lower ingroup bias in financial compensation, compared to the other two conditions. Compared to the condition in which participants were only reminded of the ingroup crime, participants in the crime reminder *plus* induced closeness condition were also more likely to favor financial compensation to Jews and less likely to endorse Jewish conspiracy theories.

(De)humanization

Emotions of victims' families. The analyses were performed only within the crime conditions. Perceived cultural closeness increased ascription of secondary emotions to the victims' families, F (1, 69) = 6.84, p = .011, partial η^2 = .09 (M = 4.79, SD = .87 in the crime reminder plus induced closeness condition; M = 4.18, SD = 1.21 in the crime reminder alone condition), whereas ascription of primary emotions remained unaffected by the closeness manipulation, F < 1(M = 5.83, SD = 1.00 vs. M = 6.02, SD = .66).

Emotions of Israeli Jews and Poles. To further examine the (de)humanization processes, a three-way ANOVA on emotions ascribed to present-day Israeli Jews and to Poles was conducted in a 3 (treatment: baseline vs. crime vs. crime plus closeness) × 2 (target: Jews vs. Poles) × 2 (emotions: primary vs. secondary) factorial design. In addition to a significant main effect of type of emotion, F (1, 103) = 8.18, p = .006, partial η^2 = .07, such that more primary emotions were ascribed (M = 4.70, SD = 1.05) than secondary emotions (M = 4.57, SD = 1.05), this analysis also showed the expected two-way Treatment × Target interaction, F (2, 103) = 15.42, p < .001, partial η^2 = .23 (see Figure 1). Simple main effects analysis failed to show the effects of treatment for the Polish targets, F < 1. However, there was an effect for Israeli Jews, F (2, 103) = 8.29, p < .001, partial η^2 = .14. The effect was due to a significant increase of Jews' perceived general emotional sensitivity (i.e., overall increase in emotion ascription regardless of their kind) in the crime plus high closeness condition both in relation to the baseline, F (1, 70) = 6.59, p = .012, *partial* η^2 = .09, and to the crime alone condition, F (1, 169) = 17.24, p < .001, partial η^2 = .18. Thus, we found that inducing cultural closeness led to the humanization of Israeli Jews on the mentalization dimension. There were no significant effects attributable to the (infra)humanization dimension.

Mediation analysis. Mediation analysis (Baron & Kenny, 1986) revealed that the relationship between perceived cultural closeness and ascription of secondary emotions to the victims' families was mediated by collective guilt. After controlling for the effects of the mediator (Sobel's z = 3.03, p = .003), the

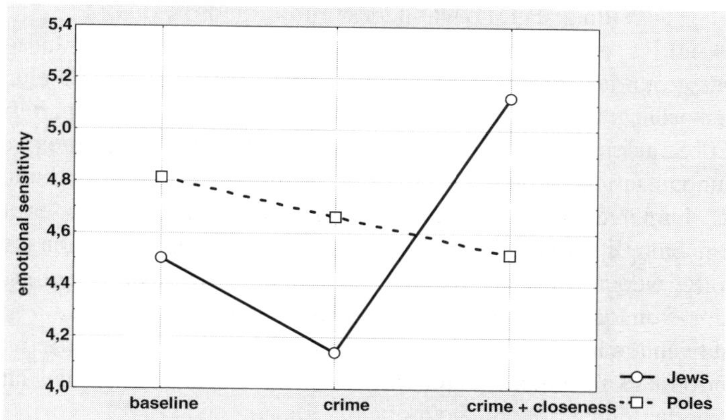

Fig. 1. Study 1: Effects of crime reminder and induced cultural closeness on general emotional sensitivity.

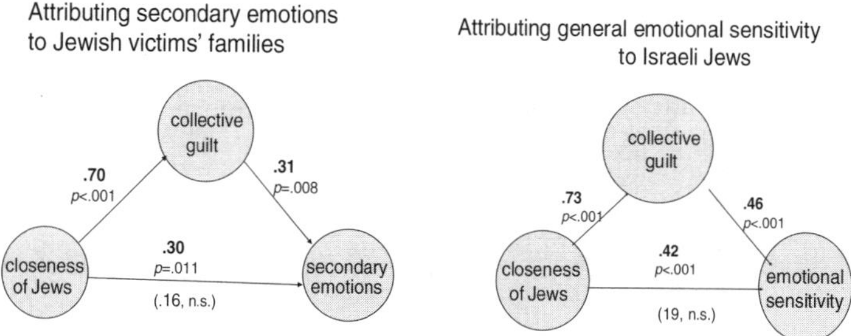

Fig. 2. Study1: Collective guilt as a mediator of the effects of perceived cultural closeness between Jews and Poles on humanization of Jews (standardized Betas).

significant predictor effect, $\beta = .30$, $p = .011$, dropped to nonsignificance, $\beta = .16$, *n.s.* (see Figure 2). Likewise, the relationship between cultural closeness and perceived emotional sensitivity of Israeli Jews was mediated by collective guilt. After partialling out the mediator (Sobel's $z = 3.85$, $p < .001$), the effect of cultural closeness on emotional sensitivity dropped from a significant effect, $\beta = .42$, $p < .001$, to nonsignificance, $\beta = .19$, *n.s.* (see Figure 2). Thus, guilt mediated the effects of cultural closeness both on (infra)humanization and (de)mentalization measures.

Discussion

The findings of Study 1 suggest that mere awareness of the ingroup's harmdoing against other groups is not sufficient to arouse guilt (e.g., Wohl et al.,

2006): when a victimized group was perceived as culturally distant (e.g., differing in values, norms, and lifestyle), the crime reminder decreased attitudes toward the victim group and only led to minimal collective guilt. Conversely, when a victimized group was viewed as culturally close, the crime reminder aroused guilt and improved attitudes toward the outgroup. Generally, the same pattern emerged for (de)humanization: without closeness induction, the crime reminder tended to increase dehumanization of a victimized group, but the crime reminder promoted the victim group's humanization in the cultural closeness condition. However, these effects were found only for ascribed emotional sensitivity and not for infrahumanization. In sum, these findings suggest that outgroup victims tend to be excluded from the moral community, but when cultural closeness is induced they are included into the moral community, with all the emotional and attitudinal consequences.

Study 2

The former study showed that, following a reminder of ingroup crime, induced cultural closeness improved attitudes toward the victim group. The question arises whether this effect results from an interaction between crime awareness and cultural closeness (as we assume), or rather due to a main effect of closeness. To address this issue, we modified the experimental design by separating two orthogonal treatments: exposure to a reminder of ingroup crime (present vs. absent) and cultural closeness of the victim group (high vs. baseline). We also added a measure of intentions to engage in intergroup contact and dialogue.

In Study 1, a remarkable difference in experienced guilt was found between induced closeness and baseline conditions. Perhaps the difference resulted not only from guilt arousal in the former condition but also from guilt suppression in the latter. This could be due to defensive denial, which is likely to accompany the moral exclusion process. To test this phenomenon, we asked our participants to evaluate the credibility of the historical account they read. It seems reasonable to assume that, in the context of crime reminder, stressing low credibility of the source would indicate ingroup-serving defensive denial.

Method

Sample

The study was conducted among 63 female and 44 male students of Warsaw University, from different majors (age: $M = 20.1$, range 19–24).

Design and Procedure

The study employed a 2 (crime reminder: present vs. absent) × 2 (cultural closeness: baseline vs. induced closeness) design. The same materials as in Study 1 were used, as well as the same participant instructions. The measure of the victim families' emotions was omitted. Measures of behavioral intentions and source credibility were added.

Measures

Collective guilt.   Participants assessed the intensity of guilt, remorse, regret, and compunction experienced while reading the account ($\alpha = .90$).

Behavioral intentions to support Polish–Jewish dialogue were assessed by a six-item scale ($\alpha = .91$), with answers ranging from 1 (*Not at all*) to 5 (*Absolutely yes*): *"I would vote for the MP candidate who supports the idea of Polish–Jewish dialogue," "I would take part in march against anti-Semitism," "I would sign up for a mailing list of an organization that promotes Polish–Jewish dialogue," "I would wear a pin that promotes Polish–Jewish dialogue," "I would attend meeting of organizations that promote Polish–Jewish dialogue"* and *"I would like to attend activities that promote Polish–Jewish dialogue, such as cleaning up an old Jewish cemetery."*

Source credibility. To test if participants denied trustworthiness of the source, differently across experimental conditions, we used a six-item scale ($\alpha = .89$), with answers ranging from 1 (*I completely disagree*) to 7 (*I completely agree*). The six items included: *"I think the content of the article is grossly exaggerated"* (reverse-coded), *"This report is, unfortunately, very well documented," "We cannot be sure of the crimes were committed by Poles"* (reverse-coded), *"One cannot trust reports that are almost solely based on witness account"* (reverse-coded), *"Reports prepared by the historians of Polish Historical Institute are not very trustworthy"* (reverse-coded), and *"The facts described in the report have been verified by many credible sources."*

Results

Manipulation check

Confirming the effectiveness of the manipulation, an ANOVA revealed the main effect of cultural closeness on the similarity measure, $F(1, 103) = 63.17$, $p < .001$, partial $\eta^2 = .38$. As expected, perceived similarity was lower ($M = 3.33$, $SD = .92$) in the control condition than in the induced closeness condition ($M = 4.90$, $SD = .99$). Additionally, a closeness × crime interaction emerged, $F(1, 103) = 34.73$, $p < .001$, partial $\eta^2 = .25$. Within the control condition, the crime reminder decreased similarity, $F(1, 43) = 22.94, p < .001$, partial $\eta^2 = .35$ ($M = 4.18, SD = .80$ in the no crime reminder condition vs. $M = 3.11, SD = .71$ in the crime reminder condition); in contrast, in the induced closeness condition, the crime reminder increased similarity, $F(1, 60) = 14.18, p < .001$, partial $\eta^2 = .19$ ($M = 4.16, SD = 1.04$ in the no crime reminder condition vs. $M = 5.39, SD = .67$ in the crime condition).

Collective guilt

Consistent with Study 1, a one-way ANOVA revealed a strong effect of cultural closeness on collective guilt, $F(1, 49) = 104.15, p < .001$, partial $\eta^2 = .37$, such that collective guilt was lower ($M = 2.26, SD = .82$) in the no closeness condition than in the closeness condition ($M = 4.72, SD = .79$).

Attitudes toward jews

A two-way MANOVA on all attitudinal measures yielded main effects for the crime reminder, Rao's $R(6, 96) = 4.75, p < .001$, partial $\eta^2 = .23$, and for cultural closeness induction, Rao's $R(6, 96) = 16.49, p < .001$, partial $\eta^2 = .51$, as well as for the interaction effect, Rao's $R(6, 96) = 6.37, p < .001$, partial $\eta^2 = .28$. Univariate analyses (see Table 2) revealed that for each measure the closeness manipulation produced main effects in the same direction (specifically, high closeness was associated with more positive attitudes than low closeness), qualified by the Closeness $\times$ Crime interactions. With exception of conspiracy approval, these interactions were statistically significant. As shown in Table 2, the interactions were such that the crime reminder decreased attitude positivity in the control condition and increased its positivity in the closeness condition. Also of interest, we found strong ingroup favoritism in regard to financial compensation in the crime plus baseline closeness condition, and outgroup favoritism in the crime plus induced closeness condition.

(De)humanization

A four-way mixed ANOVA in a 2 (crime reminder: present vs. absent) $\times$ 2 (closeness: high vs. baseline) $\times$ 2 (target: Jews vs. Poles) $\times$ 2 (emotions: primary vs. secondary) factorial design revealed a main effect of closeness on emotion ascription to Poles or Israeli Jews, $F(1, 103) = 9.42, p = .003$, partial $\eta^2 = .08$ ($M = 3.41, SD = .33$ for the baseline closeness and $M = 3.66, SD = .51$ for the induced closeness condition). We also found a Crime $\times$ Closeness interaction, $F(1, 103) = 19.10, p < .001$, partial $\eta^2 = .16$, and a Closeness $\times$ Target interaction, $F(1, 103) = 54.58, p < .001$, partial $\eta^2 = .35$, which were qualified by a predicted three-way interaction of crime, closeness, and target, $F(1, 103) = 19.30, p < .001$, partial

Table 2. Study 2: Effects of Crime Reminder and Cultural Closeness on Attitudes toward Jews

Condition	Interest in Jewish tradition M (SD)	Desire for contacting Jews M (SD)	Behavioral intentions M (SD)	Compensation to Jews M (SD)	Compensation to Poles minus to Jews M (SD)	Belief in Jewish conspiracy M (SD)
No crime + baseline closeness	4.42 (1.20)	4.52 (1.17)	2.82 (.87)	18.8 (7.5)	12.4 (22.9)	4.11 (1.34)
No crime + induced closeness	4.86 (1.40)	5.15 (1.09)	2.86 (.93)	26.5 (11.9)	4.6 (19.8)	2.99 (1.35)
Crime + baseline closeness	2.89 (.65)	3.16 (.68)	2.33(.61)	7.0 (9.7)	20.6 (24.6)	4.63 (1.15)
Crime + induced closeness	5.31 (.94)	5.55 (.91)	4.20 (.58)	33.6 (13.3)	− 5.0 (13.7)	2.64 (.93)
F for Crime	6.10[*]	6.14[*]	7.74[**]	1.62	.03	.12
Partial η^2	.06	.06	.07	.02	.00	.00
F for Closeness	40.50[***]	60.69[***]	38.67[***]	30.75[***]	17.15[***]	42.83[***]
Partial η^2	.29	.37	.27	.23	.14	.29
F for Interaction	20.05[***]	20.45[***]	36.12[***]	4.43[*]	5.03[*]	3.29
Partial η^2	.17	.17	.26	.04	.05	.03

[*]$p < .05$, [**]$p < .01$, [***]$p < .001$.

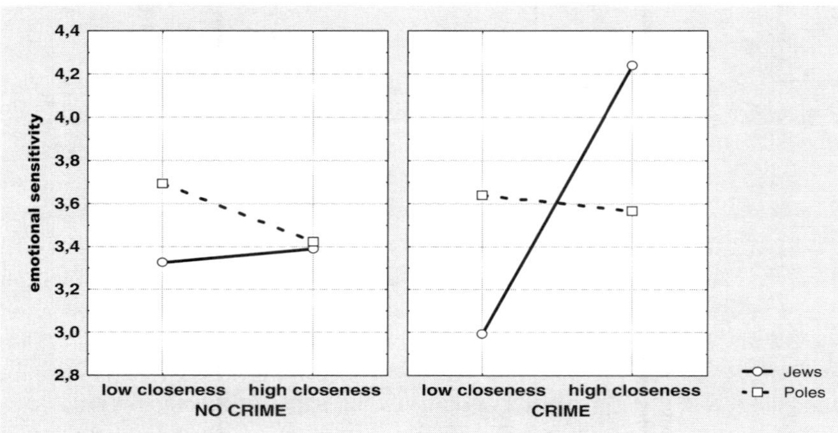

Fig. 3. Study 2: Effects of crime reminder and induced cultural closeness on ascription of general emotional sensitivity.

$\eta^2 = .16$ (see Figure 3). For Polish targets, the closeness induction did not moderate the ascription of general emotional sensitivity in the no crime ($F < 1$) or crime conditions ($F < 1$). For Jewish targets, closeness induction again did not affect ascription of emotional sensitivity in the no crime condition ($F < 1$), but did so in the crime condition, $F(1, 49) = 77.26, p < .001$, partial $\eta^2 = .62$. Compared to the respective no crime conditions (see Fig. 2), in the crime reminder only condition perceived emotional sensitivity of Jews decreased (indicating dehumanization), whereas in the crime plus induced closeness condition it increased (indicating humanization). Moreover, in the latter group participants attributed significantly more emotional sensitivity to Jews than to Poles (see Figure 3), $F(1, 26) = 27.34$, $p < .001$, partial $\eta^2 = .51$.

Additionally, an infrahumanization effect emerged, as shown by an interaction of target and primary vs. secondary emotions, $F(1, 103) = 5.84, p < .02$, partial $\eta^2 = .05$. Specifically, more secondary emotions were ascribed to Poles ($M = 3.63, SD = .50$), than to Jews ($M = 3.46, SD = .68$), $F(1, 103) = 6.77, p = .011$, while there was no difference for primary emotions, $F < 1$. However, this effect was neither qualified by a crime reminder (for the three-way interaction, $F < 1$) or closeness induction (for the three-way interaction, $F = 1, 15$, n.s.), nor by both treatments combined (for the four-way interaction, $F = 1.55$, n.s.).

Denial of source credibility

To assess the potential role of denial processes in moral responses to the ingroup's harmdoing, a one-way ANOVA with cultural closeness as the independent variable was run on source credibility within the crime condition. It revealed a significant effect, $F (1, 48) = 62.09$, $p < .001$, partial $\eta^2 = .56$, such that the historical article about ingroup crimes was viewed as less trustworthy in the baseline closeness ($M = 3.62$, $SD = .84$) than in the high closeness condition ($M = 5.31$, $SD = .68$). Also the lower the source credibility was perceived to be, the lower was the reported collective guilt, $r = .64$, $p < .001$.

Discussion

The main finding from Study 2 is that reminders of ingroup crime led to more negative attitudes toward the victimized group when cultural closeness between the ingroup and the victim group was not made salient, and to more positive attitudes when cultural closeness of these groups was induced. The same pattern was found for the ascription of emotional sensitivity to the victimized group: ingroup crime reminders increased perceptions of the victim group (Jews) as emotionally rich when closeness was induced, compared to when no such treatment was introduced. The pattern for emotion ascription strongly suggests humanization of the victim outgroup in the former condition and its dehumanization in the latter on (de)mentalization dimension (e.g., Harris & Fiske, 2009).

However, the other index of (de)humanization—preferential ascription of more secondary (but not primary) emotions to the ingroup than to the outgroup (Leyens et al., 2000)—was not modified by our experimental treatments. This suggests that the former (dementalization) but not the latter (infrahumanization) aspect of (de)humanization is critical for the discussed processes of moral inclusion and exclusion to occur. We suggest a possible answer to the question of why it could be so below.

General Discussion

In this paper, we explore how people respond to information that one's ingroup members behaved immorally against an outgroup. We propose that the perception of cultural closeness between ingroup perpetrators and outgroup victims could be a particularly important moderator of this response, complementing previously identified factors (Wohl et al., 2006).

To substantiate our hypothesis, we drew on the notion of the moral community (e.g., Opotow, 1990, 2008). Moral community means a symbolic unity with others sharing the same standards of moral conduct. We assumed that in response to the ingroup's collective crime, outgroup members could either be included into the moral community or excluded from it, resulting in different affective and attitudinal reactions toward the outgroup.

Our findings are consistent with these expectations. We found that depending on the level of perceived cultural closeness between "us" (perpetrator group) and "them" (victim group), reminders of collective crimes may cause inverted processes. When closeness is not salient, crime reminders provoked a low level of moral emotions, reduced the desire for contact and interest in outgroup culture, interfered with the willingness to compensate for the outgroup's suffering, and hampered the intention to act in support of the outgroup's interests. However, when cultural closeness was made salient, the pattern was reversed: reminding participants of atrocities committed by ingroup members resulted in increased moral emotions and more positive attitudes toward the victimized outgroup.

We also found some evidence that low moral responses in the baseline condition might be due to ingroup-defensive processes (see Leach et al., 2013). In line with this explanation, ingroup crime reminders in our studies led to an increased acceptance of the theory of Jewish conspiracy (e.g., Bilewicz & Kofta, 2011; Kofta & Sedek, 2005), albeit in Study 2 this effect was only marginally significant. Construing the outgroup as a collective, dangerous enemy (the essence of conspiracy theory) may indirectly justify the ingroup's immoral acts. Further supporting the group-defensive explanation, we found in Study 2 that within the crime condition, participants in the baseline closeness condition denied source credibility more than in the cultural closeness condition.

Infrahumanization (ascription of more secondary but not primary emotions to the ingroup compared to the outgroup) was affected by the cultural closeness treatment, albeit only for emotions ascribed to victims' families (Study 1), i.e., for more concrete attributions. When participants were asked to attribute general emotional sensitivity to national groups, which is more abstract, only the (de)mentalization component of (de)humanization was affected: the crime reminder only condition decreased perceived emotional sensitivity of Jews and increased it under the crime plus induced closeness condition (see Figs. 1 and 2). Moreover, the effect of closeness on mentalization of Jews was mediated by collective guilt, which supports the moral community explanation. Perhaps Castano and Giner-Sorolla (2006) found dehumanization and collective guilt to be unrelated because they measured infrahumanization, not dementalization.

One reason why perceiving members of the victimized group as having high or low emotional sensitivity are so critical for moral responses to ingroup-inflicted harm is because assuming victims' emotional sensitivity is a precondition for feeling empathy (see also Kozak et al., 2006). Denying that outgroup members are able to experience emotions, which is frequently observed in intergroup conflicts, may therefore inhibit empathic responses to victims and further exclude them from the moral community.

Our understanding of the role of the (de)humanization process in the context of ingroup crime is close to the approach developed by Albert Bandura (1999). In his model, Bandura proposed that dehumanization is a useful strategy of coping with moral distress experienced by the aggressor, and allows for moral disengagement such that people stop applying moral principles to their own behavior. Supplementing Bandura's approach, we show that an awareness of ingroup harmdoing may lead not only to disengagement, but—when group members believe that they share cultural worldviews with the victim group—to an intense *moral engagement*. When this is the case, the victim group may be humanized above the level of the ingroup's humanity, suggesting a guilt-based overcompensation process.

In conclusion, our research suggests that perceived cultural closeness of perpetrator and victim groups might be a critical moderator of psychological responses to the ingroup's crimes. A remaining question for future research is how permanent these effects are, which could be investigated in longitudinal studies, and how generalizable the responses of university students are to the community as a whole. These questions seem vital for successfully applying our findings to interventions aimed at improving intergroup relations in the aftermath of genocide and mass violence. Moreover, social desirability and demand characteristics are a potential limitation and need to be controlled for in future studies.

The present research also sheds light on the issue of collective memory in the aftermath of genocide and mass killings. Recently, many nations (including Poland) have started "rediscovering" their (sometimes shameful) past. Such public debates about the darker years of a nation's past may either raise blatant denial and prejudice towards the victimized group or may result in an empathetic response and sincere willingness to reconcile (see also Imhoff, Wohl, & Erb, 2013). Which of these two opposing tendencies will be in place depends significantly, as our research suggests, on the perception of cultural closeness with the victim group. Thus, understanding these dynamics may play a crucial role in future designs of intergroup educational programs and social media campaigns designed to foster reconciliation and prevent intergroup conflict in the aftermath of genocide and mass violence (see Bilewicz & Jaworska, 2013; Pearlman, 2013; Staub, 2013). Including "the other" into "our" moral universe, where the same moral rules apply, the same values are cherished, and the same emotions are felt, allows for the victim group to be perceived as "fully human." Then, one of the most fundamental moral laws, namely "Thou Shall Not Kill," also starts applying to the outgroup.

References

Aron, A., & McLaughlin-Volpe, T. (2001). Including others in the self: Extensions to own and partner's group memberships. In C. Sedekides & M. Brewer (Eds.), *Individual self, relational self, collective self* (pp. 89–108). Philadelphia, PA: Psychology Press.

Baron, R. M., & Kenny, D. A. (1986). The moderator-mediator variable distinction in social psychological research: Conceptual, strategic, and statistical considerations. *Journal of Personality and Social Psychology, 51*, 1173–1182.

Bandura, A. (1999). Moral disengagement in the perpetration of inhumanities. *Personality and Social Psychology Review, 3*, 193–209.

Bilewicz, M., & Jaworska, M. (2013). Reconciliation through the righteous: The narratives of heroic helpers as a fulfillment of emotional needs in Polish–Jewish intergroup contact. *Journal of Social Issues, 69*, 162–179.

Bilewicz, M., & Kofta, M. (2011). Less biased under threat? Self-verificatory reactions to social identity threat among groups with negative self-stereotype. *Journal of Applied Social Psychology, 41*, 2249–2267.

Branscombe, N. R., Schmitt, M. T., & Schiffhauer, K. (2007). Racial attitudes in response to thoughts of White privilege. *European Journal of Social Psychology, 37*, 203–215.

Castano, E., & Giner-Sorolla, R. (2006). Not quite human: Infrahumanization in response to collective responsibility for intergroup killing. *Journal of Personality and Social Psychology, 90*, 804–818.

Castano, E., & Kofta, M. (2009). Dehumanization: Humanity and its denial. *Group Processes & Intergroup Relations, 12*, 695–697.

Cohen, S. (2001). *States of denial.* Cambridge, U.K.: Blackwell.

Diehl, M. (1988). Social identity and minimal groups: The effects of interpersonal and intergroup attitudinal similarity on intergroup discrimination. *British Journal of Social Psychology, 27*, 289–300.

Doosje, B., Branscombe, N. R., Spears, R., & Manstead, A. S. R. (1998). Guilty by association: When one's group has a negative history. *Journal of Personality and Social Psychology, 75*, 872–886.

Dresler-Hawke, E. (2005). Reconstructing the past and attributing of responsibility for the Holocaust. *Social Behavior and Personality: International Journal, 33*, 133–147.

Gaertner, S. L., Dovidio, J. F., Nier, J. A., Banker, B. S., Ward, Ch. M., Houlette, M., & Loux, S. (2000). The common ingroup identity model for reducing intergroup bias: Progress and challenges. In D. Capozza & R. Brown (Eds.), *Social identity processes: Trends in theory and research* (pp. 133–148). Thousand Oaks, CA: Sage.

Gaunt, R. (2009). Superordinate categorization as a moderator of mutual infrahumanization. *Group Processes and Intergroup Relations, 12*, 731–746.

Gross, J. T. (2001). *Neighbors: The destruction of the Jewish community in Jedwabne, Poland.* Princeton, NJ: Princeton University Press.

Harris, L. T., & Fiske, S. T. (2009). Social neuroscience evidence for dehumanised perception. *European Review of Social Psychology, 20*, 192–231.

Iyer, A., Schmader, T., & Lickel, B. (2007). Why individuals protest the perceived transgressions of their country: The role of anger, shame, and guilt. *Personality and Social Psychology Bulletin, 33*, 572–587.

Imhoff, R., & Banse, R. (2009). Ongoing victim suffering increases prejudice: The case of secondary antisemitism. *Psychological Science, 20*, 1443–1447.

Imhoff, R., Wohl, M. J. A., & Erb, H.-P. (2013). When the past is far from dead: How ongoing consequences of genocides committed by the ingroup impact collective guilt. *Journal of Social Issues, 69*, 74–91.

Kofta, M., & Sędek, G. (2005). Conspiracy stereotypes of Jews during systemic transformation in Poland. *International Journal of Sociology, 35*, 40–64.

Kozak, M. N., Marsh, A. A., & Wegner, D. M. (2006). What do I think you're doing? Action identification and mind attribution. *Journal of Personality and Social Psychology, 90*, 543–555.

Krajewski, D. (2005). *Poland and the Jews: Reflections of a Polish Jew.* Kraków, Poland: Austeria.

Krzemiński, I. (2004). *Antysemityzm w Polsce i na Ukrainie: Raport z badań. (Anti-semitism in Poland and Ukraine: A research report).* Warsaw, Poland: Scholar.

Leach, C. W., Bou Zeineddine, F., & Čehajić-Clancy, S. (2013). Moral immemorial: The rarity of self-criticism for previous generation's genocide or mass violence. *Journal of Social Issues, 69*, 34–53.

Leidner, B., Castano, E., Zaiser, E., & Giner-Sorolla, R. (2010). Ingroup glorification, moral disengagement, and justice in the context of collective violence. *Personality and Social Psychology Bulletin, 36*, 1115–1129.

Leyens, J. P., Paladino, M. P., Rodriguez-Torres, R., Vaes, J., Demoulin, S., Rodriguez-Perez, A., & Gaunt, R. (2000). The emotional side of prejudice: The attribution of secondary emotions to ingroups and outgroups. *Personality and Social Psychology Review, 4*, 186–197.

Mirosławska, M., & Kofta, M. (2007). Zjawisko infrahumanizowania „obcych": wstępny test hipotezy generalizacji Ja (*The infrahumanization phenomenon: A preliminary test of self-projection explanation*). *Psychologia Społeczna, 2*, 52–65.

Opotow, S. (1990). Moral exclusion and injustice: An introduction. *Journal of Social Issues, 46*, 1–20.

Opotow, S. (2008). 'Not so much as place to lay our head . . .': Moral inclusion and exclusion in the American Civil War reconstruction. *Social Justice Research, 21*, 26–49.

Pearlman, L. A. (2013). Restoring self in community: Collective approaches to psychological trauma after genocide. *Journal of Social Issues, 69*, 111–124.

Powell, A. A., Branscombe, N. R., & Schmitt, M. T. (2005). Inequality as ingroup privilege or outgroup disadvantage: The impact of group focus on collective guilt and interracial attitudes. *Personality and Social Psychology Bulletin, 31*, 508–521.

Rokeach, M. (1960). *The open and closed mind*. New York, NY: Basic Books.

Staub, E. (1990). Moral exclusion, personal goal theory, and extreme destructiveness. *Journal of Social Issues, 46*, 47–64.

Staub, E. (2013). A world without genocide: Prevention, reconciliation and the creation of peaceful societies. *Journal of Social Issues, 69*, 180–199.

Wohl, M. J. A., Branscombe, N. R., & Klar, Y. (2006). Collective guilt: Emotional reactions when one's group has done wrong or been wronged. *European Review of Social Psychology, 17*, 1–37.

Wohl, M. J. A., & Branscombe, N. R. (2005). Forgiveness and collective guilt assignment to historical perpetrator groups depend on level of social category inclusiveness. *Journal of Personality and Social Psychology, 88*, 288–303.

MIROSLAW KOFTA is Professor of Psychology at the University of Warsaw, Poland. His research interests range from control deprivation and learned helplessness to intergroup phenomena. The broader framework for his research is the social cognitive context for intergroup judgment and the role of affective and motivational states in processing ingroup- and outgroup-related information. The recent foci of his research are conspiracy theories and anti-Semitism, psychological responses to threatened group identity, collective guilt, and dehumanization of outgroup members.

PATRYCJA SLAWUTA is a PhD candidate at the New School for Social Research in NYC. Her primary research interest is in intergroup conflict and intergroup relations. Recently, she has also been investigating the phenomenon of embodied morality, specifically the emotions of shame and guilt.

Journal of Social Issues, Vol. 69, No. 1, 2013, pp. 74–91

When the Past is Far from Dead: How Ongoing Consequences of Genocides Committed by the Ingroup Impact Collective Guilt

Roland Imhoff*
University of Cologne

Michael J. A. Wohl
Carleton University

Hans-Peter Erb
Helmut-Schmidt University, Hamburg

In two experimental studies, we examined how the ongoing negative consequences for victims of genocides committed by Germans influence the acceptance of collective guilt in young Germans living today. Experiment 1 showed that collective guilt is undermined when the genocide against the Herero people in Namibia is framed as having no impact on contemporary tribe members. The downstream consequence was reduced reparatory intentions. Extending these results, Experiment 2 replicated these findings in the context of Nazi crimes against Jews. In addition, we manipulated to what degree the compliance with the Holocaust was perceived as intentional, a widely debated issue in Holocaust studies. In line with predictions derived from attribution theory, collective guilt and reparatory intentions were particularly prevalent when the Holocaust was explained as the result of deliberate intentions of the ingroup. Implications for ingroup responses to historical harmdoing are discussed.

*Correspondence concerning this article should be addressed to Roland Imhoff, Department of Psychology, University of Cologne, Richard-Strauss-Str. 2, 50931 Cologne, Germany [e-mail: rimhoff@uni-koeln.de].

This research was supported by a fellowship from Evangelisches Studienwerk e.V. Villigst to Roland Imhoff. We thank Pascale Bonus, Magdalena Jasinska, and Stefanie Stein for their help with data collection.

The past is never dead. It's not even past.

–William Faulkner

Within the context of intergroup harmdoing, a considerable amount of research has outlined that group members can and do feel collective guilt for the illegitimate harm committed against other groups, including genocide (see Wohl, Branscombe, & Klar, 2006 for a review). However, this research has been fragmented into two streams: one focusing on historical harms (e.g., Branscombe, Doosje, & McGarty, 2002; Wohl & Branscombe, 2008) and the other focusing on contemporary harm (e.g., inequality between social groups; Iyer, Leach, & Crosby, 2003; Powell, Branscombe, & Schmitt, 2005). In the current research, we examine the consequences of framing past harms as "not even past." In other words, we assess the effect of making salient that an outgroup's contemporary position is the result of the historical victimization perpetrated by the ingroup.

It is a truism that people's representations and narratives of genocides show remarkable variance (Bilewicz & Jaworska, 2013; Vollhardt, 2013; but see Bilali, 2013). As one example, for most historical atrocities, the question of whether the historically victimized group continues to experience negative consequences is arguable. Are previously colonized countries' current economic hardships the result of the atrocities experienced in the past? While many theorists contend that the colonial past continues to negatively impact countries that were subject to colonization (Amin, 1973; Hoogvelt, 2001; Rodney, 1973), others claim that the reasons for current hardships lie more in today's corrupt leaders and instable political systems (Adusei, 2009; Seitz, 2009).

We argue that if ingroup harmdoing and its effects are psychologically placed in the past, then collective guilt acceptance would be undermined. In line with this contention, remarkably low levels of collective guilt have been found among contemporary Germans for the genocide committed during WWII (Imhoff, Bilewicz, & Erb, 2012; see also Leach, Zeineddine, & Čehajić-Clancy, 2013). Such low levels of collective guilt may be due, at least in part, to the fact that the Nazi past is perceived to have no contemporary negative consequences. Within Germany, placing the atrocities of the Third Reich in the distant past has been a topic of heated public debate (Zuckermann, 1998). A common sentiment in private as well as public political rhetoric concerns the need to place a "Schlusstrich" (literally: a thick line; as a more descriptive term we propose *historical closure*) between contemporary Germany and Nazi Germany (Ahlheim & Heger, 2002). Indeed, in representative surveys conducted between 1989 and 2002 large proportions of the respondents (30–60%) agreed that Germany should close the book of history on the Nazi chapter of German history by drawing a *Schlussstrich* between the past and the present (e.g., Noelle-Neumann & Köcher, 1997), implying that the past has no relevant consequences for contemporary Germans. In a series of unpublished correlational studies, Imhoff, Wohl, and Erb showed that individual differences in the degree to which historical closure (a *Schlussstrich*) is desired are systematically related to levels of collective guilt for the Holocaust and willingness to compensate the victims. Importantly, desire for historical closure fully mediated the undermining effect of defensive ingroup identification (collective narcissism; Golec de Zavala, Cichocka, Eidelson, & Jayawickreme, 2009) on collective guilt and reparation intentions.

In this context, one possible mechanism by which collective guilt might be elicited is to draw an explicit link between the past and ongoing negative consequences of that past. Recent research by Peetz, Gunn, and Wilson (2010) provides indirect evidence for this contention. Specifically, they were able to heighten the experience of collective guilt by manipulating the subjective temporal distance of the Holocaust among contemporary Germans. Participants had to locate the Holocaust on a timeline that either ranged from 1933 to 2008 (resulting in a mark close to the left end of the scale, i.e., more distant from today) or from 1900 to 2008 (moving the mark for the Holocaust further to the right, i.e. closer to today). The farther away in time the Holocaust was perceived to be, the less collective guilt was experienced.

We propose that one reason for this effect of temporal distance is its implication for the question of whether there exist ongoing consequences or not. The more time has passed, the less of an impact the genocide should have today (see Starzyk & Ross, 2008; Study 1). Colloquially, this notion is captured in the proverb "time heals all wounds." Yet, historical victimization can and does traverse generations (Klar, Shori-Eyal, & Klar, 2013; Klein-Parker, 1988; Yehuda et al., 2000). To our knowledge, however, there has been no direct empirical assessment of the influence of salient ongoing victim suffering on collective guilt. We argue that when victim suffering is thought to be ongoing, collective guilt for past wrongs should be heightened, thus increasing willingness to make amends (e.g., Swim & Miller, 1999).

Although the portrayal of continuing negative consequences for the victims may increase feelings of collective guilt, stemming from attribution theory tradition (Heider, 1958) we further reasoned that this should be particularly the case if the perpetrator behavior is attributed to controllable internal factors (e.g., Weiner, 1986). The literature on individual guilt suggests it is an emotion associated with behavioral self-blame (Janoff-Bulman, 1982). In terms of counterfactual thinking, guilt is likely to result from incidents that evoke counterfactuals beginning with "If only I hadn't" (whereas shame is expected to be more connected to characterological self-blame and counterfactuals such as "If only I wasn't").

Lickel, Schmader and Barquissau (2004) have translated this conceptualization to the group context and postulated that guilt results from negative actions— rather than characteristics—of the ingroup. Building on these ideas, we reasoned that the description of genocide as a result of conscious and controlled decisions should increase guilt—if there are ongoing consequences. In contrast, complicity with and participation in genocide may also be perceived as the result of some deeply ingrained characteristic of a group (its *essence*; Haslam, Rothschild, & Ernst, 2000). For instance, German participation in the Nazi crimes has sometimes been discussed as a result of "German aggressiveness" (e.g., Schreier, 1943) or a deeply rooted, specifically German anti-Semitism (e.g., Goldhagen, 1996) rather than the conscious decision of individuals. If negative actions are attributed to the essence of the group, these actions should be seen as a tragedy without deliberate control. In turn, less guilt should be felt—independent of potentially ongoing consequences.

The Present Research

Building on evidence for the effect of victim suffering on reparation intentions, we conducted two experiments to assess the impact of ongoing suffering as a result of genocide on the experience of collective guilt. Extending previous findings that showed increased support for reparations if victim suffering was perceived to be greater, mediated by sympathy and perceptions of injustice (Starzyk & Ross, 2008), we propose that a similar process should be observable for collective guilt. However, we also propose an important boundary condition. Ongoing victim suffering should also lead to an increase in collective guilt if the perpetrators' actions are attributed to conscious decisions (i.e., if they are seen as intentional).

In Experiment 1, young Germans were confronted with the German genocide of the Herero in 1904. Often neglected in public awareness, Germany was one of the leading colonial powers of the early 20th century (Förster, Mommsen, & Robinson, 1988). In fact, the understudied genocide against the Herero is one of the most prominent cruelties within German colonial history and is often considered to be the first genocide of the 20th century (Levi & Rothenberg, 2003), including the introduction of archetypes for the Nazi concentration camps (Zimmerman, 2001). We reasoned that making the ongoing suffering of the Herero salient should evoke feelings of collective guilt among contemporary Germans and, as a result, increase a sense of obligation to make amends for the harm done.

In Experiment 2, we tested our theoretical model within the context of Nazi Germany's systematic murder of over 6 million Jews. The Nazi extermination program against Jews, Gypsies, homosexuals, communists, disabled, and other humans labeled as "inferior" can be considered the most salient genocide in German public discourse and memory. We concentrated on Jewish victims of the Holocaust (as the largest victim group) and manipulated whether ongoing suffering of Jewish victims was implied or not. We also framed Nazi atrocities as being a result of conscious decisions of historical Germans or due to inherent ingroup attributes. We only expected an increase in collective guilt if the actions were portrayed as intentional, resulting from conscious decisions. In contrast, implying inherent ingroup attributes as the reason for the atrocities would suggest that the actions were not within ingroup members' control. For this condition it was expected that collective guilt would be undermined even if ongoing consequences were made salient.

Experiment 1

Method

Participants.　　Forty-eight students (23 men and 25 women) from a German university participated for partial course credit. They were directly addressed in the university building or the university cafeteria. Most were either students of psychology (39.6%) or computer science (33.3%). They ranged in age from 20 to 55 ($M = 24.52$, $SD = 5.77$) and all identified as German.

Design and procedure.　　Participants received a short text on the abatement of the Herero uprising in 1904. To manipulate ongoing consequences of the genocide against the Herero in Africa (ongoing consequences vs. no ongoing consequences) two different vignettes were used. In both experimental conditions the text was said to be an introductory text on German colonialism for school classes. Participants were told that the issue had been largely ignored until recently, but that the government now wanted to include it in school books and high school curricula. Before doing so, however, the Federal Headquarters for Political Education (in collaboration with various universities) wished to evaluate different versions of the text regarding quality and comprehensibility.

The text began with a quote from a national newspaper about how the first concentration camps were built in Africa and went on to describe the developments that led to the genocide. Both versions emphasized that only 12,000 of formerly 80,000 Herero survived and that the survivors were forced to work in camps with the goal of completely annihilating the tribe. The last paragraph differed between conditions. In the ongoing consequences condition, participants read that German actions against the Herero turned the tribe into a minority in Namibia and that the disproportionate unemployment and poverty rate experienced today (compared to other groups) are a direct result. In the no consequences condition, no such direct causal links to today's situation were implied. Instead, these problems were characterized as typical problems concerning the Third World in general.

Specifically, the ongoing consequences text stated: "The few successors of the Herero live in Namibia today. Due to the historical annihilation they are a minority in the state and receive little support from the government. Thus, the small tribe could never keep up with the progressive technical and economical development. Until today, this leads to difficulties of young Herero to integrate socially and establish themselves. As one indicator, the unemployment rate within this community is disproportionally high and even today Herero fight against hunger, oppression and exclusion—a late consequence of the erstwhile elimination of their collective existence by German colonists."

In contrast, in the no ongoing consequences condition the following was argued: "Over the last 100 years, many of the open wounds have healed and the Hereros have consolidated as a tribe. The third generation of Herero never had to experience hunger and genocide and does not have to suffer from the terrible consequences of the former German despotism anymore. The Herero are a minority but they live in peaceful coexistence with other tribes in Namibia today. The typical everyday worries of a third-world country have grown much more relevant than the consequences of the past."

Dependent variables. To assess collective guilt and reparation intentions, we adapted three items from the Collective Guilt Acceptance Scale (Branscombe, Slugoski, & Kappen, 2004). The two items tapping collective guilt read "I feel guilty about the things Germans did to Hereros" and "I can easily feel guilty for the bad outcomes for the Herero brought about by Germans" ($\alpha = .72$). The reparation intention item was also taken from the Collective Guilt Acceptance Scale and read "I believe that I should repair the damage caused to the Herero by Germans." These three items were included among a number of filler items (e.g., "The text was easy to comprehend"). All measures were completed on a 9-point scale ranging from 1 (*do not agree at all*) to 9 (*fully agree*).

Results

Collective guilt. In order to determine whether the ongoing victimization manipulation affected feelings of collective guilt for the Herero, a t-test for independent samples was performed. When ongoing negative consequences of the genocide were stressed, participants expressed more guilt, $M = 3.42$, $SD = 1.77$, than when this causal relation was not articulated, $M = 2.29$, $SD = 1.74$, $t(46) = 2.22$, $p = .03$, *Cohen's d* $= 0.70$ (see Figure 1).

Reparation intentions. Mirroring the results for collective guilt, a t-test for independent samples (with adjusted df due to inhomogenous variances) showed that ongoing consequences of the genocide led to a greater willingness to pay reparations to the victims, $t(40.32) = 2.09$, $p = .04$. When historical closure was implied (no ongoing consequences), participants reported less willingness to make amends, $M = 2.42$, $SD = 1.69$, compared to those in the ongoing consequences condition, $M = 3.71$, $SD = 2.51$, *Cohen's d* $= 0.60$.

Mediation analysis. To determine if the effect of our manipulation on reparation intentions could be explained by collective guilt, we conducted multiple regressions to test for mediation. As the t-tests indicated, the

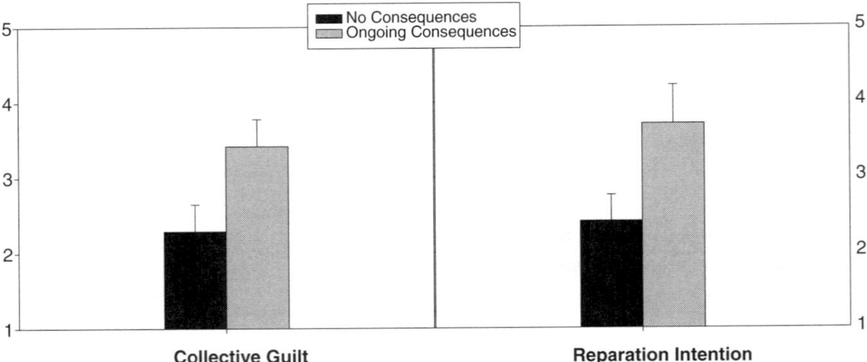

Fig. 1. Collective guilt and reparation intentions as a function of ongoing consequences manipulation in Study 1. Means (+ SE) on a scale from 1 to 9.

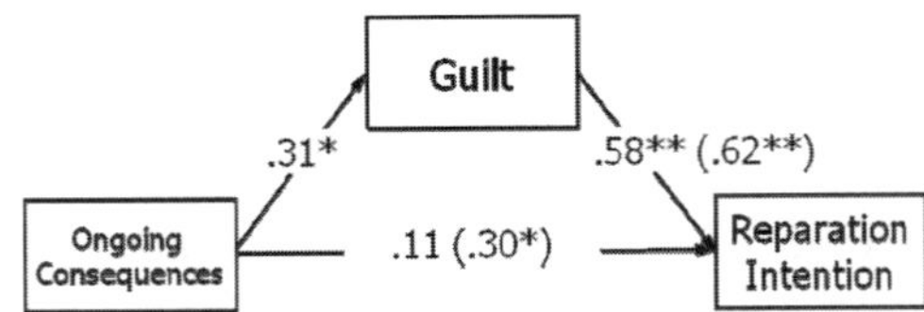

Fig. 2. Collective guilt as a mediator of the relation between manipulation of ongoing consequences and reparation intention in Study 1. Numbers show corrected standardized regression weights when predictor and mediator were entered simultaneously. Numbers in parentheses show uncorrected standardized regression weight when both variables were entered separately.

manipulation of ongoing consequences (coded as $0 =$ no ongoing consequences, $1 =$ ongoing consequences) predicted collective guilt acceptance and reparation intentions. When both predictor variables were entered (ongoing consequences manipulation and collective guilt), the regression equation accounted for substantial variance in reparation intentions, adjusted $R^2 = .36$, $F(2, 45) = 14.41$, $p < .001$. With collective guilt as a mediator, the ongoing consequences manipulation did not significantly predict reparation intentions, $\beta = .11$, $t(46) = 0.93$, $p = .39$ (Figure 2). A bootstrapping technique (with 1,000 iterations; Preacher & Hayes, 2004) showed an estimated indirect effect between 0.09 and 1.45 with 95% confidence (mean $IE = 0.78$).

Discussion

Experiment 1 demonstrated that emphasizing ongoing consequences of a historical genocide committed by the ingroup heightened the experience of collective guilt. Importantly, collective guilt for the genocide committed against the Herero increased the prosocial outcome of Germans' reparation intentions. These results offer insight into why victim suffering leads to support for reparations (see Starzyk & Ross, 2008). If the descendants of former victims continue to suffer from the crimes committed against ancestors, the descendants of the perpetrators are more likely to experience collective guilt, thus motivating the desire to repair the wrongs their ancestors inflicted.

Experiment 1 also bears some important limitations. Most obviously, reparation intentions were assessed with a single item measure. Additionally, it may be claimed that the genocide against the Herero is hardly known and thus participants' representations of it were more easily influenced by our experimental manipulation than for more accessible genocides. Experiment 2 thus sought to replicate the findings with a three-item measure of reparation intentions and a historical genocide that can be assumed to be almost chronically accessible in the German populace: the Nazi crimes against Jews. Far beyond German public discourse, Germany's Nazi-era past seems to serve as a prime example of a negative, potentially guilt-inducing history. In discussing collective guilt as a phenomenon, some authors (e.g., Doosje, Branscombe, Spears, & Manstead, 1998) anecdotally mention the heated public debate sparked by the book *Hitler's willing executioners* (Goldhagen, 1996; for an overview on the debate see Kött, 1999). Indeed, the issue of guilt has been at the core of the German *Vergangenheitsbewältigung* (coming to terms with the past) concerning the Nazi era. Exploring the effect of our manipulations in the context of Nazi crimes thus can be seen as a more conservative test of our hypotheses.

Adding to Experiment 1, we also wanted to explore a potential boundary condition of the effect of ongoing consequences. Specifically, we argue that while ongoing negative consequences for the victims fuel collective guilt, attributing the actions that led to these consequences to the essence of the perpetrators' group (as opposed to their intentional decisions) may undermine this effect. In addition to the factor *ongoing consequences* we therefore manipulated *attribution of harmdoing* as the second experimental factor in Experiment 2. We expected a fan-shaped interaction of these two factors: compared to all other groups, collective guilt and reparation intention should be highest if there exist ongoing negative consequences due to intentional harmdoing by Germans.

Experiment 2

Method

Participants.   Seventy psychology students were recruited from a German university and volunteered for partial course credit. Participants were directly approached during introductory courses for psychology as well as in the university building. The 54 women and 16 men had an average age of 24.06 years ($SD = 6.42$).

Procedure and design.   Participants were informed they would be engaging in a number of, ostensibly, independent short studies. The "first study" was explained to be about text comprehension. Specifically, participants were told that they were part of an international study on how national identities shape the comprehension of historical texts. They were instructed to read, within 5 minutes, a (fictitious) speech given by former German president von Weizsäcker to the Israeli parliament (Knesset). These texts included the two independent variables: *ongoing consequences for victims* (*ongoing consequences vs. no consequences*) and *attribution of harmdoing* (*intentional vs. unintentional*). After an introduction that was identical for all conditions and stressed the illegitimacy and horror of the Holocaust, the speaker elaborated on potential reasons for the Germans' failure to prevent the Holocaust.

In the *intentional condition* it was stressed that the goals of the Nazi movement had been known to the public more than 10 years before the Nazis received the majority vote in free elections. In addition, a large part of the German population had intentionally joined the Nazi party without any exterior pressure and many participated in the regime's crimes to benefit financially (e.g., buying Jewish property for unrealistically low prices or even stealing it). This section concluded: "As bitter as it may be, we have to see today that for many Germans it was a clear decision to participate in the Holocaust or not. The stability of the regime was not least a consequence of the great number of Germans that did not express any disagreement with what happened to the Jews." In the *unintentional condition* it was stressed that typical German characteristics (e.g., obedience to authority) had evolved over centuries and culminated in National Socialism (Goldhagen, 1996). This led to a situation where compliance with the Nazis was not so much an intentional decision but just the normal thing to do. The speaker's conclusion was: "As bitter as it may be, we have to see today that for many Germans it was never a real decision to participate in the Holocaust or not. The stability of the regime was almost a natural consequence of the typical character of a great number of Germans." To increase credibility, some of the reasoning was taken from contemporary scientific psychological literature trying to explain German behavior during the Nazi era (Bühler, 1943; Schreier, 1943).

In the ongoing consequences condition the speaker stressed the living conditions of Holocaust survivors in Israel: "Until today, numerous traumatized survivors live in Israel. Thousands wake up from nightmares. The second generation suffers from the phenomenon of secondary traumatization—their parents' suffering has been transmitted on them and they show symptoms of severe traumatization. Israel and its population are just not a society like any other but deeply affected from an endless past that overshadows other everyday worries until today." In the no-consequences condition, the times when thousands of Jews woke up screaming in nightmares were said to be in the past. "The times in which thousand woke up from nightmares are fortunately over now. The second generation of Israelis has not experienced the Holocaust and does not suffer from the terrible consequences of it anymore. Israel and its population is Western society that only marginally differs from other Western societies today. The everyday worries have long become more important than the consequences of the past."

Manipulation check. Previous research and Experiment 1 have successfully manipulated the representation of ongoing victim suffering. In order to test whether participants also accepted the *attribution* factor implied in the vignette, we included a manipulation check. The following three items measured to what extent participants attributed the compliance of most Germans with the Nazi regime to controllable causes: "Most Germans could have had more control over the historical crimes than commonly assumed," "During the Third Reich, many Germans actively decided to look the other way or even participate" and "I think Germans could have behaved differently to prevent atrocities" ($\alpha = .74$). These items were included in a set of 16 items allegedly measuring a general attitude toward German history. The other items were distracters (e.g., "Bismarck was a great statesman").

Dependent variables. Measures used in Experiment 2 were identical to those used in Experiment 1 with two exceptions. First, measures were reworded to describe Jews as the victim group. The guilt composite consisted of the same two items, $\alpha = .61$. We also included two additional items to assess support for reparation that tapped into personal compensation (apology) as well as group-based compensation (reparation payments). These items were: "We should still pay reparations for the crimes against the Jews" and "If I met a survivor I would have the need to apologize to make up for the German crimes" ($\alpha = .62$). All measures were completed on 9-point scales ranging from 1 (*do not agree at all*) to 9 (*fully agree*).

Results

Manipulation check. The 2 (*attribution*) $\times$ 2 (*consequences*) ANOVA yielded a significant main effect of *attribution*, $F(1, 66) = 5.18, p = .03$, whereas all other effects remained insignificant, all $F < 1$. Means indicate that in the control condition participants attributed the compliance with the Nazi regime more to controllable factors, $M = 7.34, SD = 1.43$, than in the essentialist condition, $M = 6.60, SD = 1.22$, *Cohen's d* $= 0.56$. The attribution manipulation was therefore successful.

Collective guilt. A two-way ANOVA yielded the predicted main effect of ongoing victim consequences, $F(1, 66) = 5.15, p = .03$. When ongoing negative consequences were mentioned, more guilt was expressed, $M = 3.97, SD = 2.01$, compared to when no such negative consequences were implied, $M = 2.92$,

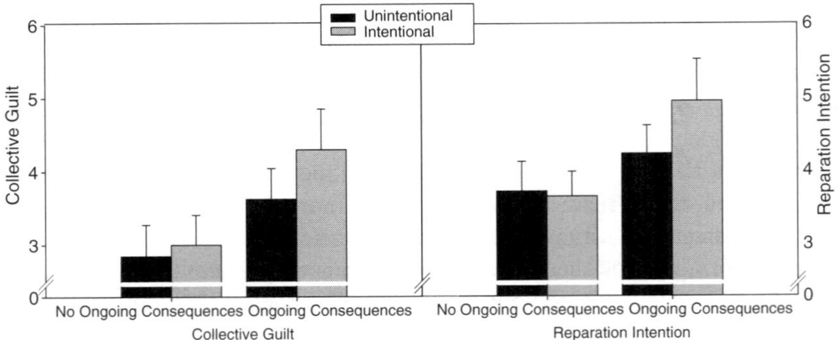

Fig. 3. Collective guilt and reparation intentions as a function of ongoing consequences and attribution manipulation in Study 2. Means (+ SE) on a scale from 1 to 9.

$SD = 1.79$, *Cohen's* $d = 0.55$. Neither the main effect of attribution, $F(1, 66) = 0.82$, $p = .37$, nor the interaction were significant, $F(1, 66) = 0.31$, $p = .58$. That said, because we predicted a fan-shaped pattern interaction (and not the crossover interaction tested by the ANOVA), a contrast analysis was conducted to test whether the data also supported the a priori specified pattern. We therefore treated our 2×2 design as a 1×4 design (see Rosenthal & Rosnow, 1985). The hypothesis that guilt should increase when atrocities are presented as intentional as well as having an ongoing effect was translated to the focal contrast with the lambda coefficient of 3 for that condition and a −1 for all other three. As expected, the focal contrast (3 −1 −1 −1) was significant, $T(66) = 2.14$, $p = .04$. However, it is important to also consider orthogonal contrasts to make sure there is no residual variance that can be better explained by a competing orthogonal hypothesis (Abelson & Prentice, 1997). The remaining two orthogonal contrasts (0 0 1 −1 and 0 −2 1 1) were nonsignificant, $ps > .20$, implying that there was no systematic residual variance.

Reparation intention. A two-way ANOVA showed the ongoing consequences manipulation to have a main effect on reparation intention, $F(1,66) = 4.38$, $p = .04$. Stressing ongoing consequences led to greater reparation intentions, $M = 4.59$, $SD = 2.03$, compared to the no-ongoing consequences condition, $M = 3.51$, $SD = 1.80$, *Cohen's* $d = 0.56$ (Figure 3). Again, neither the main effect of attribution, $F(1, 66) = 0.21$, $p = .65$, nor the interaction reached significance, $F(1, 66) = 1.23$, $p = .27$. However, akin to the collective guilt results, a contrast analysis with identical lambda weights yielded a significant effect of the predicted contrast, $T(66) = 2.14$, $p = .04$, but not for the orthogonal contrasts, $ps > .40$.

Mediation analysis. As in Experiment 1, we tested whether the effect of the ongoing consequences manipulation on reparation intentions was mediated by

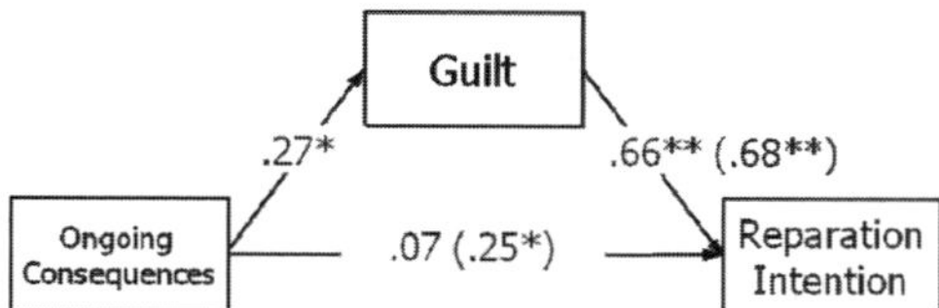

Fig. 4. Collective guilt as a mediator of the relation between manipulation of ongoing consequences and reparation intention in Study 2. Numbers show corrected standardized regression weights when predictor and mediator were entered simultaneously. Numbers in parentheses show uncorrected standardized regression weight when both variables were entered separately.

collective guilt (see Figure 4). As reported above, the ongoing consequences manipulation (coded as 0 = no-ongoing consequences, 1 = ongoing consequences) predicted both collective guilt acceptance and reparation intentions. When both predictor variables were entered (ongoing consequences manipulation and collective guilt), the regression equation accounted for substantial variance in reparation intentions, adjusted $R^2 = .48$, $F(2, 67) = 32.23$, $p < .001$. With collective guilt as a mediator, the ongoing consequences manipulation did not significantly predict reparation intentions, $\beta = .09$, $t(68) = 1.03$, $p = .31$. As in Study 1, bootstrapping (with 1000 iterations) was used to determine whether the indirect effect of the manipulation on reparation intentions was due to increased acceptance of collective guilt. The indirect effect was estimated to lie between 0.08 and 1.28 with 95% confidence (mean $IE = 0.65$).

Alternatively, it is possible that the portrayal of a lack of ongoing consequences decreased collective guilt. To account for this alternative we ran a fifth *baseline* group from the same student population ($n = 15$; 10 women, 5 men; age: $M = 26.60$, $SD = 4.93$) that only completed the questionnaire without any prior text as an additional control group. This control condition was conducted after the other conditions were completed. Participants in this condition reported the lowest levels of collective guilt compared to all other groups, $M = 2.43$, $SD = 1.41$. Particularly, more guilt was expressed in the condition *ongoing consequences/intentional*, $t(27,02) = 2.80$, $p < .01$, as well as in the *ongoing consequences/unintentional*, $t(29) = 2.14$, $p = .04$. The two *no-ongoing consequences* conditions did not differ significantly from the baseline group, $ps > .30$.

Discussion

Experiment 2 replicated the findings from Experiment 1 using a different and much more well-known genocide (the Jewish Holocaust during Nazi Germany). Specifically, the portrayal of ongoing negative consequences resulting from past atrocities committed by ingroup members led to a greater acceptance of collective guilt, and consequently to a greater willingness to pay reparations. Experiment 2 extended these findings by providing evidence that this effect depends, in part, on attributions of the perpetrators' intentionality.

In line with Lickel and colleagues (2004), collective guilt was experienced when ingroup harmdoing was framed as the result of negative actions of past ingroup members (intentional) rather than a result of negative characteristics of the ingroup (unintentional). Indeed, greater degrees of intentionality can serve as an indicator of responsibility, whereas causes of behavior that lie outside of individuals intentional decisions generally leads to less ascription of individual responsibility (Shaver, 1975). This pattern was also observed for willingness to provide reparations. Importantly, as in Experiment 1, describing historical cases of genocide as having ongoing consequences for the victimized group increased willingness to provide reparations, to the extent that collective guilt was accepted.

General Discussion

To date, collective guilt research has focused on the antecedents and consequences of this intergroup emotion for historical or contemporary harm (i.e., inequality between social groups). In two experiments, we merged these two streams by manipulating perceptions of whether historical harm has traversed generations to negatively impact contemporary members of a victimized group. In both experiments, emphasizing ongoing negative consequences of the historical crimes evoked collective guilt and willingness to compensate German atrocities committed in two genocides: against the Herero in 1904 (Experiment 1) and Jews during the Holocaust (Experiment 2). Importantly, Experiment 2 qualified this result by showing that this is particularly the case when the ingroup perpetrators are portrayed as in control of their behavior, implying intentionality and thus causal responsibility.

Our findings extend the existing literature in a number of ways. It is often the case that members of a historically victimized group experience consequences of that harm as intensely as those members who experienced the harm directly (see Klar, Schori-Eyal, & Klar, 2013; Yehuda et al., 2000), yet historical and contemporary harm have been treated separately within the extant collective guilt literature. The current research demonstrates that information about present-day consequences of historical harms elicits collective guilt from members of a perpetrator group. This research also provides a possible explanation for why collective guilt is heightened when the ingroup's negative past is perceived to be temporarily closer (as opposed to more distant; Peetz et al., 2010). Time may provide members of the perpetrator group with a sense of historical closure. Making salient that the past is not past and that the historically victimized group continues to suffer from the inflicted harm is an antecedent for the experience of collective guilt. For genocide education this implies that portraying ongoing consequences reaching from the genocidal past to today is likely to evoke feelings of guilt among members of the perpetrator group. While many would view this as a positive outcome, recent research by Imhoff and Banse (2009) also warrants some caution about trying to deliberately evoke feelings of collective guilt.

Imhoff and Banse (2009) tested the effect of ongoing victim suffering on prejudice against the victim group with an important second experimental manipulation: a bogus pipeline condition. Using a manipulation closely aligned to the one in Experiment 2, participants either learned about Jews' ongoing suffering due to the Holocaust or not. Under control conditions, the portrayal of ongoing Jewish suffering led to a decrease in anti-Semitism, which is compatible with the current findings of increased collective guilt. However, employing a bogus pipeline, and thereby reducing socially desirable but dishonest responses led to the opposite effect: reminders of ongoing Jewish suffering actually led to greater expressions of anti-Semitism under this condition (compared to a baseline measure 3 months earlier). At first glance these findings may seem difficult to reconcile with the current results. We propose two ways to interpret this discrepancy. One alternative is that in the present studies our manipulation led to a greater degree of explicit expressions of collective guilt without an accompanying authentic feeling, thus reflecting social desirability more than an actual guilt experience. A second, more interesting, explanation can be derived from Adorno's (1955) theorizing about secondary anti-Semitism. The core assumption is that the Nazi past still evokes unpleasant feelings of (collective) guilt in contemporary Germans and that this guilt fuels defensive mechanisms like secondary anti-Semitism (e.g., Bergmann & Erb, 1991; Imhoff, 2010; Rommelspacher, 1995). Future research will have to further explore this paradox as well as the relation between the constructive outcomes of collective guilt as tested in the present study (reparation intentions) and group-defensive strategies as outcomes (Imhoff & Banse, 2009; Kofta & Slawuta, 2013).

We were also able to demonstrate the role of attributions for historical harmdoing. To our knowledge, Experiment 2 is the first to manipulate the perception of past causal responsibility of ingroup members. Conscious control and explicit intentions of ingroup perpetrators have served as proxies to suggest causal responsibility of Germans living during the Nazi era for the crimes committed against Jews. In the 1970s, there was a fierce debate among Holocaust scholars about whether the Nazi extermination program was the result of conscious decisions and long-existing plans (intentionalist position) or the result of a more or less automatic dynamic of escalation into increasingly authoritarian situations that had stronger influence on individuals' behavior than their deliberate decisions (see Browning, 2000). Our results suggest that the portrayal of the Nazi past in one way or another is not only a question of historical truth but also has implications for important policy attitudes today.

Limitations, Implications, Caveats, and Conclusion

Our results provide preliminary evidence for the role of ongoing negative consequences for victims and the attribution of perpetrator actions in historical genocides in the emotional reaction to them. However, there are several methodological limitations of the present study. First of all, the reliability of both dependent variables was low and could be improved. Additionally, we interpreted reparation intentions as a behavioral outcome of collective guilt when in fact these intentions relied on self-reports as well. Future research should avoid one-item measures and provide more reliable estimates of the dependent variables, preferably actual behavioral outcomes. As an alternative, future research could also employ a bogus pipeline procedure (as in Imhoff & Banse, 2009) to distinguish authentic self-reports from responses born out of social desirability and impression management. Another weakness of the present study is that we only included manipulation checks for the attribution factor but not for the manipulation of ongoing consequences (but see Imhoff & Banse, 2009; Starzyk & Ross, 2008 for previous successful manipulations).

Our results suggest that the portrayal of ongoing victim suffering may be a key factor for evoking collective guilt—an aversive emotion that group members actively avoid (Leach et al., 2013; Wohl et al., 2006)—as well as willingness to pay reparations. Despite these positive outcomes, some caution about such strategies seems warranted. Examples of positive consequences of collective guilt beyond verbal support for reparations are sparse. In fact, collective guilt has been reported as a generally weak predictor for any actual behavioral intentions (Harth, Kessler, & Leach, 2008; Leach, Iyer, & Pedersen, 2006). Similarly, guilt had no relation to positive views of the victim group or the willingness to engage in contact with them when regret was adjusted for (Imhoff et al., 2012).

In addition to the doubts whether collective guilt has any incremental validity over and above other group-based emotions, recent evidence suggests that emphasizing ongoing victim suffering may actually backfire. Bilewicz (2007) showed that only touching the subject of a conflicted common history can undermine the positive effects of intergroup contact. Imhoff and Banse (2009) even provided support for the idea that under specific conditions (bogus pipeline) the portrayal of ongoing Jewish suffering actually can lead to greater degrees of anti-Semitism. Taken together, these results suggest that precautions should be taken against an instrumental use of the portrayal of ongoing consequences for the victims to improve intergroup relations in the aftermath of genocide.

References

Abelson, R. P., & Prentice, D. A. (1997). Contrast tests of interaction hypothesis. *Psychological Methods, 2*, 315–328.

Adorno, T. W. (1955). Schuld und Abwehr [Guilt and defense]. In F. Pollock (Ed.), *Gruppenexperiment [Group experiment]* (pp. 278–428). Frankfurt: Europäische Verlagsanstalt.

Adusei, A. (2009, November 24). What is wrong with African leaders? *Modern Ghana News.* Retrieved January 16, 2010, from http://www.modernghana.com/news/251029/1/what-is-wrong-with-african-leaders.html

Ahlheim, K., & Heger, B. (2002). *Die unbequeme Vergangenheit. NS-Vergangenheit, Holocaust und die Schwierigkeiten des Erinnerns [The unpleasant past. The history of National Socialism, the Holocaust and the difficulties of remembering].* Schwalbach: Wochenschau-Verlag.

Amin, S. (1973). *Neo-Colonialism in West Africa* Harmondsworth: Penguin.

Bergmann, W., & Erb, R. (1991). *Antisemitismus in der Bundesrepublik Deutschland: Ergebnisse der empirischen Forschung von 1946–1989 [Anti-Semitism in West Germany: Results of empirical research from 1946–1989].* Opladen: Leske und Budrich.

Bilali, R. (2013). National Narrative and Social Psychological Influences in the Turkish Denial of the Armenian Genocide. *Journal of Social Issues, 69,* 16–33.

Bilewicz, M. (2007). History as an obstacle: Impact of temporal-based social categorizations on Polish-Jewish intergroup contact. *Group Processes & Intergroup Relations, 10,* 551–563.

Bilewicz, M., & Jaworska, M. (2013). Reconciliation through the righteous: The narratives of heroic helpers as a fulfillment of emotional needs in Polish−Jewish intergroup contact. *Journal of Social Issues, 69,* 162–179.

Branscombe, N. R., Doosje, B., & McGarty, C. (2002). Antecedents and consequences of group-based guilt. In D. M. Mackie & E. R. Smith (Eds.), *From prejudice to intergroup emotions: Differentiated reactions to social groups* (pp. 49–66). Philadelphia, PA: Psychology Press.

Branscombe, N., Slugoski, B., & Kappen, D. M. (2004). The measurement of collective guilt: What it is and what it is not. In N. Branscombe & B. Doosje (Eds.), *Collective guilt: International perspectives* (pp. 16–34). Cambridge: Cambridge University Press.

Browning, C. R. (2000). *Nazi policy, Jewish workers, German killers.* Cambridge, UK: Cambridge University Press.

Bühler, C. (1943). Why do Germans so easily forfeit their freedom? *Journal of Abnormal and Social Psychology, 38,* 149–157.

Doosje, B., Branscombe, N. R., Spears, R., & Manstead, A. S. R. (1998). Guilty by association: When one's group has a negative history. *Journal of Personality and Social Psychology, 75,* 872–886.

Förster, S., Mommsen, W., & Robinson, R. (Eds.). (1988). *Bismarck, Europe, and Africa. The Berlin Africa Conference 1884–1885 and the onset of partition.* Oxford: Oxford University Press.

Goldhagen, D. J. (1996). *Hitler's willing executioners: Ordinary Germans and the Holocaust.* New York, NY: Knopf.

Golec de Zavala, A., Cichocka, A., Eidelson, R., & Jayawickreme, N. (2009). Collective narcissism and its social consequences. *Journal of Personality and Social Psychology. 97,* 1074–1096.

Harth, N. S., Kessler, T., & Leach, C. W. (2008). Advantaged group's emotional reactions to intergroup inequality: The dynamics of pride, guilt, and sympathy. *Personality and Social Psychology Bulletin, 34,* 115–129.

Haslam, N., Rothschild, L., & Ernst, D. (2000). Essentialist beliefs about social categories. *British Journal of Social Psychology, 39,* 113–127.

Heider, F. (1958). *The psychology of interpersonal relations.* New York, NY: Wiley.

Hoogvelt, A. M. M. (2001). *Globalization and the postcolonial world: The new political economy of development.* Baltimore, MD: Johns Hopkins University Press.

Imhoff, R. (2010). Zwei Formen des modernen Antisemitismus? Eine Skala zur Messung primären und sekundären Antisemitismus [Two forms of anti-Semitism? A scale for the measurement of primary and secondary anti-Semitism]. *Conflict and Communication Online, 9.* Retrieved April 17, 2010, from http://www.cco.regeneronline.de/2010_1/pdf/imhoff.pdf

Imhoff, R., & Banse, R. (2009). Ongoing victim suffering increases prejudice: The case of secondary antisemitism. *Psychological Science, 20,* 1443–1447.

Imhoff, R., Bilewicz, M., & Erb, H.-P. (2012). Collective regret versus collective guilt: Different emotional reactions to historical atrocities. *European Journal of Social Psychology, 42,* 729–742.

Iyer, A., Leach, C. W., & Crosby, F. J. (2003). White guilt and racial compensation: The benefits and limits of self-focus. *Personality and Social Psychology Bulletin, 29*, 117–129.

Janoff-Bulman, R. (1982). Esteem and control bases of blame: "Adaptive" strategies for victims versus observers. *Journal of Personality, 50*, 180–192.

Klar, Y., Shori-Eyal, N., & Klar, Y. (2013). The "Never Again" State of Israel: The emergence of the Holocaust as a core feature of Israeli identity and its four incongruent voices. *Journal of Social Issues, 69*, 125–143.

Klein-Parker, F. (1988) Dominant attitudes of adult children of Holocaust survivors toward their parents. In J. P. Wilson, Z. Harel, & B. Kahana (Eds.), *Human adaptation to extreme stress: From the Holocaust to Vietnam* (pp. 193–218). New York, NY: Plenum.

Kofta, M., & Sławuta, P. (2013). Thou shall not kill... your brother: Victim-perpetrator cultural closeness and moral disapproval of Polish atrocities against Jews after the Holocaust. *Journal of Social Issues, 69*, 54–73.

Kött, M. (1999). *Goldhagen in der Qualitätspresse: Eine Debatte über "Kollektivschuld" und "Nationalcharakter" der Deutschen [Goldhagen in the quality press: A debate on German "collective guilt" and "national character"]*. Konstanz: UVK Medien.

Leach, C. W., Iyer, A., & Pedersen, A. (2006). Anger and guilt about ingroup advantage explain the willingness for political action. *Personality and Social Psychology Bulletin, 32*, 1232–1245.

Leach, C. W., Zeinnedine, F. B., & Čehajić-Clancy, S. (2013). Moral immemorial: The rarity of self-criticism for previous generation's genocide or mass violence. *Journal of Social Issues, 69*, 34–53.

Levi, N., & Rothenberg, M. (2003). *The Holocaust: Theoretical readings*. New Brunswick, NJ: Rutgers University Press.

Lickel, B., Schmader, T., & Barquissau, M. (2004). The evocation of moral emotions in intergroup contexts: The distinction between collective guilt and collective shame. In N.R. Branscombe & B. Doosje (Eds.), *Collective guilt: International perspectives* (pp. 35–55). New York, NY: Cambridge University Press.

Noelle-Neumann, E., & Köcher, R. (1997). *Allensbacher Jahrbuch der Demoskopie, Band 10: 1993–1997 [Allensbach Institute. Almanac of public opinion survey, Volume 10: 1993–1997]*. München: Saur.

Peetz, J., Gunn, G. R., & Wilson, A. E. (2010). Crimes of the past: Defensive temporal distancing in the face of past in-group wrongdoing. *Personality and Social Psychology Bulletin, 36*, 598–611.

Powell, A. A., Branscombe, N. R., & Schmitt, M. T. (2005). Inequality as ingroup privilege or outgroup disadvantage: The impact of group focus on collective guilt and interracial attitudes. *Personality and Social Psychology Bulletin, 31*, 508–521.

Preacher, K. J., & Hayes, A. F. (2004). SPSS and SAS procedures for estimating indirect effects in simple mediation models. *Behavior Research Methods, Instruments, & Computers, 36*, 717–731.

Rodney, W. (1973). *How Europe underdeveloped Africa*. London: Bogle-L'Ouverture Publications.

Rommelspacher, B. (1995). *Schuldlos – schuldig? Wie sich junge Frauen mit Antisemitismus auseinandersetzen [Guiltless – guilty? How young women deal with anti-Semitism]*. Hamburg: Konkret Literatur Verlag.

Rosenthal, R., & Rosnow, R. L. (1985). *Contrast analysis: Focused comparisons in the analysis of variances*. Cambridge: Cambridge University Press.

Schreier, F. (1943). German aggressiveness—its reasons and types. *Journal of Abnormal and Social Psychology, 38*, 211–224.

Seitz, V. (2009). *Afrika wird armregiert oder Wie man Afrika wirklich helfen kann [Africa is being governed to poverty or how one can really help Africa]*. München, Germany: dtv.

Shaver, K. G. (1975). *An introduction to attribution processes*. Cambridge: Winthrop Publishers.

Starzyk, K. B., & Ross, M. (2008). A tarnished silver lining: Victim suffering and support for reparations. *Personality and Social Psychology Bulletin, 34*, 366–380.

Swim, J. K., & Miller, D. L. (1999). White guilt: Its antecedents and consequences for attitudes toward affirmative action. *Personality and Social Psychology Bulletin, 25*, 500–514.

Vollhardt, J. R. (2013). "Crime against humanity" or "crime against Jews"? Acknowledgment in construals of the Holocaust and its importance for intergroup relations. *Journal of Social Issues, 69,* 144–161.

Weiner, B. (1986). *An attributional theory of motivation and emotion.* New York, NY: Springer.

Wohl, M. J. A., & Branscombe, N. R. (2008). Remembering historical victimization: Collective guilt for current ingroup transgressions. *Journal of Personality and Social Psychology, 94,* 988–1006.

Wohl, M. J. A., Branscombe, N. R., & Klar, Y. (2006). Collective guilt: An emotional response to perceived ingroup misdeeds. *European Review of Social Psychology, 17,* 1–36.

Yehuda, R., Bierer, L. M., Schmeidler, J., Aferiat, D. H., Breslau, I., & Dolan, S. (2000). Low cortisol and risk for PTSD in adult offspring of holocaust survivors. *American Journal of Psychiatry, 157,* 1252–1259.

Zimmerman, A. (2001). *Anthropology and antihumanism in Imperial Germany.* Chicago, IL: University of Chicago Press.

Zuckermann, M. (1998). *Zweierlei Holocaust: Der Holocaust in den politischen Kulturen Israels und Deutschlands [Twofold Holocaust: The Holocaust in the political cultures of Israel and Germany].* Göttingen: Wallstein.

ROLAND IMHOFF (PhD, Bonn, 2010) is an assistant professor for social cognition at the University of Cologne, Germany. His dissertation research focused on representations of history and consequences for group-based emotions and intergroup relations. Other lines of his research are dedicated to the development of indirect measures of intergroup bias, dehumanization, and the role of implicit cognition in partnership and sexuality.

MICHAEL J. A. WOHL (PhD, Alberta, 2003) is an Associate Professor of Psychology at Carleton University in Ottawa, Canada. His research focuses on the causes and consequences of harmdoing at both the interpersonal (one person transgressing against another) and intergroup level (historical and contemporary harm experienced by members of one group at the hands of another group). Wohl's research has also focused on the factors that contribute to addiction (smoking, gambling) and refusal to seek treatment.

HANS-PETER ERB (PhD, Heidelberg, 1996) is Professor of Social Psychology at the Helmut-Schmidt University Hamburg. He received his habilitation at the University of Jena in 2004. He has worked at several universities including Mannheim, Würzburg, Maryland, Halle, Jena, Bonn, Chemnitz, and Magdeburg. His research interests include judgment and social influence in a wide variety of social phenomena.

Journal of Social Issues, Vol. 69, No. 1, 2013, pp. 92–110

Child Survivors of the 1994 Rwandan Genocide and Trauma-Related Affect

Suzanne Kaplan[*]

Uppsala University

This article reports findings from an interview study of orphans who were street children in Rwanda after the genocide in 1994. During two study visits in Rwanda in 2003 and 2004, in-depth videotaped interviews, follow-up interviews, and observations were carried out. Specifically, this article addresses how 10 teenage boys dealt with their memories and affects. The affect regulation of these Rwandan child survivors is elaborated and explained in a theoretical model referred to as the "affect propeller". This model emerged in previous studies of life histories of Holocaust child survivors, using grounded theory, and has been further developed based on the findings from these follow-up studies of Rwandan teenagers. One key finding that is described is the theme of retraumatization and revenge fantasies, which are obstacles in efforts toward resilience, as well as counterforces that facilitate a positive development in the aftermath of the genocide.

During the 1994 genocide, Rwandan children were exposed to extreme levels of violence, often witnessing the murder of close family members. Children's reactions were associated with loss, violence exposure, and, most importantly, persistent feelings that their lives were in danger (Dyregrov, Gupta, Gjestad, & Mukanoheli, 2000; Schaal & Elbert, 2006). A Human Rights Watch (2003) report estimated that 400,000 children—more than 10% of all Rwandan children at the time—were orphaned as a result of the genocide and of HIV/AIDS in the aftermath of genocide-related rapes. Attempts to trace possibly surviving family members were met with almost insurmountable obstacles. Street children in Rwanda were predominantly adolescent boys, almost half of whom were homeless (42%), and

---

*Correspondence concerning this article should be addressed to Suzanne Kaplan, The Hugo Valentin Centre, Uppsala University, Box 521, SE-75120 Uppsala, Sweden [e-mail: kaplan.suzanne@gmail.com].

The author would like to thank the Rwandan boys who agreed to be interviewed and Ellen Meisels for her help with linguistic suggestions and formatting of an earlier draft of this article.*

a high proportion of whom were orphaned or had lost at least one parent (Veale & Doná, 2003). In 1997, the authorities decided to regularly sweep the city and clear the streets and public spaces of persons they regarded as undesirable, such as street children, who were sent to reception centers far from the capital. Since 2003, Rwandan government policy has favored reducing the number of centers assisting unaccompanied children and increasing the placement of children with foster families. In some cases, children continue to live on the streets because they prefer life there (Human Rights Watch, 2006). Organized foster programs have proven to be an effective means of providing care for separated children in Rwanda (Doná, 2011).

This article examines how 10 child survivors who were teenage boys during interviews conducted in 2003 (Interview 1) and 2004 (Interview 2) dealt with their affect. These boys had lived in the streets for several years following the genocide. A few of them had stayed for shorter periods of time with a single surviving relative, but then returned to the streets because of the lone relative's poverty and insufficient care-giving. From 2002, they received help in a foster home, with a medical doctor as caregiver. This arrangement provided a unique opportunity to interview the boys in a safe context and within a relatively short time following the genocide.

Genocidal Trauma, Affect Regulation, and Attachment

Genocide often evolves from persistent conflict between groups (Melvern, 2000; Staub, 2011, 2013). The central aim of the 1994 Rwandan genocide was the extermination of an entire people, the Tutsis. Measures to this end had been planned for years in advance. The Hutu extremists in Rwanda began spreading their propaganda of ethnic hatred mainly through the radio (Mamdani, 2001). Among the Hutus, an ideology of "Hutu Power" developed and was propagated by elements of the government and media, intensifying fear and devaluation of Tutsis. A number of degrading and dehumanizing labels paved the way for the persecution. For example, Tutsi children were described in the media as "small rats" (Doná, 2011). The perpetrators also used expressions such as "pulling out the roots of the bad weeds" to refer to the killing of women and children (Gourevitch, 1998). Any possibility of a new generation of Tutsis was to be eliminated. From April to July 1994, Hutu extremists killed approximately 700,000 people, mostly Tutsis, as well as approximately 50,000 politically moderate Hutus.

Human beings exposed to extremely severe traumas feel first and fore-most completely terror-stricken. The concept of trauma has its roots in the Greek term for "wound," and mental trauma symbolizes bodily injuries and is defined as an event that overwhelms the individual's coping resources. For example, the concept of *perforating* (Kaplan, 2006) describes a puncture in the psychic shield.

The psychic membrane has figuratively and literally become "full of holes," for example, by an invading frightening voice, a tearing away (from family members, important objects, and routines), and "body markings" (both actual and symbolic, e.g. having "T" for Tutsi imprinted on an identity card and being the object of fabricated racial differences) (Kaplan, 2006, 2008). The individual feels an intense, urgent need to regain control over life but lacks the capacity to cope with the intensity of feelings. The traumatic events are registered as a panicky feeling— a fear—in the body. These bodily registered memories may be activated and recur during the course of the afflicted person's life, as the so-called flashbulb memories (Schore, 2003). During interviews with traumatized individuals, the concept of time and the time-related memory function can be seen as damaged. It is as if the trauma did not happen a long time ago, but instead is happening again and again every day (Laub & Auerhahn, 1993). A split in the self appears as a result of the difficulties in dealing with the fear and anxiety. This dissociation refers to a compartmentalization of experience, which is stored in memory as isolated fragments, sensory perceptions, affective states, or behavioral re-enactments (van der Kolk & Fisler, 1994).

From work with different populations separated geographically and in time— the Holocaust and Rwanda (Kaplan, 2006, 2008)—I have concluded that extreme traumatization resulting from unexpected, abnormal events is experienced in similar ways, regardless of culture. However, each individual's personal vulnerability, life history, and culture have a bearing upon how he or she *regulates anxiety* in connection with the traumatic moment and its aftermath. For example, the likelihood of surviving psychological damage and humiliation increases if there is a capacity for *reflective functioning* that results from secure attachment during the first years of one's life (Fonagy, Gergely, Jurist, & Target, 2002). Moreover, it is important that the traumatized individual has a safe psychic space in which to reflect about the fear and destructive fantasies that may follow the traumatic experience (Böhm & Kaplan, 2011). Van der Kolk (1993, p. 222) stresses that "fear needs to be tamed before proper integration of experience can occur (. . .) so that people are able to think and be conscious of current needs."

Recent findings on affect regulation come from neuroscience (Tutté, 2004). The awareness of one's affects fulfills a regulatory function that benefits the individual (Damasio, 1999). Loss of the ability to regulate the intensity of affect and impulses is possibly the most far-reaching effect of trauma and neglect (van der Kolk & Fisler, 1994). Ultimately, this regulatory function is designed to help us keep our inner psychic balance, and avoid loss of integrity and threat of death. Moreover, while exposure to war trauma may contribute to cognitive impairment (Dyregrov et al., 2000), the ability to self-regulate or modulate emotions is a "key predictor of academic or social success" (Masten & Coatsworth, 1998, p. 208). The aim of this article is to examine how affect regulation impacts the psychological well-being of 10 orphans in the aftermath of the Rwandan genocide in the present.

Theoretical Framework: The "Affect Propeller"

In the following, I present two directions that the psychic process can take for traumatized individuals: *trauma linking* and *generational linking*. These concepts have been developed in research with Holocaust survivors (Kaplan, 2002), using the method of grounded theory (see Glaser, 1978), and they are continuously further developed by studying new groups of survivors (Kaplan & Laub, 2009). In the present article, I examine these concepts among a group of Rwandan orphans. The theoretical framework for this analysis is the "affect propeller" model (see Figure 1), which is a theoretical model of affect regulation (Kaplan, 2005a, 2006) based on findings from studies of Holocaust survivors and Rwandan survivors. As we can learn to recognize even subtle emotional reactions in the most extreme affective states, such as in life histories of survivors, the "affect propeller" can also be applied to general emotional reactions.

The shape of a propeller illustrates and emphasizes the various dynamic processes of affect regulation related to trauma within each individual. Each blade represents a main category of such processes, which I refer to as *affect invading, affect isolating, affect activating*, and *affect symbolizing*.

Affect invading refers to wordless emotions—such as a body movement or a cry—preceding contents of traumatic memories. Victims repeatedly re-experience the events in their imagination, thereby re-experiencing the trauma (see also Allen, Fonagy, & Bateman, 2008, pp. 217-218). *Affect isolating* is characterized by a distanced, sometimes contained narrative in a closed part of the self. In a similar vein, Hopper (1991) describes the process of utilizing encapsulation (i.e., hiding oneself unconsciously in a fantasized capsule) as a defense against the fear of annihilation. The dynamic between affect invading and affect isolating corresponds to Herman's description of the two contradictory responses of intrusion and constriction "established as an oscillating rhythm" in the aftermath of overwhelming trauma, which she calls the "dialectic of trauma" (Herman, 1992, p. 47).

Affect activating refers to the risk of becoming moved and possibly feeling anxiety when talking about traumatic experiences. Conversely, in *affect symbolizing*, the person may feel freer in relation to the past. The trauma is no longer dissociated and contained in a closed part of the self, but is to a certain degree integrated into the individual's life and may be expressed in art, writing, lecturing, etc.

The affect propeller model poses that the regulation of trauma-related affect occurs as an oscillation between these four categories. In other words, the blades of the propeller pivot around the central point, *affect regulating*. While individuals oscillate between these blades at any given time, people differ individually in regard to how much they gravitate toward one blade or the other. Additionally, each blade includes three different levels of the so-called linking processes: two forms of trauma linking, and generational linking. Linking refers to the associative connections between affective states and major narrative elements of the

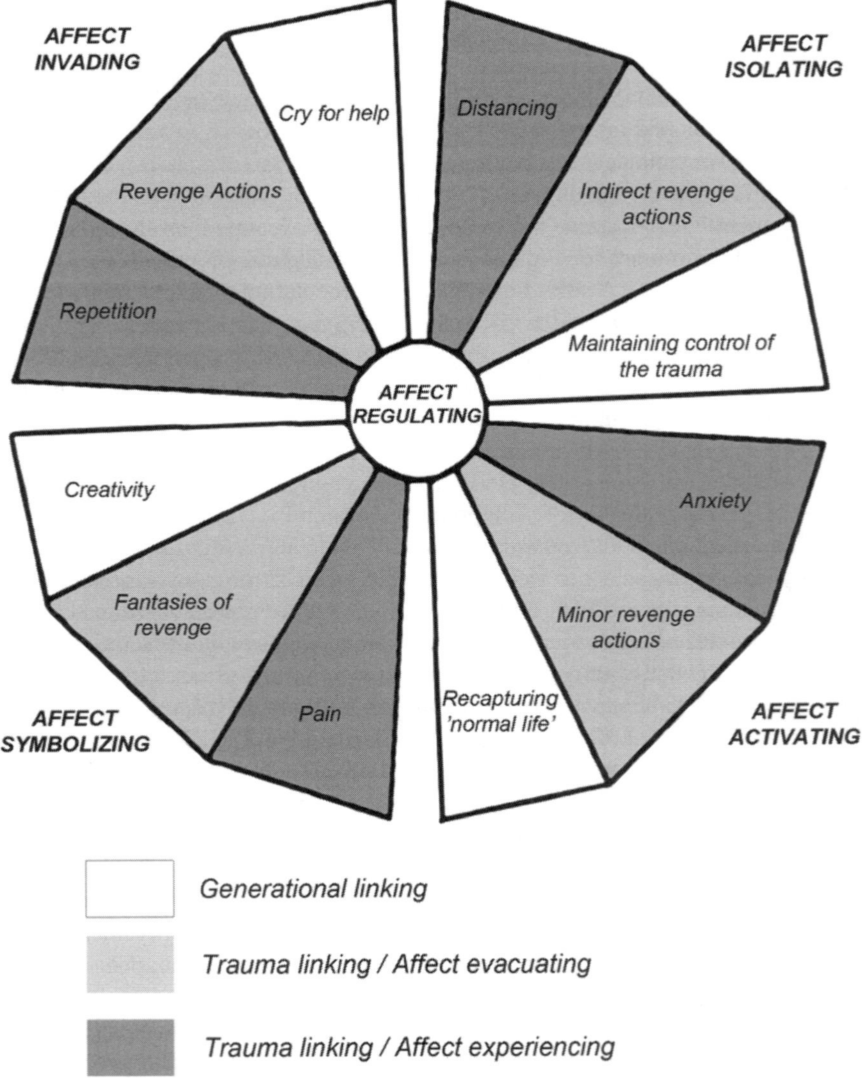

Fig. 1. The "Affect Propeller" (first published in Suzanne Kaplan (2010): Wenn Kinder den Völkermord überleben. Giessen (Psychosozial-Verlag), p. 258, © Psychosozial-Verlag, Giessen (Germany 2012).

individual's account. *Trauma linking* means that traumatic experiences are easily evoked associatively in the interview as well as by events in everyday life. One form of trauma linking is *affect experiencing* (relating to the trauma), the other is a more destructive process called *affect evacuating* (rejecting the trauma, as in revenge). *Generational linking* is a constructive process and indicates that the interviewees have their attention directed towards significant people and objects in the past and in the present. This facilitates the feeling of living in a safe societal context with less anxiety.

The blades rotate around the pivot and may overlap or lie separately, similar to the way in which emotions fluctuate. An interview with a survivor may start at any level or blade. The affect propeller model has proven to be a useful analytic tool for conceptualizing the interplay between affective states, both related to trauma and in general (e.g., Kaplan & Laub, 2009).

The Present Study

Context

The child survivors were interviewed during two research visits to Rwanda within a safe context, in order to reduce the risk of re-traumatization. Specifically, boys were interviewed who lived in a private orphanage established in 2002 by a doctor—referred to as Dr. Y to maintain anonymity—for orphaned and begging street children. At the time, he cared for seven boys. He provided for them and helped them with their schooling. By 2009, the operation had grown to include 55 boys. This context for conducting a study with the child survivors was optimal. The doctor was in a position to observe delayed reactions to the interviews and to follow up on these in a supportive way after the interview process had been completed.

Sample

In-depth, videotaped interviews were carried out with seven boys in 2003 and with the same boys and three additional boys in 2004. The boys were between 14 and 19 years old at the time of the interviews. One boy was only 8 years old, born after the genocide. Three of the boys were born in Kigali, and the others in rural areas. The boys had almost all experienced the unbearably painful loss of having their parents and most of their siblings murdered during the genocide (only one boy's parents had died of AIDS before the genocide, and the youngest had a surviving mother who died of malaria), after which they lived in the streets.

Interview Method and Analysis

The boys decided to be interviewed individually, in order not to be influenced by the thoughts of the others and most likely not to reveal very personal and vulnerable feelings to each other. The interviews lasted 30−45 minutes and usually began by asking, "You do fun things like dancing, but there are also problems you deal with. *What kind of thoughts return to you when you are by yourself?*" The interviews were conducted in French, English, and Kinyarwanda, the national language, with the help of a local interpreter. The interviews were videotaped and later translated in detail into English by a Rwandan research assistant. All names of the participants have been changed, in order to protect their identities.

The interviews were analyzed thematically. Affect categories were derived from the affect propeller model and enriched by this new data. Both verbal and nonverbal expressions of affect among the 10 Rwandan orphans were taken into account. In addition, I remained open to new, emerging themes.

Key Findings

The interviews revealed pronounced *affect invading* (i.e., re-traumatization) in both categories of trauma-linking, *affect experiencing* and *affect evacuating* (Figure 1). The boys also showed *generational linking*, by talking in detail about good memories from early childhood. In the following, examples from the boys' narratives within each affect category are presented.

Affect Invading/Affect Experiencing

Violence and humiliation.   All of the boys had been victims of extremely cruel violence and abuse. For example, Phil (Interview 1) described one such experience: "They had a fire nearby and were roasting meat on small metal sticks. They brought these hot metal sticks and burnt my forehead." We are reminded that genocide is about situations that we cannot imagine experiencing ourselves, "unique in the collective descent into an unimaginable primitivity of affect," in the words of Grubrich-Simitis (1981, p. 415).

The role and significance of humiliation in human-caused traumatic experiences, long overlooked (Lindner, 2001), need to be emphasized here. Phil asked before the interview: "How do you Europeans see us? As some kind of crazy animals?" People who have been forced to endure extreme traumatization often express feelings of shame. Wurmser (1981) speaks of the shame experience as a spectrum of emotions, from the mildest twinge of embarrassment to the searing pain of mortification.

There are many examples of humiliating experiences during genocide that involve the loss of one's values, such as to be betrayed by those believed to be one's friends, to be characterized as racially inferior or as an animal, and to be ordered to perform demeaning tasks. Jean (Interview 1) spoke intensely about this: "What hurt me most, was that the man who killed (my sister) used to be our neighbour, roasting meat near our home." Fred (Interview 1) showed me the palm of his hand:

> One of them told us to show our hands because they could tell from the palm of our hands. He said that Hutu do not have the middle line in the hands, while Tutsi have the middle line straight . . . They threw me in burning coffee husks and I got burned everywhere while they were just laughing . . . I cried loudly and one of them said, "Why don't we finish that fool and stop having him make trouble for us?"

Phil (Interview 1) said, "One of these men got hold of my brother and told him to put his tongue in his nose or in his eyes." This order to perform an impossible task can be regarded as humiliating.

Witnessing killing.   All of the boys had witnessed someone being killed or wounded, which is representative of children's experiences in Rwanda during the genocide (Human Rights Watch, 2003). Paul (Interview 1) reported that ". . . the Interahamwe (i.e., the Hutu militia, 'those who work/attack together') then started kicking and stepping on the chest of the man . . . one of the Interahamwe started killing small babies." Fred (Interview 1) said, "The smell of the dead bodies became too much." The boys also witnessed fear among the perpetrators as a precursor to killing. Paul (Interview 1) recounted,

> One of the Interahamwe asked, "what should we do if we are overpowered by the Tutsi?" The leader got very angry and quickly threw this man in the burning tires. As he tried to get out with all his clothes burning, the leader pulled out a machete and stabbed him to death.

Fear.   The boys reported a constant fear of dying during the genocide. Paul (Interview 1) said,

> I wanted to shout for help but my elder brother covered my mouth with his hands . . . my heart started then pumping a lot because I thought we would be killed in the same way . . . We moved slowly from our hiding place and I went crying all the way to the well . . . When I saw how they killed them, I took a very deep breath and made some noise. One of the Interahamwe said, "Eh!!! Who has made that noise?"

Phil (Interview 1) described his experience as follows:

> It became obvious that they were killing people . . . We became very scared and escaped to Nyarushishi . . . I stood up and started running for my life . . . One of these men immediately jumped and stepped on my brother's chest. He made a lot of noise which scared me and I also fell down. When I could not hear the noise any more, I woke up to find him already dead.

For the boys recounting their traumatic experiences and fears, these invasions of sounds during the persecutions seemed to be happening in the present. This is in line with research showing that traumatized people do not habituate, because their central nervous system does not block out stimuli as nonthreatening (van der Kolk, 1993). This means that fear prevails among traumatized people.

The threat of loss.   The boys described many instances of loss of close others, and the struggle to hold on to someone. Paul (Interview 1) cried and imitated his mother's voice while putting his head between his knees. "After mama discovered that her child was dead, she started crying 'Oh dear Lord God, my child is dead' . . . As we went out of the house . . . we found also our mother lying dead." Fred (Interview 1) said, "I started debating with myself whether I should leave my mother or stay and die with her . . . I decided to go with the baby on my back and prayed that my mother should be allowed to survive." Phil (Int. 1) told us, "The Inkotanyi (Tutsi rebels) took us away to a lorry, but I refused to go in and instead stayed behind with my dead mother."

The intensely painful loss of siblings was also described in many interviews. Jean (Interview 1) said, "What keeps coming back to my mind is the way my sister died." Fred (Interview 1) described how he tried to keep his baby brother alive: "I would uproot cassava tubes and eat them raw. As for the baby, I would chew the tube and spit in his little mouth so as to keep him alive." There is a strain on child survivors to become responsible adults prematurely (Kaplan, 2008).

Trauma triggers in everyday life.   Like other Rwandan genocide survivors, the boys reacted with anxiety when they heard sounds that reminded them of the whistling that perpetrators used to communicate with each other in the darkness. The boys also expressed a constant fear that the perpetrators would show up; they were seeing killers everywhere. When one of the boys came for his first visit to the group, everybody ran and hid, because they thought he looked like a perpetrator. Fred (Interview 2) explained and showed with his body movements what triggered his traumatic memories. "I fear when I see someone lying down, being beaten and punched. And that reminds me how we were being killed. They were laid down and cut with machetes, or any weapons they came across."

Affect Invading/Affect Evacuating

Rage and revenge.   Feelings of rage and murderous revenge fantasies are normal reactions to abuse (Herman, 1992), and fury and violence may become a response to shame-induced experiences (Schore, 2003). Thoughts about revenge can arise out of fear after having been put in an inferior position, that is, a traumatic event consisting of external violations and internal vulnerability (Böhm & Kaplan, 2011). While revenge acts were not reported in the interviews, two of the boys presented examples of pronounced revenge fantasies. Jean's face twisted in rage and he held his finger tips on his forehead as he said,

> Whenever I thought about that man who had killed my sister . . . I felt like . . . I could hunt him down and kill him. I felt that, even if they found me out there and killed me, I would have been able to take revenge for my sister and that was what mattered.

However, at the end of the interview, he suddenly looked considerably more relaxed and said,

> I no longer think the way I used to because those who are dead can't come back to this life that we're living in. I just hope for a better future with a wife and children. I'll tell them about everything I have gone through.

This example shows a rapid fluctuation of emotions—from affect-evacuating trauma linking to constructive generational linking.

In contrast, Fred (Interview 2) expressed an unsuccessful attempt to overcome his affect-evacuating trauma linking:

> The days I feel happy is when I'm with "Daddy" [Dr. Y], happily together. When a month goes by without him getting angry with me, I get so happy. But when he gets annoyed with me, my heart becomes like that of an animal. I feel like killing someone. My life depends on him, and making your own daddy annoyed is not very nice. Especially when he is responsible for you.

Affect Isolating/Affect Experiencing

Denial of affect. In some instances of trauma linking, the boys created a distanced narration that denied the impact of their life histories. For example, Alain (Interview 2) said, "For me, it is OK. I go to school, I live a normal life, I do not have any problems." This is in line with previous research showing that traumatized children have difficulty knowing how to express feelings (van der Kolk, 1998). Herman (1992) stresses that human beings always experience a conflict between the desire to deny loathsome events and the desire to speak openly about them. However, it is often the former urge that takes the upper hand.

Affect Isolating/Affect Evacuating

Denial of affect by action. In affect isolating, there is a risk of indirect actions of revenge—avoidance of trauma by flight into exile or suicide attempts (Kubai, personal communication, 2011). Stephane (Interview 2) said, "My dream is to go abroad, and this would help me to forget all that I have gone through." Patrick (Interview 1) said simply, "I dance to forget." Dance had become a distraction from trauma-related memories and affects.

Affect Activating/Affect Experiencing

Feeling abandoned. The interviews revealed that the boys' sense of safety was very fragile. Feeling abandoned was the most painful condition. Phil (Interview 1) explained,

> That is why whenever someone hurts me or abuses me, I start thinking of my family . . . and now that I am left all alone, it makes me very sad . . . I see no future for myself unless I study . . . and graduate and become able to work and look after myself.

Similarly, Fred (Interview 2) said, "I never remember anything except when someone shouts, abuses or talks to me in a harsh way. That is when I remember that I actually have no parents or relatives."

The relationship with Dr. Y was a lifeline for the boys. Stephan (Interview 1) told us, "I feel so happy that if he ever sent me away I would commit suicide." Paul (Interview 1) also said, "Where would I go when I know nobody on this earth?" The threat of loss can be described as an attachment trauma. Developmental traumatology describes the effects of profound stress and social isolation or defeat on the central nervous system (Koehler, 2010).

Affect Activating/Affect Evacuating

Reparation fantasy.   Within affect activating, there are "small revenge acts," such as not greeting a perpetrator. Alain (Interview 1) said, "In my heart [with a gesture to his chest], the sadness and rage will always be there. I will not be able to reconcile, but to accept." The emphasis shifted from doing destructive acts to regaining a sense of dignity. Alain (Interview 2) said, "I would like to go and study outside my country . . . and then I will come back here and then I am beyond them, my mind is beyond them . . . You become an important person when you come back to Rwanda." He tried to assume a superior position rather than enacting destructive revenge. Alain showed a mixture of triumph over others and constructive goals. He wanted to repair his self-image which had been hurt by the genocide, by coming back "beyond them" —a constructive reparation fantasy. He also expressed an interest in learning English.

Affect Symbolizing/Affect Experiencing

For short moments, the interviewees seemed to feel freer in relation to the past. One could say that for those moments, the trauma no longer existed only as something contained in a closed part of the self, but to a certain degree had been integrated into a broader time perspective on the course of their lives. For example, Phil (Interview 1) said, "I started acrobatics at the age of 8 . . . I was happy and started practicing more and it made my whole body feel good." Moreover, Phil imagined a normal future life with a real home: "I would like to live a normal life, have a permanent place that I would call my own with an address."

In Interview 2, Phil talked with pain about surviving in Lake Kivu while a boat sank during the genocide. He attempted, by his choice of words, to symbolize this horrible event:

> I was swimming for three hours [biting his lip repeatedly]. I came out crying, also happy that I survived . . . I was afraid and part of me was dead, like half of my body was numb, then I started to get normal again . . . I always think about this. There is a meaning that I did not die. I think that God has something for me.

Phil seemed to be able to express in words and metaphors how he felt. He shared his burden of pain in a constructive way.

Generational Linking

In the interviews there were also some, but considerably fewer, examples of the more adaptive generational linking that may function as counterforces to the traumatic experiences. These experiences tended to disappear in the boys' narratives of traumatic events. It also seemed very painful for them to remember their losses and lives before the genocide. However, most of the boys described some experiences that suggested a secure base during their first years of life. For example, Paul (Interview 1) said,

> I was my mother's favorite child, and was put in a kindergarten. Whenever I came home from school, she would lift me, hug me and kiss me and take me to the house. She was always waiting for me from school.

Similarly, Stephane (Interview 1) reported, "My father would buy me very nice clothes, and he bought me a bicycle one time." Leo (Interview 1) was only seven years old when his parents and sisters were killed. He and his four small brothers were protected by a neighbor Hutu family who pretended that the children were their own. The boys were later separated, but eventually managed to find each other. Thus, there are positive examples in which generational linking dominates over trauma linking. Likewise, the boys managed to maintain their reflective functioning and continuity in their contact with their caregiver, Dr. Y, and with me as a researcher who came to interview them twice.

Caring for the future.   Several boys also expressed the desire to overcome the consequences of trauma and to provide for a better future, both for themselves and for the country in general. Phil (Interview 2), who was successful at school, stressed, "I also deeply think of what I can do so this will not happen again. What I think and wish is to study so hard outside Rwanda so that I can get a solution for this problem." Jean (Interview 2) expressed a similar idea: "If I am lucky enough and pass my exams, then I will get a job and try to build my country." These examples also show efforts toward affect symbolizing and generational linking.

Follow-Up Interviews after 1 Year

The purpose of the follow-up interviews was to investigate how living in the foster home would contribute to healing the experiences of extreme trauma. The focus of the interviews was the boys' development after 1 year. Most boys managed well, but there was one case of continuous problems concerning the experience of social exclusion and maladaptation.

After 1 year of staying with Dr. Y, Fred had to move to another foster family. During the second interview, his continued suffering was apparent and intensified by the social exclusion he had experienced—first when the group living with the doctor expanded, and then when his behavior and regular conflicts with the doctor and the other boys, caused by his stealing from them, forced him to move from the house. However, he came back to the house for the interview—remarkably moved and concerned. Giving examples from his current situation when he felt tempted to steal, Fred explained:

> For me, I do such things because I like to do things that children like to do that need a little money. This is not a character that I was born with. I have no problems with food, nor accommodation or schooling. But when I see other children riding bicycles, I want to ride a bicycle as well. So if I find money, maybe on the table, then I get tempted to take it ... But I think it is wrong to steal, but I do it because I'm afraid to ask daddy. Because he meets all my needs, then I fear to ask him for such small things.

Fred's capacity for affect tolerance seemed to have been destroyed as a result of having been exposed to horrific traumatic cruelties. He acted instead of talking about his feelings, but during the follow-up interviews he was able to reflect on the situation. Fred was the first boy to get help from Dr. Y, and Dr. Y talked about their very first meeting. This was a moment of generational linking—a mutual reconciliation.

Retraumatization through Commemoration of the Genocide

Aside from the development that had occurred over the past year, another crucial influence on the second interview was an important event that occurred at the time of the interviewing. Specifically, the second interview with the boys was conducted on April 7, 2004, the 10th commemoration of the genocide.

The memory of the genocide is kept alive in Rwanda through memorials and annual commemorations. However, there may be a contradiction between unity and commemoration (Doná, 2010). A Rwandan psychologist explained:

> We are confronted during the genocide commemoration week with a kind of collective crisis of trauma, where about 100 people fall down at the same time during a two-hour ceremony of commemoration [at The National Stadium]. Some survivors were falling down, they were crying, trying to escape, they were reporting that they are seeing killers everywhere in the stadium ... and we ourselves felt at this moment strong emotions like fear ... It is as if the population is called by the government to focus during the whole year on the obligation of cohabitation, unity and reconciliation and rebuilding the country. During commemorations, things are reversed; to express their emotions is still difficult even if years have gone. In this particular space, the society allows them to say what they have to say, but there are no words to express the lived experience ... The rest of the year, they have to do a sort of repression of emotions. The work on unity, reconciliation, reconstruction of the country takes precedence over the rest of the year. (Gishoma, personal communication, 2010)

When the second interview was conducted in the boys' home, the television in the room next to ours broadcasted from the Kigali Stadium. All the boys were very affected and somewhat restless during the interview, and their accounts became even more fragmented. Jean (Interview 2) said, "A lot comes into my mind. I remember when they cut people into pieces with machetes, sometimes shot at them, threw them into pit-latrines alive or buried them alive. All this I witnessed with my own eyes." Similarly, Patrick (Interview 2) also said, "I remember how the Interahamwe murdered people. I saw it with my own eyes" (rubbing his eyes). Stephane (Interview 1) had told me, "I only remember them [my family] when there is a national mourning . . . The songs which are sung remind me that out of us 12 in the family, it is only me who is still alive and that makes me very sad."

The commemoration day re-traumatized the boys and actualized their wishes to "be taken away from Rwanda." Flight and efforts to forget were of major concern to them on this special day. Phil (Interview 2) told me, "I can't stay there by the TV . . . I leave the room to keep from thinking too much . . . I decided not to watch because it makes me remember." Patrick (Interview 2) said, "I feel sad when I think of my family and miss them immensely. I don't even want to watch television. I remember that someone ran after me." And Stephane (Interview 2) said, "This day is a terrible day and nobody will forget it, it can remind you what you might have forgotten. If possible, the government should abolish this commemoration day . . . it reminds me of all my close relatives who died [coughs] . . . ." Fred (Interview 1) commented, "When one tries to forget the genocide, they start announcing on the radio that they are going to officially mourn . . . that cannot allow me to forget." These statements confirm the concerns of the Rwandan therapist.

Jean was initially calm and serious. He did not talk about revenge, as he did during the first interview. He had a friendly smile and looked the interviewer in the eyes when he spoke. He said that ever since he had the chance to live at Dr. Y's, "things have developed in a good way." What he thought about most was school. "In this world there's a lot to do in the future." His dream was to work at a hospital. "I hope to become a doctor . . . And I want to work for my country," he added. Jean's ability to accept Dr. Y's help made things look bright and hopeful for him. Even though his dreams about the future were to some extent a defense strategy, there seemed to be hope for Jean for a constructive development—a generational linking, which in the long term would dominate over trauma linking. He was able to accept help, he completed his school work, and he adequately regulated the affects that were evoked when he saw pictures and heard sounds on TV that reminded him of the past. The oscillation between trauma linking and generational linking may actually be part of the healing process.

Discussion

The interviews show that affect matters a lot in the aftermath of extreme trauma, and the affect propeller allows us to systematize and understand some of these affective reactions. Both destructive and constructive dynamics become apparent in the interviews. The hope is that trauma-linking processes, with their accompanying temptations to take revenge, will gradually be covered over by generational linking processes—the latter then becoming the dominating links. At that stage, the individual feels a greater wholeness of being, has achieved restoration, has regained his or her dignity, and therefore does not have the urgency to take revenge.

Destructive Aspects

In some interviews, revenge fantasies came up and showed how thin the membrane is between perpetrators and victims, especially if the strain is too hard due to insufficient caregiving and lack of an empathetic listener for the victim's rage and destructive thoughts. If a person cannot mourn, as a result of being overwhelmed by the inconceivable losses of genocide, and cannot wipe out the horrifying memories, the rage may trigger an urge to kill, as in the cases of Jean and Fred. Probably the boys' fears that the killing would start again resulted in an attitude of "attack is the best defense." It seems that revenge fantasies have the purpose of restoring the inner psychic balance (Böhm & Kaplan, 2011).

Constructive Aspects

The boys who were able to meet the demands of Dr. Y most likely had a good emotional start in life. However, the role of fear after traumatic events cannot be underestimated. One may assume that the boys' strong emotional expressions—both verbal and physical—reflected the fact that they were young. They were vulnerable teenagers who still needed caring adults as they reflected on their futures. Moreover, they were once again neighbors of the perpetrators and were expected to be part of a united people—"Rwandans"—at the same time as daily events triggered memories of the genocide. Supportive help within a safe context, above all a social network, is invaluable. But helpers cannot have unrealistic expectations and underestimate the boys' ongoing experience of trauma as they return to "normal life." This process takes time, perhaps generations. They need to be able to talk about the trauma, in order to mourn their losses, while also trying to build new lives in a unified country. The boys' ambitions to further their educations and their willingness to share their experiences in the two interviews can be seen as counterforces to further re-traumatization and also as indications of resilience.

Practical Implications for Interventions

In 1980, the characteristic syndrome of psychological trauma became a formal diagnosis, an important recognition (Herman, 1992). The relevance of the

PTSD (post-traumatic stress disorder) diagnosis has, however, been increasingly questioned as a static label. Children affected by war must not be stigmatized as permanently damaged (Summerfield, 1998). The affect propeller's focus on affect regulation may open up possibilities to highlight the ongoing, dynamic process within each individual. Awareness of trauma linking and generational linking phenomena may be helpful in orienting therapeutic work with traumatized individuals. Either linking phenomenon may be dominant among these individuals. By picking up on themes associated with generational linking phenomena, and highlighting them—even when their presence is subtle and not obvious—the helper can support the individual's predilection for creativity and resilience (Kaplan, 2008).

All of the 10 boys, to different degrees, showed evidence of having a reflective capacity (Fonagy & Target, 1997)—reflecting their self-images—as illustrated in Paul's comment (Interview 2) about being humiliated: "It is a double conflict, because I don't want to be angry either" or Fred's comment (Interview 2) about stealing: "This is not a character that I was born with." These kinds of comments give hope. An opportunity to talk about emotions in a safe context may result in a calmer state and lessen the risk of spreading panic. Sharing with others may help in the process of becoming liberated from feelings of shame. The process of mentalizing, that is, reflecting about one's experiences, may change one's self-image and attitudes and diminish anxiety-driven behavior (Kaplan, 2006).

This has implications for educational settings in the aftermath of violent conflict. Schools can be structured such that they provide significant positive contact across group lines, and students may also develop critical consciousness and moral courage in these settings (Staub, 2013). The socialization of children for inclusive caring is highly important (Staub, 2011, 2013). Research and practice in the United States have demonstrated the importance of building *trauma-sensitive schools*, which can help children who have suffered trauma to develop the social skills that help them build positive identities and relationships (Cole, O'Brien, Gadd, Ristuccia, Wallace, & Gregory, 2005). This psychological work could be done in Rwandan schools and in community-based interventions (see also Pearlman, 2013; Wessells & Monteiro, 2004), where the lessons learned about the fear of both victims and perpetrators can be applied to reparative work. Moreover, Western approaches to trauma may learn from healing rituals, as we might need more supportive structures of symbolizing in order to achieve what is not always possible to verbalize after major traumas (Kaplan, 2005b). African researchers stress the importance of going from describing the problems to finding solutions (Donald, Dawes & Louw, 2000).

Let us return to the Rwandan situation. How should the Rwandan people cope with the contradiction presented by the Day of Commemoration recalling a collective crisis of trauma, and the need during the rest of the year to emphasize unity and reconciliation? Perhaps if the contrast between talking and not talking about the genocide is not emphasized, if there is more openness to talk about the past in organized group discussions during the year, the commemoration may become less of an exceptional state. It is worth reminding ourselves that forgiveness is usually a one-way process, whereas reconciliation is reciprocal, meaning that both the perpetrator and the victim are involved. Certain actions are unforgivable and they require acknowledgement in order to make reconciliation possible (Böhm & Kaplan, 2011). Maybe acceptance of history is a better concept. As Phil (Interview 2) said, "When I realized that I didn't have anybody, I had to *accept this life.*"

References

Allen, J. G., Fonagy, P., & Bateman, A. W. (2008). *Mentalizing in clinical practice.* Arlington, VA: American Psychiatric Publishing.

Böhm, T., & Kaplan, S. (2011). *Revenge: On the psychodynamics of a frightening urge and its taming.* London: Karnac Books.

Cole, S. F., O'Brien, J. G., Gadd, M. G., Ristuccia, J., Wallace, D. L., & Gregory, M. (2005). *Helping traumatized children learn: Supportive school environments for children traumatized by family violence.* Boston, MA: Massachusetts Advocates for Children.

Damasio, A. (1999). *The feeling of what happens: Body, emotion and the making of consciousness.* London: Heinemann.

Doná, G. (2010). Collective suffering and cyber-memorialisation in post-genocide Rwanda. In M. Broderick & A. Traverso (Eds.), *Trauma, media, art: New perspectives* (pp. 16–35). Newcastle on Tyne: Cambridge Scholars Press.

Doná, G. (2011). Researching children and violence in evolving socio-political contexts. In J. Pottier, L. Hammond, & C. Cramer (Eds.), *Caught in the crossfire: Ethical and methodological challenges to researching violence in Africa* (pp. 16–35). Leiden: Brill Publishers.

Donald, D., Dawes, A., & Louw, J. (Eds.). (2000). *Adressing childhood adversity.* Cape Town: David Philip.

Dyregrov, A., Gupta, L., Gjestad, R., & Mukanoheli, E. (2000). Trauma exposure and psychological reactions to genocide among Rwandan children. *Journal of Traumatic Stress, 13,* 3–21.

Fonagy, P., Gergely, G., Jurist, E. L., & Target, M. (2002). *Affect regulation, mentalization and the development of the self.* New York, NY: Other Press.

Fonagy, P., & Target, M. (1997). Attachment and reflective function: Their role in self-organization. *Development and Psychopathology, 9,* 679–700.

Glaser, B. G. (1978). *Theoretical sensitivity: Advances in the methodology of grounded theory.* MillValley, CA: Sociology Press.

Gourevitch, P. (1998). *We wish to inform you that tomorrow we will be killed with our families.* New York: Farrar, Strauss & Giroux.

Grubrich-Simitis, I. (1981). Extreme traumatization as cumulative trauma: Psychoanalytic investigations of the effects of concentration camp experiences on survivors and their children. *Psychoanalytic State of the Child, 36,* 415–450.

Herman, J. (1992). *Trauma and recovery: The aftermath of violence—from domestic abuse to political terror.* New York, NY: Basic Books.

Hopper, E. (1991). Encapsulation as a defense against the fear of annihilation. *International Journal of Psychoanalysis, 72,* 607–624.

Human Rights Watch. (2003). *Rwanda's lasting wounds: Consequences of genocide and war for Rwanda's children.* New York, NY.

Human Rights Watch (2006). *Swept away: Street children illegally detained in Kigali, Rwanda.* New York, NY.

Kaplan, S. (2002) *Children in the Holocaust—Dealing with affects and memory images in trauma and generational linking.* Unpublished doctoral Thesis, Stockholm University Department of

Education in cooperation with The Uppsala Programme for Holocaust and Genocide Studies, Uppsala University.

Kaplan, S. (2005a). *Kindheit im Schatten von Völkermord. Massives seelisches Trauma in der Kindheit und seine Folgen.* Nierstein: Iatros Verlag.

Kaplan, S. (2005b). *Children in Africa with experiences of massive trauma. A research review.* Stockholm: SIDA Department for Research Cooperation.

Kaplan, S. (2006). Children in genocide: Extreme traumatization and the "affect propeller". *International Journal of Psychoanalysis, 87,* 725–746.

Kaplan, S. (2008). *Children in genocide: Extreme traumatization and affect regulation.* London: International Psychoanalysis Library and Karnac Books.

Kaplan, S. (2010). *Wenn Kinder Völkermord überleben—Über extreme Traumatisierung und Affektregulierung.* Giessen: Psychosozial Verlag.

Kaplan, S., & Laub, D. (2009). Affect regulation in extreme traumatization—fragmented narratives of survivors hospitalized in psychiatric institutions in Israel. *Scandinavian Psychoanalytic Review, 33,* 95–106.

Koehler, B. (2010, November). Schizophrenia in the 21st century: Integration of recent research from brain, mind and culture. *Lecture delivered at the ISPS-US Eleventh Annual Meeting* (Austin Riggs, Stockbridge, New England).

Laub, D., & Auerhahn, N. C. (1993). Knowing and not knowing massive psychic trauma: Forms of traumatic memory. *International Journal of Psychoanalysis, 74,* 287–302.

Lindner, E.G. (2001). Humiliation and human rights: Mapping a minefield. *Human Rights Review, 2,* 46–63.

Mamdani, M. (2001). *When victims become killers.* Princeton, NJ: Princeton University Press.

Masten, A. S., & Coatsworth, J. D. (1998). The development of competence in favorable and unfavorable environments. *American Psychologist, 5,* 205–220.

Melvern, L. (2000). *A people betrayed—The role of the West in Rwanda's genocide.* London: Zed Books.

Pearlman, L. A. (2013). Restoring self in community: Collective approaches to psychological trauma after genocide. *Journal of Social Issues, 69,* 111–124.

Schaal, S., & Elbert, T. (2006). Ten years after the genocide: Trauma, confrontation and posttraumatic stress in Rwandan adolescents. *Journal of Traumatic Stress, 19,* 95–105.

Schore, A. N. (2003). *Affect dysregulation and disorders of the self.* New York, NY: Norton.

Staub, E. (2011). *Overcoming evil: genocide, violent conflict, and terrorism.* New York, NY: Oxford University Press.

Staub, E. (2013). A world without genocide: Prevention, reconciliation and the creation of peaceful societies. *Journal of Social Issues, 69,* 180–199.

Summerfield, D. (1998). Children affected by war must not be stigmatized as permanently damaged. *British Medical Journal, 317,* 1249.

Tutté, J. C. (2004). The concept of psychical trauma: A bridge in interdisciplinary space. *International Journal of Psychoanalysis, 85,* 897–921.

van der Kolk, B. A. (1993). Biological considerations about emotions, trauma, memory, and the brain. In S.L. Ablon, D. Brown, E. Khantzian, & J.E. Mack (Eds.), *Human feelings: Explorations in affect development and meaning* (pp. 221–240). Hillsdale, NJ: Analytic Press.

van der Kolk, B.A. (1998). Psychology and psychobiology of childhood trauma. *Praxis der Kinderpsychologie und Kinderpsychiatrie, 47,* 19–35.

van der Kolk, B. A., & Fisler, R. E. (1994). Childhood abuse and neglect and loss of self-regulation. *Bulletin of the Menninger Clinic, 58,* 145–168.

Veale, A., & Doná, G. (2003). Street children and political violence: A socio-demographic analysis of street children in Rwanda. *Child Abuse and Neglect: The International Journal, 27,* 253–269.

Wessells M., & Monteiro C. (2004). Healing the wounds following protracted conflict in Angola: A community-based approach to assisting war-affected children. In U. P. Gielen, J. Fish, & J. G. Draguns (Eds.), *Handbook of culture, therapy, and healing* (pp. 321–341). Mahwah, NJ: Erlbaum.

Wurmser, L. (1981). *The mask of shame.* Baltimore, MD: Johns Hopkins University Press.

SUZANNE KAPLAN is Associate Professor of Education and researcher at The Hugo Valentin Centre/Holocaust and Genocide Studies, Uppsala University, Sweden. She is a psychologist and child and training psychoanalyst, and a recipient of the Hayman Prize for published work pertaining to traumatized children and adults (2001 and 2007). Publications include *Children in genocide: Extreme traumatization and affect regulation* (2008) and (with T. Böhm) Revenge – On the dynamics of a frightening urge and its taming (2011).

Journal of Social Issues, Vol. 69, No. 1, 2013, pp. 111–124

Restoring Self in Community: Collective Approaches to Psychological Trauma after Genocide

Laurie Anne Pearlman*

Trauma Research, Education, and Training Institute, Inc.

Recovery from the profound negative psychological and spiritual effects of geno-cide is essential for individuals to live fulfilling lives, engage in reconciliation, and prevent future violence. This article discusses community approaches to trauma recovery that focus on individuals within their social context. It briefly identifies common psychological problems that follow genocide. It then presents construc-tivist self development theory (CSDT) as a foundation for understanding these effects and the RICH (Respect, Information, Connection, and Hope) framework, based in CSDT, for designing and assessing the effects of post-genocide psychoso-cial interventions. The article reviews three approaches to collective recovery: a multifamily group approach, a psychoeducational program focused on youth, and a public education program aimed to promote trauma recovery and prevent future violence. The RICH framework is applied to each approach.

Genocide and other forms of group violence create a wide range of negative aftereffects for individuals, communities, and societies. Constructive functioning at each level, including effective involvement in efforts to reconcile and prevent fu-ture violence, requires some trauma recovery, as well as mourning losses. Because genocide is a group process, community (rather than solely individual) recovery is an essential focus. While theory informs several evidence-based treatment models for survivors of individual violence and victimization, there is a dearth of theory-based or empirically tested models for recovery from massive group violence. Such models would allow for more effective responses to communities' psychosocial needs following mass violence, when needs often far outstrip available resources.

*Correspondence concerning this article should be addressed to Laurie Anne Pearlman, PO Box 1367, Holyoke, MA 01041, USA [e-mail: lpearlmanphd@comcast.net].

Laurie Anne Pearlman, Trauma Research, Education, and Training Institute, Inc., Holyoke, Mas-sachusetts. The author would like to thank Jamie Sullivan, B.A., for research assistance.

I focus here on trauma recovery of individuals in their larger social context, taking a community rather than a clinical approach. That is, I address group approaches that may contribute to individual and community recovery.

Collective recovery is not the same as clinical treatment conducted with groups of people. While helping people understand trauma and woundedness, collective recovery promotes resilience and reengagement with community. It may best be done through population-based processes such as public education, community forums, large-scale ceremonies and rituals, institution-based programs (e.g., set in faith communities, schools, and work places), and the media. Some whom genocide harms may not respond to these approaches. Their wounds will require more individualized, intensive, interventions. Yet, collective approaches can reach large numbers of affected persons and contribute to individual recovery through community restoration.

Wessells (1999) offered a useful analysis of the psychosocial effects of armed conflict. He gave 17 suggestions for outside consultants wishing to provide psychosocial support following such conflict. These included self-awareness and awareness of cultural and political issues, partnership with local people, sustainability, and capacity building.

Norris, Stevens, Pfefferbaum, Wyche, and Pfefferbaum (2008) described a network of adaptive capacities that require attention following mass violence. These include such elements as reducing risk and resource inequities, engaging local people in mitigation, creating organizational linkages, enhancing social supports, cultivating reliable information resources, and enhancing decision-making skills. They suggest that these capacities augment other interventions such as those described below.

With those observations in mind, this article opens with a brief description of some of the psychological and spiritual effects of genocide and a theoretical framework for understanding and responding to those effects. The second part of the article presents three evidence-based models for community recovery following genocide, considered in the context of the proposed theoretical framework.

Collective Responses to Genocide

An extensive literature documents individual responses to collective violence (e.g., Bar-Tal, Chernyak-Hai, Schori, & Gundar, 2009; Boris et al., 2008; Brown & Cehajic, 2007; Danieli, 1985, 2010; Erber, 2002; Jacob, 2009; Kaplan, 2013; Macek, 2009; Sajjad, 2009, Staub, 2011; Vollhardt, 2009). Some of these responses are as follows. Denial (Stanton, 1998) may take a variety of problematic forms, including denying genocide on the part of harm doers (Akcam, 2007; Bilali, 2013; Staub, 2011) or silencing dissent (Buckley-Zistel, 2006; Stefansson, 2010). Shame can motivate violence to restore the group's self worth or its image (Lindner, 2009; Lu, 2008; Scheff, 2000; Staub, 2011). Fear may inhibit people from participating effectively in societal matters (Kantowitz & Riak, 2008) or lead to aggression (Pettigrew, 2003). Psychological wounds can give rise to unnecessary defensive violence (Staub, 2011). Post-genocide identity disruptions may include victim identity (Bar-Tal et al., 2009), victim beliefs (which may be constructive or destructive; Vollhardt, 2009), or the collective adaptation of a "chosen trauma" (Volkan, 1996). In her interviews with 10 teenage boys following the Rwandan genocide, Kaplan (2013) found indications of humiliation, fear, insecurity, and damaged self-worth.

The multitudinous individual responses take shape and interact within the post-genocide social/cultural context. In addition to aspects of the violence and the person's connection to it (Green, 1993), these responses relate to " . . . culture, political, economic, environmental as well as worldview and large-group identity issues . . . " (Hart, 2008, p. 120). While these responses may be understandable and some have some adaptive value, they pose various problems.

Theoretical Framework: Constructivist Self Development Theory

A theoretical framework for psychological interventions allows for the generation of hypotheses and a deeper understanding of evaluation findings (including why interventions may not work as planned), beyond whether an intervention reduces particular symptoms. Constructivist self development theory (CSDT; McCann & Pearlman, 1990; Pearlman, 2001) describes areas of the self that violence and victimization can disrupt. These realms include self capacities (abilities that enhance self-regulation), ego resources (skills to manage the interpersonal world), psychological needs (such as security, trust, esteem, intimacy, and control) and related cognitive schemas, frame of reference (including identity, world view, and spirituality), and body and brain. The theory emphasizes that trauma responses take place in a particular social/cultural context that is the foundation for the individual's self development, specific expressions of traumatic bereavement (which encompasses both trauma and grief; Pearlman, Wortman, Feuer, Farber, & Rando, in press), and the recovery process. The wounds in these realms of the self give rise to culturally shaped symptoms and other problematic adaptations that recovery must address.

Collective Recovery after Genocide

When Ervin Staub and I began to work in Rwanda in 1999, I observed many of the same individual trauma adaptations that I saw in complex trauma psychotherapy clients in the United States. Thus, it seemed possible to use CSDT and its RICH treatment model as a foundation for trauma work in Rwanda, as described below.

RICH: A Theoretical Framework for Recovery Models

The Risking Connection trauma training curriculum (Saakvitne, Gamble, Pearlman, & Lev, 2000) translates CSDT into an approach to trauma recovery. The curriculum received empirical support in one study of 30 Risking Connection training participants (Giller, Vermilyea, & Steele, 2006) and another of 261 participants (Brown, Baker, & Wilcox, 2012). It has also received preliminary support in a study of 15 primary health care providers and 207 medical patient respondents (Green et al., 2010). Within Risking Connection, the acronym RICH captures the essential elements of recovery: Respect, Information, Connection, and Hope. The premise is that trauma recovery requires RICH relationships. Developed for use with individual survivors of childhood sexual abuse and neglect, RICH is not a treatment model, but a philosophy of or framework for treatment, based in CSDT, that can encompass many models and be adapted to a range of social/cultural contexts. The Rwandans with whom we worked embraced it and together we found it broad enough to allow for cultural adaptation and application to their collective trauma recovery needs. This application was perhaps aided by the coincidence that the acronym could readily be translated into French, as RIChE, for Respect, Information, Connection, et Espoir, or "hope" in French (the French word *riche* means rich in English). The effectiveness of our approach among 194 Rwandan research participants was reported in a carefully controlled study (Staub, Pearlman, Gubin, & Hagengimana, 2005).

In the context of the aftermath of genocide or other forms of mass violence, we can operationalize the RICH acronym as follows. Respect, broadly construed, could include, for example, acknowledgment by others of the injustice of the violence and its damage (addressing esteem needs), justice (through formally acknowledging responsibility for wrongdoing, justice demands respect for survivors, thereby addressing their disrupted world view), agency (by including the voice of the victim group in material and psychological recovery and justice processes), and restitution (such as restoring property to its owners or providing victim compensation). Information could include facts about what happened, how and why genocide comes about (e.g., Staub, 1989, 2011), the potential effects of violence (psychological trauma, traumatic bereavement, psychological wounds), what to expect in the aftermath of mass violence (symptoms, natural course of these problems), paths to healing, and how to help oneself and others as well as finding both material and social resources (such as trauma recovery assistance and community-based opportunities to rebuild civil society). Information confirms or corrects one's judgment (an ego resource), and can address self-trust (through validation), both physical safety and psychological security, and control (through an enhanced ability to make informed decisions). Connection takes both intrapersonal and interpersonal forms: acknowledging to oneself what happened (losses as well as one's behaviors during the violence and their consequences, addressing self-worth and world view), connecting with experience (remembering and talking about what happened while feeling the emotions, addressing affect tolerance), connecting with the greater community (repairing rifts among survivors, harm doers, and bystanders, addressing intimacy needs), reestablishing community (addressing security and intimacy needs), and receiving support and validation from others (addressing disrupted self-esteem). Hope arises from all of these dimensions—respect, information, and connection—as well as from developing a life worth living, investing in the future, contributing to others' well-being, and finding or creating meaning (Frankl, 1984). Hope, restored through meaning, is an antidote to disrupted spirituality.

The above elaboration of the RICH elements allows for a delineation of the links between RICH and CSDT. Respect could contribute to the restoration of self-capacities, which CSDT defines as aspects of the self that include affect regulation, self-worth, and object constancy (Pearlman, 1998). Information could help to restore ego resources, such as judgment, decision-making, establishing boundaries, and understanding the consequences of one's actions (Pearlman, 2001). Connection with self (among thoughts, feelings, and needs) could support psychological needs and related cognitive schemas (Pearlman, 2003), while connection with others might contribute to self-capacities. Hope is likely to contribute to meaning, life purpose, and spiritual connection, all aspects of frame of reference (Pearlman, 2001).

Sample Collective Recovery Models

In this section, I briefly present three models of collective recovery and comment on them within the RICH framework. Readers may also want to review other excellent training and nonclinical intervention approaches to addressing psychosocial needs following group violence such as those of the International Trauma Studies Program (Saul, 2009) and the Transcultural Psychosocial Organization (de Jong, 2002).

My focus is on individuals within their communities, with a steady gaze on the community's overall well-being. A public health or community psychology model, rather than a psychopathology or clinical model, is the foundation for a collective recovery approach. The emphasis is on prevention of further psychological harm and on strengths. In order to ensure cultural appropriateness, community members must participate in shaping the approach (Wessells, 2009a).

Coffee and family education and support for Bosnian families (CAFES).
Stevan Weine and colleagues developed an approach to supporting refugee families after the genocide in the former Yugoslavia. They based their work on the observation that refugees from Bosnia and Kosovo were not using available services, despite high levels of psychosocial need. The program " . . . is a structured

multi-family discussion group program aimed at building upon family strengths" (Weine, 2000). Weine described the approach as aimed at the family, an important unit between the individual and the collective, which, according to his Bosnian refugee informants, is the locus of post-genocide social life. Weine wrote that the approach "emphasizes what remains strong and intact in survivors and in particular survivor families and aims to help them build on that." Its goals are "1) to help families ... draw upon their strengths and resources to cope together under the stresses of survival and exile; 2) to give families information that will make it easier for them to obtain appropriate care and services." They did this by setting up 9 to 15 weekly meetings with Bosnian facilitators who assisted groups of about seven families in learning from and supporting each other in addressing the problems they faced as refugees in a new culture and community. Groups focused on networking, education, and support. They adapted the model to work with Kosovar refugees, renaming it TAFES (tea replacing coffee for cultural suitability; Raina et al., 2006). Both programs had the additional goals of increasing participants' awareness of trauma-related mental health issues and available resources.

Weine et al. (2004) used grounded theory to assess the effects of this approach. Participants were 125 Bosnian families. Their evaluation yielded two major dimensions of concern to the families. They termed these "Displaced Families of War," representing the negative effects of war and its aftermath for families, and "Families Rebuilding Lives," which reflects families' thoughts about how to move forward constructively in response to the negative effects. This rich analysis contrasts with a strict clinical perspective by illustrating the complex intertwining of negative and positive dimensions of post-genocide family life, both the losses and families' determination, resilience, and creativity. Research on the model has found that it may be effective with refugee families post-war in increasing networking, trauma mental health knowledge and attitudes, utilization of mental health services, family hardiness, and to a lesser extent, social support (Weine et al., 2004; Weine, Knafl, & Feetham, 2005; Weine et al., 2008).

This model includes some of the RICH elements noted above. It offers respect by including local people in its design process, honoring the Bosnian café culture, responding to expressed needs, drawing upon the mutual support potential of participants, using leadership skills of facilitators from the community, and highlighting the creative responses of participant families to the deprivations they experienced. It provides information to families to address their life problems. It provides connection with other families and to community resources. Through these elements, it may well provide hope to families in overcoming their isolation and daily struggles. The program does not address trauma or grief directly, but in focusing on strengthening the family, a core unit in society, provides a strong platform for doing so as needed.

Wessells's model. Michael Wessells and his colleagues have developed a model for supporting communities after group violence (Wessells & Monteiro, 2006). They have applied their model in Angola and Sierra Leone, among other places affected by mass violence. While the model has not yet been applied in a post-genocide context, it seems well suited to it. The focus is on people between approximately 13 and 18 years of age, because this group is in developmental transition and has a particular opportunity to break continuing cycles of violence. The stated goal of the program was to improve the social integration of youth into their communities. Its specific objectives were "(1) to reinforce key adults' knowledge of youth's psychosocial needs, (2) to improve youths' life skills, and (3) to strengthen youths' positive role in the community" (p. 9). The program "taught youth life skills, provided peer support and peace education, educated adults about youth, and engaged youth as workers on community development projects" (p. 1). Evaluation research methods included open-ended questions, focus groups, and youth self-reports that were corroborated by adults. They revealed positive outcomes, including "increased adult awareness of the situation and needs of youth, improved youth-adult relations, reduced perceptions of youth as troublemakers, reduced fighting between youth, increased community planning, and increased perceptions that youth make a positive contribution to the community" (p. 1).

In Sierra Leone, Wessells and colleagues applied a related approach to promote reconciliation between returning child soldiers and their communities (Wessells, 2009b). Working with local partners in 20 communities, the Christian Children's Fund used a superordinate goals approach which, through dialogue, identified a project in each community on which participants agreed to collaborate. Examples of projects are rebuilding a school and repairing a bridge. Both recruited and nonrecruited youth from different sides of the conflict each committed 20 hours of work in exchange for $27/participant. At the end, extensive interviews and focus groups revealed that both groups of youth and community elders reported positive effects related to intervillage unity and reconciliation.

This program reflects elements of the RICH approach. It provided respect through collaboration with local participants to design the program and cofacilitate groups and through attention to strengths and resilience-building. It provided information about life skills, peace education, and the needs of youth. It provided connection through peer support and community development projects. All of these elements may contribute to hope for a more peaceful future. While the program elements do not address trauma per se, to the extent that they address the four RICH elements, they may be contributing to trauma recovery.

Staub-Pearlman-La Benevolencija approach. In 2001, Ervin Staub, George Weiss, Anneke van Hoek, and I initiated a public education program intended to promote trauma recovery and prevent future violence in Rwanda. The programs began broadcasting in Rwanda in 2004 and expanded broadcasting to

Burundi in 2005 and to the Democratic Republic of Congo in 2006. The project is described in detail elsewhere (Staub, 2011; Staub, Pearlman, & Bilali, 2008; see also Staub, 2013). Its basis is an approach to addressing post-genocide trauma and psychological wounds, promoting reconciliation, and preventing future conflict based on Staub's theoretical work on the origins and prevention of group violence and reconciliation (1989, 2011) and Pearlman and colleagues' constructivist self development theory (McCann & Pearlman, 1990; Pearlman, 2001) and RICH approach to trauma recovery (Saakvitne et al., 2000), described briefly above.

We implemented and tested a training program in Rwanda based on this approach. The research, using an experimental design, demonstrated a reduction in trauma symptoms in members of community groups led by facilitators whom we trained in comparison to those in groups led by nontrained facilitators and those who received no intervention (Staub et al., 2005).

The three primary objectives of the public education project are to promote (1) reconciliation and the prevention of group violence by fostering understanding of the influences that contribute to the evolution of mass killing and genocide, (2) understanding of the impact of group violence (trauma and psychological woundedness) and of the RICH approach as a path to trauma recovery, and (3) awareness and knowledge that can help listeners become active bystanders who intervene to prevent the evolution of group violence.

The project conveys information about the origins of group violence, psychological trauma, recovery, reconciliation, and violence prevention through entertaining radio dramas and informational programs. It encourages pluralism, active bystandership, and a neighbor-to-neighbor approach to trauma recovery. It also has a grassroots component in which trained community members help resolve conflicts among people in their communities that come to their attention. Local and international staff collaboratively develop the overall design of each program and specific story lines within the dramas, which include evidence-based educational messages, transformed to apply to each local culture. Examples of the trauma messages, as described in the project training manual (Staub, Pearlman, Haven, Bilali, & Vollhardt, 2007), are as follows:

- Group violence has profound effects on all parties: victims or survivors, perpetrators or harm doers, and bystanders or witnesses.
- There are individual differences in how people are affected by violence. These include changes in identity, self-concept, attitudes toward others, empathy, meaning, and trauma responses such as fear, sleep difficulties, aggression, nightmares, alcohol use, and social withdrawal. Some of these responses can increase the likelihood that people will contribute to future violence, or be unable to help stop it as it begins to unfold.
- Trauma is not madness. It can be understood.
- Many traumatized people function adequately in their daily lives.

- Healing is a long, slow process that can be facilitated by RICH relationships (Respect, Information, Connection, and Hope).
- It is important to share one's trauma story. This process is most constructive when the person who is sharing the story controls what, how, when, and with whom s/he shares it, and when others listen with empathy.
- People who have suffered traumatic losses must mourn those losses. Ceremonies, commemorations, community rituals, and testimonials that connect people to each other, to the past, and to the future can support this mourning and promote recovery.
- Retraumatization is less likely with preparation for encountering reminders of traumatic experiences, support during those encounters, and discussion afterward of what it was like to encounter reminders.
- Neighbors can help neighbors heal by empathic listening and demonstrating compassion and tolerance, respecting and not judging others' experiences, creating ceremonies together, and inviting neighbors into daily activities.

Local scriptwriters create the program scripts, incorporating these messages. Staff then translates the scripts into English for an international "academic team" who reviews them for fidelity to the educational messages. Local actors and production teams bring the programs to the air in the local languages. A call-in phone option, public events, listener groups, and evaluation studies have documented the programs' popularity (about 67% of the population listens in Burundi: La Benevolencija, 2010; and DRC: Helbig, 2011, April; and 84% in Rwanda: La Benevolencija, 2011).

Research on the project in post-genocide Rwanda has shown it to be effective in increasing empathy for various groups including survivors, leaders, and perpetrators; increasing people's willingness to speak their beliefs; heightening their awareness of trauma; and increasing their independence of authority (Paluck, 2009; see also Staub & Pearlman, 2009). Those in an experimental group who listened to the radio drama tended more to engage in reconciliation behaviors, approaching people who harmed them or whom they had harmed. In contrast, people not exposed to the drama talked more about reconciliation without engaging in such action (Paluck, 2009; see also Staub & Pearlman, 2009). A follow-up study revealed that listeners who were primed with the voice of a character from the drama were also more likely to report historical perspective-taking in regard to the other group's conflict narrative, and less likely to report mistrust and competitive victimhood than those listeners who were not reminded of the drama's messages (Bilali & Vollhardt, 2013). While this does not directly speak to the reduction of trauma, it seems likely that such attitudes and actions require some recovery from trauma.

This project includes elements of the RICH approach. It provides *respect* by collaborating with local stakeholders and partners to develop and translate the concepts into the culture, emphasizing a neighbor-to-neighbor approach to trauma recovery (suggesting that each person can help others, meaning that everyone has something to contribute and that professionals are not the only potential helpers), placing trauma in a broader context (not pathologizing those affected by violence, but acknowledging the inevitable wounds that genocide inflicts on all parties), and asserting the importance of justice. It provides information on the origins and prevention of group violence, its potential traumatic effects, paths to recovery, and essential elements of reconciliation. It supports connection by suggesting that neighbors can help neighbors heal, emphasizing the importance of acknowledging what happened and expressing its impact, and promoting active bystandership. It also encourages connection through its venue, radio, to which most people in the region listen in natural community groups. It suggests that meaning is an essential component of the recovery process, and orients people to reconciliation and the development of a peaceful future, which all contribute to hope.

Unlike the other collective recovery models described earlier, this project also specifically addresses trauma and psychological wounds (CAFES aims to guide participants to trauma recovery resources in the community but does not address trauma as directly as this approach). It aims to educate people about traumatic stress (but not post-traumatic stress disorder, which certainly exists in Rwanda, but is too narrow a conceptualization for what people often experience after genocide: e.g., Priebe et al., 2010). This project includes harm doers among the groups affected by group violence and points to their need to heal as part of violence prevention. Finally, the project addresses bereavement, suggesting the importance of mourning rituals for moving through grief, which many trauma-focused interventions neglect.

Future Directions for Research, Practice, and Policy

There is much to learn about the best approach to restoring meaning and hope after genocide, and there are great challenges to learning what works for whom. Testing the effectiveness of post-genocide interventions is very challenging be-cause of the many complexities of field research, often including cross-cultural issues. Some relevant cultural issues include the use of Western approaches that have not been validated in other cultures and the use of culturally unsustainable approaches (Wessells, 1999), a misunderstanding of the meanings of loss and trauma, and neglect of local approaches to recovery and prevention. Nonetheless, prospective helpers and funders should include impact assessments in all inter-ventions and publish their findings to contribute to the evidence base of collective recovery models in post-genocide societies.

Each culture will require its own approach. Yet there are certainly common elements to successful approaches. Practitioners have engaged in heated debates about the best paradigm—trauma, resilience, individual, family, clinical, community (Summerfield, 2004; Wessells, 1999). There may be a place for each approach. Linkages among scholars who bring a familiarity with the evidence base and evaluation methods, community partners who know their cultures (including current needs, traditional practices, and meanings of harm, help, resilience, and sustainability) and local resources; nongovernmental organizations with expertise in relief and other field work as well as in creating partnerships; and governmental bodies with access to local resources have the potential to create programs that can be tested with the hopes of both empowering and assisting community and individual recovery and providing templates for use in other situations of the aftermath of genocide and mass violence.

References

Akcam, T. (2007). *A shameful act: The Armenian genocide and the question of Turkish responsibility.* New York: Holt Paperbacks.

Bar-Tal, D., Chernyak-Hai, L., Schori, N., & Gundar, A. (2009). A sense of self-perceived collective victimhood in intractable conflicts. *International Review of the Red Cross, 91,* 229–258. doi: 10.1017/S1816383109990221

Bilali, R. (2013). National narrative and social psychological influences in Turks' denial of the mass killings of Armenians as genocide. *Journal of Social Issues, 69,* 16–33.

Bilali, R., & Vollhardt, J. R. (2013). Priming effects of a reconciliation radio drama on historical perspective-taking in the aftermath of mass violence in Rwanda. *Journal of Experimental Social Psychology, 49,* 144–151. doi: 10.1016/j.jesp.2012.08.011

Boris, N., Brown, L., Thurman, T., Rice, J., Snider, L, Ntaganira, J., & Nyirazinyoye, L. (2008). Depressive symptoms in youth heads of household in Rwanda: Correlates and implications for intervention. *Archives of Pediatrics & Adolescent Medicine, 162,* 836–843. doi: 10.1001/archpedi.162.9.836

Brown, R., & Cehajic, S. (2007). Dealing with the past and facing the future: Mediators of the effects of collective guilt and shame in Bosnia and Herzegovina. *European Journal of Social Psychology, 38,* 669–684. doi: 10.1002/ejsp.466

Brown, S. M., Baker, C. N., & Wilcox, P. (2012). Risking Connection trauma training: A pathway toward trauma-informed care in child congregate care settings. *Psychological Trauma: Theory, Research, Practice and Policy, 4,* 507–515. doi: 10.1037/a0025269

Buckley-Zistel, S. (2006). Remembering to forget: Chosen amnesia as a strategy for local coexistence in post-genocide Rwanda. *Africa: The Journal of the International African Institute, 76,* 131–150. Project MUSE. Available online January 21, 2011, from http://muse.jhu.edu/

Danieli, Y. (1985). The treatment and prevention of long-term effects and intergenerational transmission of victimization: A lesson from Holocaust survivors and their children. In C. R. Figley (Ed.), *Trauma and its wake* (pp. 295–313). New York: Brunner/Mazel.

Danieli, Y. (2010). Fundamentals of working with (re)traumatized populations. In G. H. Brenner, D. H. Bush, J. Moses, G. H. Brenner, D. H. Bush, & J. Moses (Eds.), *Creating spiritual and psychological resilience: Integrating care in disaster relief work* (pp. 195–210). New York: Routledge/Taylor & Francis Group.

de Jong, J. T. (2002). Public mental health, traumatic stress and human rights violations in low-income countries: A culturally appropriate model in times of conflict, disaster and peace. In J. T. de Jong (Ed.), *Trauma, war, and violence: Public mental health in socio-cultural context* (pp. 1–91). New York: Plenum Publishers.

Erber, R. (2002). Perpetrators with a clear conscience: Lying, self-deception, and belief change. In L. S. Newman & R. Erber (Eds.), *Understanding genocide: The social psychology of the Holocaust* (pp. 285–300). New York: Oxford University Press.

Frankl, V. (1984). *Man's search for meaning [originally published in 1946].* New York: Washington Square Press/Simon & Shuster.

Giller, E., Vermilyea, E., & Steele, T. (2006). Risking Connection: Helping agencies embrace relational work with trauma survivors. *Journal of Trauma Practice, 5,* 65–82. doi:10.1300/J189v05n01_05

Green, B. (1993). Identifying survivors at risk: Trauma and stressors across events. In J. P. Wilson & B. Raphael (Eds.), *International handbook of traumatic stress syndromes* (pp. 135–144). New York: Plenum Press.

Green, B., Saunders, P., Power, E., Dass-Brailsford, P., Bhat Schelbert, K., Giller, E., Wissow, L., & Hurtado, A. (2010). Improving communication between primary care providers and their trauma patients. *Poster presented at the 26th annual meeting of the International Society for Traumatic Stress Studies,* Montreal, Quebec, Canada.

Hart, B. (2008). Peacebuilding leadership in traumatized societies. In B. Hart (Ed.), *Peacebuilding in traumatized societies* (pp. 108–128). Lanham, MD: University Press of America.

Helbig, H. (2011, April). *Kumbuka kesho: Etude d'audience [Kumbuka kesho: Audience survey.] Unpublished report.* Amsterdam, The Netherlands: La Benevolencija.

Jacob, N. (2009). Consequences of traumatic stress in Rwandan genocide survivors: Epidemiology, psychotherapy, and dissemination. Doctoral dissertation, University of Konstanz, Badem-Wurttemberg, Germany. Available online http://d-nb.info/1000485595/34 (Downloaded January 2, 2013.)

Kantowitz, R., & Riak, A. (2008). Critical links between peacebuilding and trauma healing: A holistic framework for fostering community development. In B. Hart (Ed.), *Peacebuilding in traumatized societies* (pp. 3–26). Lanham, MD: University Press of America.

Kaplan, S. (2013). Child survivors of the 1994 Rwandan genocide and trauma-related affect. *Journal of Social Issues, 69,* 92–110.

La Benevolencija. (2010). *Etude d'audience et d'impact du feuilleton radiophonique Murikira Ukuri* [Survey of the audience and the impact of the radio drama Murikira Ukuri]. Unpublished report. Amsterdam, The Netherlands: La Benevolencija.

La Benevolencija. (2011). *Musekeweya impact evaluation and popularity survey.* Unpublished report. Amsterdam, The Netherlands: La Benevolencija.

Lindner, E. G. (2009). Genocide, humiliation, and inferiority: An interdisciplinary perspective. In N. A. Robins & A. Jones (Eds.), *Genocides by the oppressed: Subaltern genocide in theory and practice* (pp. 138–158). Bloomington, IN: University of Indiana Press.

Lu, C. (2008). Shame, guilt and reconciliation after war. *European Journal of Social Theory, 11,* 367–383. doi: 10.1177/1368431008092568

Macek, I. (2009). The plight and fate of women during the crisis in the former Yugoslavia. In S. Totten (Ed.), *The plight and fate of women during and following genocide* (pp. 83–106). New Brunswick, NJ: Transaction Publishers.

McCann, I. L., & Pearlman, L. A. (1990). *Psychological trauma and the adult survivor: Theory, therapy, and transformation.* New York: Brunner/Mazel.

Norris, F., Stevens, S., Pfefferbaum, B., Wyche, K., & Pfefferbaum, R. (2008). Community resilience as a metaphor, theory, set of capacities, and strategy for disaster readiness. *American Journal of Community Psychology, 41,* 127–150. doi: 10.1007/s10464-007-9156-6

Paluck, E. (2009). Reducing intergroup prejudice and conflict using the media: A field experiment in Rwanda. *Journal of Personality and Social Psychology, 96,* 574–587. doi: 10.1037/a0011989; 10.1037/a0011989.supp (Supplemental)

Pearlman, L. A. (1998). Trauma and the self: A theoretical and clinical perspective. *Journal of Emotional Abuse, 1,* 7–25. doi: 10.1300/J135v01n01_02

Pearlman, L. A. (2001). The treatment of persons with complex PTSD and other trauma-related disruptions of the self. In J. P. Wilson, M. J. Friedman, & J. D. Lindy (Eds.), *Treating psychological trauma & PTSD* (pp. 205–236). New York: The Guilford Press.

Pearlman, L. A. (2003). *Trauma and Attachment Belief Scale (TABS) manual*. Los Angeles, CA: Western Psychological Services.

Pearlman, L. A., & Caringi, J. (2009). Living and working self-reflectively to address vicarious trauma. In C. A. Courtois & J. D. Ford (Eds.), *Treating complex traumatic stress disorders: An evidence-based guide* (pp. 202–224). New York: The Guilford Press.

Pearlman, L. A., Wortman, C. B., Feuer, C. A., Farber, C. H., & Rando, T. A. (in press). *Treating traumatic bereavement in survivors of sudden death*. New York: The Guilford Press.

Pettigrew, T. (2003). People under threat: Americans, Arabs and Israelis. *Peace and Conflict: Journal of Peace Psychology, 9*, 69–90. doi: 10.1207/S15327949PAC0901_03

Priebe, S., Bogic, M., Ajdukovic, D., Franciskovic, T., Galeazzi, G. M., Kucukalic, A., Lecic-Tosevski, D., Morina, N., Popovski, M., Wang, D., & Schutzwohl, M. (2010). Mental disorders following war in the Balkans: A study in 5 countries. *Archives of General Psychiatry, 67*, 518–528.

Raina, D., Weine, S., Kulauzovic, Y., Feetham, S., Zhubi, M., Huseni, D., & Pavkovic, I. (2006). A framework for developing and implementing multiple-family groups for refugees. In G. Reyes & G. A. Jacobs (Eds.), *Handbook of international disaster psychology: Vol. 3. Refugee mental health* (pp. 37–64). New York: Praeger Publishers.

Saakvitne, K. W., Gamble, S. J., Pearlman, L. A., & Lev, B. T. (2000). *Risking connection: A training curriculum for working with survivors of childhood abuse*. Lutherville, MD: Sidran Foundation and Press.

Sajjad, T. (2009). The post-genocidal period and its impact on women. In S. Totten (Ed.), *The plight and fate of women during and following genocide* (pp. 219–248). New Brunswick, NJ: Transaction Publishers.

Saul, J. (2009). International trauma studies program. In C. E. Stout (Ed.), *The new humanitarians: Inspiration, innovations, and blueprints for visionaries* (pp. 209–230). Westport, CT: Praeger Publishers.

Scheff, T. (2000). Shame and the social bond: A sociological theory. *Sociological Theory, 18*, 84–98. doi.org/10.1111/0735-2751.00089

Stanton, G. H. (1998). The 8 stages of genocide. Available online http://www.learning4u2.com/HAL/ Independent%20study%20pages/Anne_Frank/Genocide%20Watch.pdf (Downloaded January 2, 2013.)

Staub, E. (1989). *The roots of evil: The origins of genocide and other group violence*. Cambridge, U.K.: Cambridge University Press.

Staub, E. (2011). *Overcoming evil: Genocide, violent conflict, and terrorism*. Oxford, U.K.: Oxford University Press.

Staub, E. (2013). A world without genocide: Prevention, reconciliation and the creation of peaceful societies. *Journal of Social Issues, 69*, 180–199.

Staub, E., & Pearlman, L. A. (2009). Reducing intergroup prejudice and group conflict: A commentary. *Journal of Personality and Social Psychology, 96*, 588–593. doi: 10.1037/a0014045

Staub, E., Pearlman, L. A., & Bilali, R. (2008). Psychological recovery, reconciliation, and the prevention of new violence: An approach and its uses in Rwanda. In B. Hart (Ed.), *Peacebuilding in traumatized societies* (pp. 131–153). Lanham, MD: University Press of America.

Staub, E., Pearlman, L. A., Gubin, A., & Hagengimana, A. (2005). Healing, reconciliation, forgiving, and the prevention of violence after genocide or mass killing: An intervention and its experimental evaluation in Rwanda. *Journal of Social and Clinical Psychology, 24*, 297–334. doi: 10.1521/jscp.24.3.297.65617

Staub, E., Pearlman, L. A., Haven, T. J., Bilali, R., & Vollhardt, J. (2007). Promoting healing and reconciliation in the Great Lakes Region. La Benevolencija Public Education Project Training Manual. Unpublished work, La Benevolencija, Amsterdam, The Netherlands.

Stefansson, A. H. (2010). Coffee after cleansing? Co-existence, co-operation, and communication in post-conflict Bosnia and Herzegovina. *Focaal, 57*, 62–76. doi:10.3167/fcl.2010.570105

Summerfield, D. (2004). Cross-cultural perspectives on the medicalization of human suffering. In G. Rosen, *Posttraumatic stress disorder: Issues and controversies* (pp. 233–245). Sussex, U.K.: Wiley.

Volkan, V. D. (1996). *Intergenerational transmission and "chosen" traumas: A link between the psychology of the individual and that of the ethnic group.* In L. Rangell & R. Moses-Hrushovski (Eds.), *Psychoanalysis at the political border: Essays in honor of Rafael Moses* (pp. 257–282). Madison, CT: International Universities Press.

Vollhardt, J. (2009). The role of victim beliefs in the Israeli-Palestinian conflict: Risk or potential for peace? Peace and Conflict: *Journal of Peace Psychology, 15,* 135–159. doi:10.1080/10781910802544373

Weine, S. (2000). Survivor families and their strengths: Learning from Bosnians after genocide. Other Voices: *The (e) Journal of Cultural Criticism, 2.*

Weine, S. M., Knafl, K., & Feetham, S. (2005). A mixed-methods study of refugee families engaging in multiple-family groups. *Family Relations, 54,* 558–568. doi: 10.1111/j.1741-3729.2005.00340.x

Weine, S., Kulauzovic, Y., Klebic, A., Besic, S., Mujagic, A., Muzurovic, J., Spahovic, D., Sclove, S., Pavkovic, I., Feetham, S., & Rolland, J. (2008). Evaluating a multiple-family group access intervention for refugees with PTSD. *Journal of Marital and Family Therapy, 34,* 149–164. doi: 10.1111/j.1752-0606.2008.00061.x

Weine, S., Muzurovic, N., Kulauzovic, Y., Besic, S., Lezic, A., Mujagic, A., Muzurovic, J., Spahovic, D., Feetham, S., Ware, N., Knafl, K., & Pavkovic, I. (2004). Family consequences of refugee trauma. *Family Process, 43,* 147–160. doi: 10.1111/j.1545-5300.2004.04302002.x

Wessells, M. G. (1999). Culture, power and community: Intercultural approaches to psychosocial assistance and healing. In K. Nader, N. Dubrow, & B. H. Stamm (Eds.), *Honouring differences: Cultural issues in the treatment of trauma and loss* (pp. 276–282). New York: Taylor and Francis.

Wessells, M. G. (2009a). Do no harm: Toward contextually appropriate psychosocial support in international emergencies. *American Psychologist, 64,* 842–854. doi:10.1037/0003-e066X.64.8.842

Wessells, M. (2009b). Community reconciliation and post-conflict reconstruction for peace. In J. de Rivera (Ed.), *Handbook on building cultures of peace* (pp. 349–361). New York: Springer Science +Business Media. doi:10.1007/978-0-387-09575-2_24

Wessells, M. G., & Monteiro, C. (2006). Psychosocial assistance for youth: Toward reconstruction for peace in Angola. *Journal of Social Issues, 62,* 122–139. doi:10.1111/j.1540-4560.2006.00442.x

LAURIE ANNE PEARLMAN, Ph.D., is a clinical psychologist in independent practice in Massachusetts. She is co-founder and former co-director and research director of the Traumatic Stress Institute/Center for Adult & Adolescent Psychotherapy, LLC, in South Windsor, CT. She has been working with Ervin Staub in Rwanda since 1999. She is a senior psychological consultant for the Headington Institute and immediate past president of the Trauma Research, Education, and Training Institute, Inc.

Journal of Social Issues, Vol. 69, No. 1, 2013, pp. 125–143

The "Never Again" State of Israel: The Emergence of the Holocaust as a Core Feature of Israeli Identity and Its Four Incongruent Voices

Yechiel Klar[*]
Tel Aviv University

Noa Schori-Eyal
University of Maryland

Yonat Klar
Tel Aviv University

For the vast majority of contemporary Israelis, the Holocaust is an acquired memory. However, over the years its presence has not diminished but rather is on the rise. We describe how perceptions of the Holocaust have changed from "what Israeliness is not" in the 1940s and 1950s to a core element in Israeli identity. Inspired by Bauer, we present four different and sometimes incompatible voices related to the Holocaust that greatly affect the Israeli society. They are: Never be a passive victim; never forsake your brothers; never be passive bystander; and never be a perpetrator. Experimental evidence related to these voices is also described.

Almost immediately after its establishment in May 1948, the State of Israel, still enmeshed in a difficult war for its survival, became the home for the largest community of Holocaust survivors. About 330,000 Jewish refugees from

---

[*]Correspondence concerning this article should be addressed to Yechiel Klar, School of Psychological Sciences, Department of Psychology, Tel Aviv University, Ramat Aviv 69978, Israel [e-mail: yklar@post.tau.ac.il].

This research was supported by a grant from the Israel Science Foundation to Yechiel Klar, a grant from the Tami Steinmetz Center for Peace Research at Tel Aviv University to Yechel Klar, and by a research prize from the Tami Steinmetz Center for Peace Research at Tel Aviv University to Noa Schori-Eyal. The authors thank Hadas Laor and Tami Sunensein for their help with this article.

devastated Europe joined the 600,000 members of the Jewish community in Israel in a massive immigration influx. Thus, in 1949, almost every third person in the newborn country was a Holocaust survivor (Yablonka, 1999). The Holocaust survivors' background was not so different from most of the veteran Israelis (who came to the country before WWII). Basically, both groups emigrated from the same, primarily Eastern European localities, and many if not most of the veteran Israelis also had to cope with the news that the families they had left in Europe had perished in the Holocaust. Yet despite this common background and misfortune, there was an unbridgeable divide between the veteran Israelis and the survivors. The Holocaust clearly "belonged" to the survivors and was alien to those who lived in Israel when it transpired. The survivors were not asked to share their stories with others or dwell on their experiences. They were expected to go on with life, rehabilitate themselves, adopt the Israeli identity and become new Israelis. The Holocaust in those days was perceived as something that had happened to the passive and cowardly Jews of the Diaspora who had gone "like sheep to the slaughter" (e.g., Segev, 2000). It was seen as antithetical to the identity of the "new Israeli," who was active, free, and daring. The Holocaust was something that happened "there" in the Jewish Diaspora and by no means could happen "here" in the new and independent state of Israel.

Today, more than 65 years after the end of WWII, the number of living Holocaust survivors has naturally dwindled (currently less than 3% of the Israeli population). For the vast majority of contemporary Israelis, the Holocaust is an acquired rather than a living memory. However, the presence of the Holocaust and its place in Israeli collective identity has not faded in the last 65 years but is rather on the rise (e.g., Bar Tal 2007; Ofer, 2009). For example, most of Oron's (1993) respondents, college students, endorsed the statement that "all Jewish people must see themselves as Holocaust victims." Most recently, 98.1% of the respondents in a 2009 survey of the Jewish–Israeli adult population (Arian, 2012) have stated that remembering the Holocaust is a guiding principle in their life; in fact, more important principle than other guiding principles such as "Feeling part of the Jewish people," "Feeling part of Israeli society," "Living in Israel" or even "Having a family."

In this article we first describe the omnipresence of the Holocaust in Israeli life today. Then we delineate how the Holocaust has gradually been transformed from "what Israeliness is not" into one of the core elements of Israeli identity. Next, we argue (inspired by Bauer, 2002) that the *Never Again* imperative derived from the Holocaust invokes not one but at least four powerful and frequently conflicting voices. They are: (1) *never be a passive victim;* (2) *never forsake your brothers;* (3) *never be passive bystander;* and (4) *never be a perpetrator.* We will demonstrate how these voices impact major arenas of Israeli life today. Finally, we will present experimental evidence pertaining to the first and fourth voices.

The Omnipresence of the Holocaust in Contemporary Israeli Life

Political scientists Liebman and Don-Yihya (1983) were among the first to observe (. . .) the centrality of the Holocaust as the primary political myth of Israeli society, the symbol of Israel's present condition and the one which provides Israel with legitimacy and the right to its land. (. . .) Its memory is omnipresent, cutting across differences in age, education and even country of origin (pp. 137–138).

This observation appears even more compelling today. The Holocaust is a predominant issue in all areas of Israeli social and cultural life, including literature (Feldman, 1992), film (Gertz, 2004), visual arts (Katz-Freiman, 2003), and even humor (Zandberg, 2006). A comprehensive account of the Holocaust in current Israeli life is beyond the scope of this article, but a number of examples can demonstrate this point.

Daily mentions in the media. Rinkevich-Pave (2008) calculated how often the word Holocaust (*Shoah* in Hebrew) appeared in 12 months (October 2007– September 2008) in *Haaretz*, a leading Israeli newspaper. She compared this historical event with the number of mentions of the term *Israeli–Arab conflict* (in different versions such as Israeli/Jewish/Palestinian conflict), the major issue Israeli society confronts day in and day out. The term *Holocaust* appeared 132 times, on average, every month, and *Israeli–Arab conflict* appeared roughly the same number of times (140 times being the monthly average).

New Hebrew Holocaust titles. According to the National Library of Israel's (2011) statistics, books related to the Holocaust are the largest thematic category of newly published Hebrew titles, even more than titles related to the Israeli–Arab conflict and wars, the second most prevalent category.

In the Israeli school curriculum. In 1980, an amendment to the State Education Law defined "Holocaust and Heroism awareness" as one of the official goals of the state educational system. Seventy-six percent of the high school students in a recent survey indicated that "the Holocaust affects their world view," and 94% stated that they "are committed to preserving the memory of the Holocaust" (Cohen, 2010).

Holocaust remembrance day (Yom haShoah). Since the 1960s, Yom haShoah has been an official memorial day in Israel. A siren is sounded throughout the country for 2 minutes in the morning, during which all activities in Israel come to a complete halt and the entire public stands at silent attention. All places of entertainment are closed, media programming is devoted exclusively to the Holocaust, and ceremonies are conducted in schools, military bases, and public places (see Ben-Amos & Bet-El, 1999). Since 2005, International Holocaust Remembrance day is also officially commemorated on January 27.

Organized trips to Holocaust sites.   Every year since 1988, 10,000 Israeli high school students accompanied by Holocaust survivors embark on intensive 8-day trips to death camps and other Holocaust sites, mainly in Poland (see Bilewicz & Jaworska, 2013; Feldman, 2008; Hazan, 2001). The rate of participation on these trips is remarkable. Although they are voluntary and their costs are mostly paid for by the students' families, about 16% of the entire cohort every year participates, and there is constant public pressure to view these trips as a basic right of every Israeli youngster (Zelikovitz, 2010).

The Israeli army (IDF) also organizes trips for thousands of officers every year to the death camps in Poland. One of the prime goals of this project, called *Witnesses in Uniform,* is "strengthening the sense of commitment of the commander to the State of Israel as a democratic state and to the Jewish people" (Edim Be-madim, 2011).

The Holocaust presence scale.   Rinkevich-Pave (2008) conducted a survey study among 378 Jewish Israelis (245 women, 133 men), ranging in age from 18 to 71. The highly diverse sample included respondents from all over Israel, from different ethnic backgrounds, people of different socioeconomic status and levels of religious observance. About two thirds of the respondents had no direct family ties to the Holocaust. The respondents were presented with 27 specific behaviors and attitudes reflecting the place of the Holocaust (if at all) in their personal lives. For each of these items they were asked to indicate their level of agreement or disagreement. Table 1 lists the 18 most widespread attitudes or behaviors, with the percentage of those expressing strong and strong to moderate agreement. The items indicating interest in acquiring knowledge about the Holocaust were endorsed by most interviewees. In addition, more than half of the respondents also indicated that they found themselves occasionally contemplating how they would have behaved during the Holocaust, that the Holocaust affects their attitudes and beliefs, that they are afraid the Holocaust could happen again, and that many events in the news make them mull over it.

Together with findings reported by Oron (1993) and Cohen (2010), these data suggest the ubiquity of the Holocaust in Israeli life, not just in the public but also in the private sphere (see also Schuman, Vinitzky-Seroussi, & Vinokur, 2003).

Perceptions of the Holocaust in the First Postwar Decades in Israel

Numerous historians and social scientists have dealt with perceptions of the Holocaust in Israel and how it has affected Israelis (e.g., Bar-Tal, 2007; Grodzinsky, 2004; Liebman & Don-Yihya, 1983; Ofer, 1996, 2009; Segev, 2000; Shapira,

Table 1. Items from the Holocaust Presence Scale

	Strong agreement (%)	Strong to moderate agreement (%)
On Holocaust remembrance day (Yom HaShoah) I make sure to watch the programs on television about the Holocaust.	51.1	78
I consider myself to have a lot of knowledge about the Holocaust.	38.1	81
I think about how I would have behaved if I had found myself in certain situations that happened during the Holocaust.	35.8	78
It is important for me to meet people who experienced the Holocaust in order to hear their stories.	35.8	68
When I think of the Holocaust I feel that it overwhelms me emotionally.	32.4	69
I have a habit of going to Holocaust museums in Israel or outside of Israel (Yad VaShem, Anne Frank's house, etc.).	32.3	62.7
When I see elderly people, I ask myself if they were in the Holocaust.	31.7	61.3
When I am in Europe, I think about the Holocaust.	31.7	62.5
The Holocaust affects my beliefs and attitudes on different issues.	28.5	63
I am afraid the Holocaust will be repeated.	26.6	54.6
Because of the Holocaust it is hard for me to visit countries like Germany and Austria.	24.7	43
I often choose to watch movies and plays related to the Holocaust.	23.9	50
Because of the Holocaust, I don't take being alive for granted.	22.3	47.6
Many events in the news make me think about the Holocaust.	17.9	56
The Holocaust comes into my thoughts, both when I intend to and when I don't.	16.4	42
Sometimes I feel that the memory of the Holocaust influences my behavior.	14.7	48.5
The memory of the Holocaust causes me to worry more about the security and future of my children.	14.4	48.5
When I think about the future, I sometimes have thoughts about the Holocaust.	12.5	30.6

1998; Yablonka, 1999; Zertal, 2005; Zuckerman, 1993). As noted by Shapira (1989), from 1945 until the 1961 Eichmann trial the Holocaust was not a defining feature of Israeli collective identity. Israelis who were not survivors "knew and did not know about the Holocaust; ached and did not ache given the disaster" (p. 325). Perceptions of the Holocaust at that time were mainly governed by the conceptions, capacities, and needs of the newly founded State. They were filtered through three partially overlapping prisms: the traditional (Jewish) perspective, the Zionist perspective, and the perspective of the Israeli–Arab conflict.

The traditional (Jewish) perspective.   Jewish historical remembrance stretches back thousands of years and is replete with memories of historical calamities, persecution, exile, deportations, and pogroms. According to this perspective, the biblical Pharaoh, Amalek, and Haman of Persia all attempted to annihilate the Jewish people, followed by a long sequence of enemies, massacres, deportations, inquisitions, and pogroms characterizing Jewish history. Through the Jewish prism, the Holocaust is the latest in this series of catastrophes (see Bar-Tal & Antebi, 1992; Hareven, 1983).

The Zionist perspective.   From the Zionist perspective (the most dominant ideology in Israel), the Holocaust was the ultimate (albeit tragic) testimony of the impossibility of Jewish life in the Diaspora, and proof of the Zionist ideology that Israel was the only way to ensure Jewish existence. This point of view, however, cast retrospective blame on the Holocaust victims and the survivors who failed to come to Israel when this was still possible. From this perspective, the Holocaust confirmed and even reinforced the image of Diaspora Jews who went to their death "like sheep to the slaughter" (e.g., Zertal, 2005).

The nation building and conflict framework.   After WWII, the struggle for a Jewish state in Palestine was immediately rekindled. Consequently, the perception of the Holocaust became to a large extent subordinated to the needs of the nation-building process and the ensuing Israeli–Arab conflict. Most of the energy of both veteran Israelis and the incoming survivors was channeled to the pressing issues of the present. The survivors, who arrived in Israel amidst the 1948 war, fought side by side local Israelis and shed their blood for their new country (Yablonka, 1999). The Holocaust in Europe was portrayed soon after its occurrence as something of the past with little relevance to the challenging present (Shapira, 1998). In addition, for Israelis enmeshed in a difficult war with the entire surrounding Arab world, dwelling too much upon the massive extermination of Jews in Europe just several years earlier would have been highly intimidating. One way of distancing the terrifying implications of the Holocaust was to portray it as the *antithesis* of the Israeli condition. The Holocaust was possible—so went the reassuring, popular account—because Diaspora Jews were unarmed, unprepared, and unwilling to fight; Israelis, on the other hand, are fully armed, well-prepared, and heroic.

The grand dichotomies in Holocaust discourse.   Holocaust perception in Israel during the postwar years was governed by two powerful dichotomies. One was "Holocaust and Heroism" (Ofer, 2009; Stauber, 2007; Zertal, 2005). Heroism during the Holocaust referred mainly to the Ghetto and concentration camps uprisings. The small group of Ghetto fighters was symbolically separated from the rest of the victims. The Israeli postwar public mainly wanted to hear the story of the fighters and not that of other survivors (Shapira, 1989).

The other dichotomy was "from Holocaust to Rebirth," conveying the notion that the Holocaust led to rebirth of the sovereign state of Israel. Thus, the creation of Israel was seen as compensation for the great loss of the Holocaust. Some survivors may have found some limited consolation in this idea, but its main aim was giving the creation of Israel as equal symbolic weight as the Holocaust.

Thus, the Holocaust was perceived through several abstract and simplifying conceptual prisms. It instantly became a historical event that had happened to the "Jewish people" (in the traditional framework), or to the "Jews of the Diaspora" (in the Zionist and national frameworks). This created a sharp distinction between what was "there" in the Diaspora (Holocaust) and what is "here" (Heroism and Rebirth). The testimonies of the survivors were largely absent from these pictures and little if at all sought after.

The Encounter of Israeli Society with the Survivors

The encounter of Israeli society with Holocaust survivors was a complex issue (Yablonka, 1999). The great reluctance or inability to hear the survivors' stories in the first postwar decades is well-documented (e.g., Segev, 2000; Zertal, 2005). Shapira (1998) wrote: "... the veterans chose not to ask ... The new immigrants preferred not to speak ... then the big silence set in" (p. 51). This imposed silence was by no means unique to Israeli society. Danieli (1982, 1984) observed a conspiracy of silence in survivors' families in America and even survivors' dealings with mental health professionals (see also Solomon, 1995).

Blaming the survivors.   In addition to being sometimes blamed for not coming to Palestine when this was still possible and for not openly fighting their persecutors, the survivors had to face another painful question: "How did you survive?" This question was motivated by a negative and ill-informed stereotype of the survivors: that the better and moral people were the first to perish, and that those who survived were selfish and unscrupulous (Segev, 2000). Thus, for the general Israeli public there was a negative aura surrounding the survivors, which increased their tendency not to talk about their experiences.

The Merging of the Holocaust with the Core Israeli Identity

How was Holocaust transformed from a Diaspora reality into an Israeli event? And how was it transformed from an event that was irrelevant and even contradictory to the new Israeli identity to one of the major components of the Israel heritage and identity? In the following we first discuss the internalization of the Holocaust, starting with the Eichmann trial, and continue with the impact of the survivors and their offspring on Israeli society. Next, we discuss the effects of the recurring Arab–Israeli wars and the growing geopolitical threats, which led to an erosion of the belief that Israeli heroism is an ultimate safeguard to survival and made the Holocaust closer to the Israeli concerns.

The Internalization of the Holocaust

The Eichmann trial.   The 1961 Eichmann trial in Jerusalem is generally considered one of the major turning points in the way that Israelis perceived the Holocaust (e.g., Segev, 2000; Shapira, 1998; Yablonka, 2004). Over one hundred Holocaust survivors testified at the trial, turning it into a classroom for the entire Israeli public (who listened intensively to the radio trial's broadcasts) and serving as a form of "national group therapy" (Segev, 2000, p. 351). The trial also showed officially that Israel recognized the Holocaust as part of its heritage. Perhaps most importantly, the personal stories of the survivors underlined the human dimensions of the Holocaust. The trial provided Israelis with a new understanding of the great human strength and courage demanded of people just to survive in the ghetto or camps. The allegations regarding the paucity of physical resistance, so prevalent before the trial, gradually subsided (Ofer, 2010).

The growing impact of the survivors on Holocaust awareness.   Over the years, the survivors played a greater role in shaping Israeli Holocaust memory. They founded museums and Holocaust memorial institutions, academic and teaching programs. In later years, many survivors volunteered to be "witnesses" telling their personal stories on commemoration days in the media, schools, and army camps. Survivors became visible as writers, poets, painters, sculptors, musicians, stage, and cinema artists (see Ofer, 2009).

The second and third generations.   The term "second generation" was first used by clinical psychologists looking for signs of secondary trauma among the offspring of Holocaust survivors. In general, little evidence was found in this regard (van Ijzendoorn, Bakermans-Kranenburg, & Sagi-Schwartz, 2003). However, members of the second (and third) generation became significant carriers of the Holocaust legacy and memory (Vardi, 1992). The impact of second and third-generation authors, educators, and artists on public life is massive (e.g., Milner, 2003). With the changing social climate in Israel, many of them introduced more humanistic and universalistic tones into Holocaust discourse in Israel, and some were critical of the "nationalization" of the Holocaust (Gutwein, 2009). Above all, with their unquestioned native Israeli identity they have contributed to the perception of the Holocaust as an integral part of Israeli life. Thus, the (Diaspora) Holocaust became "our Holocaust" (see Gutfreund, 2007).

The Effects of Recurring Wars and Existential Threats

The Holocaust discourse in Israel reveals a fundamental Israeli existential paradox: Israelis commonly argue that the Holocaust happened because Jews failed to come to Palestine at the time and that the Diaspora can never be a safe place for Jews. At the same time, Israelis are painfully aware of the fact that Israel is one of the least safe places for Jews today. Initially, this paradox was conceptually resolved by the assertion that Israeli independence, military strength, and readiness to fight (allegedly absent in Diaspora life) is the ultimate safeguard of Israel's survival, even in a hostile environment. However, this belief has frequently been shaken over the years. Shapira (1998) described the role of the Six-Day War of 1967 and the Yom Kipur War of 1973 in changing the relation of Israel to the Holocaust. The Six-Day War is remembered as a swift and glorious Israeli victory over its Arab neighbors, but this war was preceded by a 3-week waiting period in which Israelis and Jews all over the world listened with much trepidation to Arab public statements that they were determined to "wipe Israel off the map," "drive the Jews into the sea," etc. (Novick, 1999, p. 148). For Israelis, "the sense of helplessness, of there being no way out, that had hitherto been identified only with the Holocaust and life in exile was seen now as being possible in the free Jewish state as well" (Shapira, 1998, p. 41). The Yom Kipur War, 6 years later, further contributed to the erosion of the dichotomy between "there" and "here."

The 1991 Gulf War provided Israelis with yet another demonstration of their basic geopolitical vulnerability. Although Israel was not directly involved in the Gulf crisis, the Iraqis (led by Saddam Hussein) launched missiles directed at Israeli cities. To defend citizens against possible chemical warfare, all Israelis were hurriedly provided with gas masks and syringe with an antidote against nerve gas, and were instructed to seal a room in the house and wear the gas masks when sirens were sounded. Although the number of casualties was minimal, it undermined life in Israel for 6 weeks. Unlike previous wars, this was an antiheroic war, directed only at the population with no Israeli military response. Family members sat together in the "sealed rooms" in their (now unsafe) homes, waiting for the daily strike and fearing gas attacks. Many left their homes to seek refuge in the less vulnerable Israeli periphery. The association with the Holocaust became almost inescapable, and it was indeed formulated excessively. To top this association, Israelis were angered that Western companies, many of them German, were selling Iraq war materials, including deadly chemicals. References to Europe in the past were abundant (Zuckerman, 1993). The intimate encounter with fear, the sight of thousands of Israelis fleeing Tel-Aviv, and the relatively calm reactions of Holocaust survivors made the dichotomy between the "fearful Holocaust Jews" and the "brave new Israelis" obsolete (Porat, 2008).

More recently, the developing Iranian nuclear capability has increasingly captured Israeli fears and anxieties. The ghastly term "second Holocaust" now

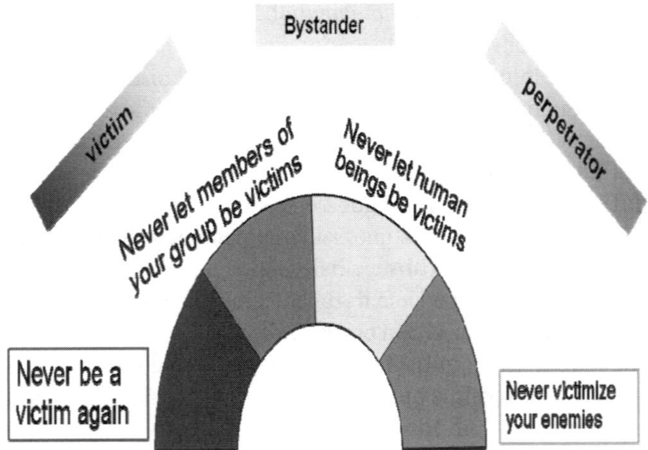

Fig. 1. Four different lessons that former victims may draw from their past victimization.

appears frequently in the media and in private conversations (e.g., Morris, 2007). Studies show that the Israeli public views Iran as an existential danger for the survival of Israel and that Iranian nuclear capabilities are perceived as an extreme danger (Ben Meir & Shaked, 2007). It is also noteworthy that 80% of those questioned by Rinkevich-Pave (2008) endorsed the view that "Most Arab people have not accepted the existence of Israel and would destroy us if they could." For many Israelis the Holocaust does not seem merely an issue of the past (e.g., Bar-Tal & Antebi, 1992).

The Four Conflicting Voices of the Holocaust

What are the personal and collective lessons that Israelis draw from the Holocaust? Historian Yehuda Bauer suggested adding three additional commandments to the original Ten Commandments relating to the Holocaust and other genocides: "Thou shalt not be a victim, thou shalt not be a perpetrator, but, above all, thou shalt not be a bystander" (2002, p. 67). Inspired by these moral imperatives, we devised Figure 1, which is descriptive rather than prescriptive, and presents four different lessons (or voices) that individuals and groups targeted by a human perpetrated calamity such as the Holocaust may draw from the events. The first and second voices, *never to be a victim again,* and *never to forsake other members of the group when they are in jeopardy,* are the more particularistic voices focusing on the protection of members of one's own group. The third and fourth voices voices, *never to be a passive bystander when other human are in jeopardy,* and *never to become a victimizer yourself* are the more universalistic voices, shifting the focus of protection to outgroup members and even to one's enemies or rivals. These four voices are somewhat incompatible with each other in that protecting another group member, nongroup members and enemies may detract from one's own self-preservation.

First Voice: Never Be a Passive Victim Again

This is perhaps the most dominant Holocaust voice for most Israelis (see also Bar-Tal & Antebi, 1992; Elon, 1971; Hareven, 1983). For example, Israeli Prime Minister Benjamin Netanyahu addressed the nation on Holocaust Remembrance Day in 2010, saying: "'In every generation there are those who stand against us. And in this generation we must fortify our strength and independence so that we will be able to prevent the current enemy from carrying out its plan" (Netanyahu, 2010).

For most Israelis, building military strength is the prime lesson of the Holocaust and this connection is often symbolically reinforced. For example, when the first Israeli female fighter pilot was qualified, the media emphasized that she was the granddaughter of two of the most revered leaders of the Warsaw Ghetto uprising (Gross, 2001). In 2003 the Israeli Air force organized a ceremonial flyover of the Auschwitz death camp. The three jets were flown by six pilots, all descended from Holocaust survivors (O'Sullivan, 2003). Visitors at the office of General Meir Dagan, the former head the Mosad (the Israeli intelligence agency), could see a photograph of an old Jew standing next to a trench, a rifle aimed at him by an SS officer. "This old Jew was my grandfather," said Dagan. "We should be strong, use our brain, and defend ourselves so that the Holocaust will never be repeated" (cited in Mahnaimi, 2010).

Second Voice: Never Forsake Your Brothers

A second voice that originates from Holocaust memory revolves around the Biblical question of "Am I my brother's keeper?" (Genesis 4:9). After the Holocaust, the veteran Israeli community was left with troubling questions regarding its own conduct during the Holocaust years. Had they done everything they could have done to save their brethren? (Segev, 2000). The sense of shame and guilt was coupled with the conviction that the Holocaust was possible because the Jews had no homeland, and almost no country in the world was willing to give them shelter. Therefore, the 1950 Israeli *Law of Return* summarized immigration policy in one line: "Every Jew has the right to come to this country as an *ole* (i.e. Jew immigrating to Israel)." Acting on this commitment, Israel took in almost 700,000 Jewish immigrants in its first 3 years. In some cases entire communities were airlifted to Israel in what looked like a semimilitary rescue operation, involving top army units. Although urgency in some of these cases was undeniable, these operations had a powerful symbolic message: "Now we have the ability to rescue Jews in jeopardy and bring them to Israel. Had we had a strong independent Jewish state at the time of the Holocaust, things might have been different."

Third Voice: Never Be a Passive Bystander

The third voice emanating from Holocaust memory (admittedly, less powerfully than the previous two) is related to "You shall not stand idly by the blood of your neighbor" (Leviticus 19:16), an obligation that extends to every human being in jeopardy. Israeli Holocaust memory is accompanied by a sense of moral contempt and outrage toward the bystander nations for their lack of help during the Holocaust (e.g., Firer, 1989). This moral outrage created a need to demonstrate that Israelis have higher humanitarian values than other countries (e.g., Elon, 1971). In the 1960s, Israelis took great pride in the aid and expertise it provided to dozens of new African and Asian countries. In 1977, a group of Vietnamese refugees stranded at sea were refused help from several ships from various countries, except for an Israeli crew. The newly elected Israeli Prime Minister Menachem Begin (as the first act of his government) granted them Israeli citizenship, comparing their situation to the plight of Jewish refugees seeking refuge during the Holocaust (Hurwitz, 2004).

This humanitarian voice, however, sometimes clashes with other interests. For example, in recent years there has been a stream of thousands of African refugees and work seekers who enter the country through the Egyptian border. Few are granted temporary refugee status (mainly those from Sudan and Eritrea), but many are refused or detained. Israeli governments and the Israeli found themselves in quandary: on the one hand, they are unwilling to grant the refugees permanent status, but on the other hand many Israelis feel that it is impossible for Israel to take steps such as deportation, which elicit associations with the countries that closed their borders to the Jewish refugees at the time of the Holocaust (Derfner, 2008; The Combat Genocide Association, 2008).

Fourth Voice: Never Be a Perpetrator

The fourth voice emanating from the Holocaust is the moral obligation not to harm other human beings, even if they are rivals or enemies. This voice is in fact a derivative of the ethical Silver Rule (i.e., *"Do not do unto others what you do not want others to do unto you."* see Terry, 2004). Some former victims contemplating on the evil done to them may also bring to mind the ensuing "do not do unto others" clause (e.g., Staub & Vollhardt, 2008; Vollhardt, 2009).

This theme is particularly relevant in the context of the intractable Israeli–Palestinian conflict (for a detailed account see Morris, 1999). While many Israelis view the Israeli actions as legitimate self-defense, others are more critical of Israel's role in the conflict. Whereas condemning one's own group or feeling guilt over its deeds is always difficult (Leach, Zeineddine, & Čehajić-Clancy, 2013; Roccas, Klar, & Livitan, 2006; Wohl, Branscombe, & Klar, 2006; see also Imhoff, Wohl, & Erb, 2013), it is even more difficult when a group's past victimization (such as the Holocaust) is made salient (Wohl & Branscombe, 2008). Nevertheless, can the memory of the Holocaust make Israelis less tolerant of transgressions perpetrated by Israel? This is sometimes the case. For example, on the seventieth anniversary of the 1938 *Kristallnacht*, the first orchestrated attacks against Jews in Germany and Austria, a letter to the newspaper Haaretz stated: "I was born in Berlin and was three years old when the rioting occurred on Kristallnacht... For me, stories about Kristallnacht necessarily evoke the actions of the Israeli occupation army in the occupied territories" (Spiro, 2008). In Israel, any reference to Nazi Germany in a context critical to Israeli conduct instantaneously enrages the Israeli public. Consequently, many critical responses to Israeli policies toward Palestinians make use of less specific references, such as "it is reminiscent of dark periods in history" (e.g., Blatman, 2010).

Yet, the Holocaust memory may evoke protest against groups' moral violations. A recent sociological study of women's protest and human right movements in Israel (such as *Women in Black* and *Makhsom Watch*) found an unusually high representation of second-generation women and even Holocaust survivors in their eighties. A common reason for joining these activities expressed in these studies was the fear of becoming passive bystanders "like the Germans" (Benski & Katz, 2013). Activist women said that although it is impossible to compare the Holocaust to the situation in the occupied territories, "we would desecrate the memory of the Holocaust if we did not compare the processes leading to it" (Saar, 2008).

This particular Holocaust influence is also evident in protest activities of younger Israelis. For example, Yehuda Shaul, the founder of *Breaking the Silence,* a grassroots group of veteran Israeli soldiers "working to raise awareness about the daily reality in the occupied territories" told about the army experiences that led him to found the group:

> When we entered Hebron we realized the settlers could do whatever they wanted and no one would stop them.... There is a huge ideological gap between me and a person who can walk up to an Arab's door and spray paint the Star of David or write "Arabs out". The historical memory is unnerving. We all know what symbols did to Jews' storefronts and whose symbols those were. We all know the writing when "Arabs" is replaced with "Jews". We know this history. (Justvision, 2008)

Connecting Past Group Trauma to Current Conflicts: Experimental Demonstrations

Schori-Eyal, Klar, and Roccas (2013) conducted several studies on the Holocaust "voices." Related to the first voice, they conceptualized the *perpetual ingroup victimhood orientation* (PIVO), the belief that one's group is persecuted continually by different enemies (see also Bar-Tal & Antebi, 1992; Vollhardt, 2009; Wohl & Branscombe, 2008). PIVO involves a sense of ongoing threat that links past and present. Contemporary enemies are experienced as a reincarnation of former adversaries. High levels of PIVO involve a strong belief in the uniqueness of the group's trauma, unparalleled by the painful experiences of any other group, and a strong sense of mistrust of outgroups. The construct was measured using a 12-item scale (e.g., *All our enemies throughout history share a common denominator—the will to annihilate us*). This scale was tested on multiple samples and was found to have high reliability. Before answering the questionnaire, respondents were asked to recall an event in which the ingroup was harmed by another group. The most commonly mentioned event (mentioned by 40– 50% of respondents, depending on the sample) was the Holocaust.

The second construct in these studies was the *fear of victimizing* (FOV), which is related to the fourth voice. This is the fear that due to past suffering, one's group may loose its moral sensitivity to the plight of its adversaries. FOV was measured using a 10-item scale (sample item: *We are in danger of treating other people in the same way that we were treated by our worst enemies*). FOV was also found to have high reliability.

In a series of studies, PIVO and FOV were both found to be associated with a variety of intergroup outcomes, including a sense of moral entitlement, group-based guilt, behavioral tendencies, and cognitive processes. PIVO was positively correlated and FOV negatively correlated with a sense of moral entitlement: the belief that one's group is allowed to do anything in self-defense, even commit acts that can be considered moral transgressions (e.g., *Harming innocents is certainly justified when our existence is being threatened*). Moral entitlement was shown to mediate the relationship between PIVO as well as FOV and outcome variables such as group-based guilt and moral decision making: the higher the sense of moral entitlement, the less group-based guilt was experienced over harm caused to enemy outgroup members and the greater the support was for actions that result in severe damage to outgroup civilians (Schori-Eyal et al., 2013). The results indicate that the Holocaust still plays a role in Jewish–Israelis' attitudes, emotions, and behavioral tendencies in relation to current conflicts. The first voice ("never be a victim again") as reflected by PIVO is associated with greater willingness to engage in morally questionable actions against enemy outgroup members and lessened group-based guilt over the results of such actions (see also Wohl & Branscombe, 2008). In contrast, FOV, which reflects the fourth voice ("never be a perpetrator"), is associated with greater moral sensitivity and greater group-based guilt.

PIVO and FOV were also found to affect several cognitive processes such as memory and categorization. In one study (Schori-Eyal, 2013), participants were asked to categorize national-ethnic groups according to two criteria: a neutral criterion and a "hostility" criterion (whether or not the group was hateful toward Israel). PIVO was associated with categorizing more outgroups as hostile and with shorter response times when using the hostility criterion compared to the neutral criterion. The higher the level of PIVO, the longer it took participants to declare a group "non-hostile."

In other studies (Schori-Eyal, 2011), participants read descriptions of historical persecution and attacks against ingroup members. They were then presented with several open-ended stories describing ambiguous social interactions between ingroup and outgroup members, followed by three endings for each story, representing either hostile, neutral, or benevolent intentions of the outgroup actors. With higher levels of PIVO, participants tended to attribute more hostile intentions to outgroup members in these situations. When reminded of historical group trauma, high-PIVO participants attributed more negative intentions to outgroup members compared to the unreminded group. Low-PIVO participants reminded of historical group trauma attributed fewer hostile intentions to outgroup members. Thus, the "first voice" (operationalized by the PIVO measure) affects the way intergroup interactions are interpreted, and increases the attribution of hostile intentions to outgroup members.

PIVO and FOV are both associated with memory biases in intergroup conflict. In the study by Schori-Eyal et al. (2013), participants read about the plight of a family in Gaza whose home was hit by an IDF missile, and were later asked to recall the text and answer a series of questions. The higher the level of PIVO was, the less accurately participants recalled details of information they had read earlier. Both details of the damage and trivial information were affected, indicating that PIVO acted as a filter that deflected participants' attention to all types of information about the outgroup. In contrast, the higher FOV was, the more accurately the information about the Palestinian family was recalled.

These studies indicate that the "never be a victim again" voice is associated with a perception of rival outgroups as hostile, and with downplaying damage to outgroup members. The "never be a victimizer" voice, on the other hand, is related to a more accurate perception of the suffering of other groups (see also Vollhardt, 2013).

In another study (Schori-Eyal, 2011), participants were subliminally primed with either a neutral stimulus or a reminder of group trauma (swastika). They then completed a measure of group-based guilt toward the Palestinians. High but not low PIVO participants experienced *less* group-based guilt when primed with group trauma compared with a neutral prime. High but not low FOV participants experienced *more* group-based guilt when primed with group trauma compared with the neutral prime. These findings indicate that implicit reminders of trauma may strengthen each of the two voices. If the perception of eternal victimhood is predominant, subliminal reminders of trauma reinforce this belief, resulting in less group-based guilt about harming others. If fear of victimizing is predominant, subliminal reminders of trauma increase this perception, resulting in more group-based guilt.

Conclusion

Israelis (those who did not experience the Holocaust personally) very slowly and reluctantly acknowledged the Holocaust as part of their collective identity. For them, the Holocaust represented the ultimate realization of the tragic Jewish destiny in the Diaspora, the destiny they had sought to break away from. The social and historical processes by which the Holocaust was gradually turned into a core feature in the Israeli identity are complex and multilayered, and we could only briefly touch here upon some of them. Time was involved in several processes, such as the growing impact of the survivors on Holocaust awareness, and the role of second and third generations who were born in Israel yet unashamed in their Holocaust heritage. Israel's difficult geopolitical situation and the recurring wars also had enormous effects on the continued impact of the Holocaust on Israeli collective identity. One dominant voice of the Holocaust is to *Never be a victim again*, which many Israelis learned to identify as a source of resilience and inventiveness. And there are also the other Holocaust voices urging group members to become better human beings and, even more difficult, to refrain from victimizing other groups. These different voices are often incongruent and disharmonic. It seems that the future vitality of the Israeli society—and probably of any other society that survives massive trauma—greatly depends on how well these voices will be orchestrated and played.

References

Arian, A. (2012). *A portrait of Israeli Jews: Beliefs, observance, and values of Israeli Jews, 2009*. Jerusalem, Israel: The Israel Democracy Institute and the AVI CHAI– Israel Foundation.

Bar-Tal, D. (2007). *Likhiot im ha-sikhsukh* [Living with the conflict: Socio-psychological analysis of the Jewish society in Israel]. Jerusalem, Israel: Carmel.

Bar-Tal, D., & Antebi, D. (1992). Siege mentality in Israel. *International Journal of Intercultural Relations, 16*, 251–275. doi: 10.1016/0147-1767(92)90052-V

Bauer, Y. (2002). *Rethinking the Holocaust*. New Haven, CT: Yale University Press.

Ben-Amos, A. & Bet-El, I. (1999). Holocaust Day and Memorial Day in Israeli schools: Ceremonies, education and history. *Israel Studies, 4*, 258–284.

Ben Meir, Y., & Shaked, D. (2007). The people speak: Israeli public opinion on national security 2005-2007. *Memorandum No. 90*. Tel Aviv, Israel: Institute for National Security Studies.

Benski, T., & Katz, R. (2013). Women's peace activism in Israel and the reversal of the hegemonic Holocaust discourse in Israel. In I. Levine, C. Lenz, O. Kopperud, & M. L. Seeberg (Eds.), *Active memory: Public and private perspectives*. Oslo, Norway: Unipub publishing.

Bilewicz, M., & Jaworska, M. (2013). Reconciliation through the righteous: The narratives of heroic helpers as a fulfillment of emotional needs in Polish-Jewish intergroup contact. *Journal of Social Issues, 69*, 162–179.

Blatman, D. (2010). 1932 is already here. *Haaretz*. Available online http://www.haaretz.com/print-edition/opinion/1932-is-already-here-1.332974 (Downloaded January 6, 2013.)

Cohen, E. H. (2010). *Hora'at Ha-shoah be-batei sefer mamlakhtiyim be-Israel: Mekhkar khinukhi 2007–2009* [Teaching the Holocaust in Israeli State Schools: An educational study 2007–2009. School of Education.] Bar Ilan University, Israel. Available online http://education.biu.ac.il/files/education/%201_.pdf (Downloaded January 6, 2013.)

Danieli, Y. (1982). Families of survivors of the Nazi Holocaust: Some short- and long-term effects. In C. D. Spielberger, I. G. Sarason, & N. Milgram (Eds.), *Stress and anxiety* (Vol. *8*, pp. 405–421). New York: McGraw-Hill/Hemisphere.

Danieli, Y. (1984). Psychotherapists' participation in the conspiracy of silence about the Holocaust. *Psychoanalytic Psychology, 1*, 23–42.

Derfner, L. (2008). African refugees pose a dilemma for Israel. *US News and World Report.* Available online http://www.usnews.com (Downloaded January 6, 2013.)

Edim Bemadim (2011). *Matrot ha-mishlakhat* [Goals of the delegation]. Available online http://www.aka.idf.il/edim/theProj/TheProj.asp (Downloaded January 6, 2013.)

Elon, A. (1971). *The Israelis: Founders and sons.* London, U.K.: Weidenfeld & Nicolson.

Feldman, J. (2008). *Above the death pits, beneath the flag: Youth voyages to Poland and the performance of Israeli national identity.* New York: Berghahn.

Feldman, S. Y. (1992). Whose story is it anyway? Ideology and psychology in the representation of the Shoah in Israeli literature. In S. Friedlander (Ed.), *Probing the limits of representation: Nazism and the 'final solution'* (pp. 223–239). Cambridge, MA: Harvard University Press.

Firer, R. (1989). *Sokhnim shel ha-lekakh* [Agents of Holocaust lesson]. Tel Aviv, Israel: Hakibbutz Hameuchad.

Gertz, N. (2004). *Mak'hela Aheret [Holocaust survivors, aliens and others in Israeli cinema and literature].* Tel Aviv, Israel: Am Oved.

Grodzinsky, Y. (2004). *In the shadow of the Holocaust: The struggle between Jews and Zionists in the aftermath of World War II.* Monroe, ME: Common Courage Press.

Gross, T. (2001). Female fighter pilot joins Israel's top guns. *Telegraph.* Available online http://www.telegraph.co.uk/news/worldnews/middleeast/israel/1333264/Female-fighter-pilot-joins-Israels-top-guns.html (Downloaded January 6, 2013.)

Gutfreund, A. (2007). *Our Holocaust.* New Milford, CT: Toby Press.

Gutwein, D. (2009). The privatization of the holocaust: memory, historiography, and politics. *Israel Studies, 14*, 36–64. doi: 10.1353/is.0.0024

Hareven, A. (1983). Victimization: Some comments by an Israeli. *Political Psychology, 4*, 145–155.

Hazan, H. (2001). *Simulated dreams: Israeli youth and virtual zionism.* New York: Berghahn.

Hurwitz, H. Z. (2004). *Begin, his life, words, and deeds.* Jerusalem, Israel: Gefen.

Imhoff, R., Wohl, M. J. A., & Erb, H.-P. (2013). When the past is far from dead: How ongoing consequences of genocides committed by the ingroup impact collective guilt. *Journal of Social Issues, 69*, 74–91.

Justvision (2008). *Interview with Yehuda Shaul.* Available online http://www.justvision.org/he/ portrait/76159/highlights (Downloaded January 6, 2013.)

Katz-Freiman, T. (2003). Don't touch my Holocaust – analyzing the barometer of responses: Israeli artists challenging the Holocaust taboo. In S. Hornstein, L. Levitt, & L. J. Silberstein (Eds.), *Impossible images: Contemporary art after the Holocaust* (pp. 129–154). New York: New York University Press.

Leach, C. W., Bou Zeineddine, F., & Čehajić-Clancy, S. (2013). Moral immemorial: The rarity of self-criticism for previous generation's genocide or mass violence. *Journal of Social Issues, 69*, 34–53.

Liebman, C. S., & Don-Yihya, E. (1983). *Civil religion in Israel: Traditional Judaism and political culture in the Jewish state.* Berkeley, CA: University of California Press.

Mahnaimi, U. (2010). Meir Dagan: The mastermind behind Mossad's secret war. *The Sunday Times.* Available online http://sudhan.wordpress.com/2010/02/21/meir-dagan-the-mastermind-behind-mossads-secret-war/ (Downloaded January 6, 2013.)

Milner, I. (2003). *Kire'y Avar: Biographia, Ze'hut Vezicharon Be'siporet Ha-dor ha-sheni* [Past present: Biography, identity and memory in second generation literature]. Tel-Aviv, Israel: Am Oved.

Morris, B. (1999). *Righteous victims: A history of the Zionist-Arab conflict, 1881–1998.* New York : Knopf.

Morris, B. (2007). The Second Holocaust. *The New York Sun*. Available online http://www.nysun.com (Downloaded January 6, 2013.)

National Library of Israel (2011). *Israeli book statistics*. Available online http://jnul.huji.ac.il/eng/lgd-statistics-2011.html#netunim (Downloaded January 6, 2013.)

Netanyahu, B. (2010). Prime Minister Benjamin Neytanyahu's speech at the Holocaust and Heroes' Remembrance Day ceremony. Available online http://en.netanyahu.org.il (Downloaded January 6, 2013.)

Novick, P. (1999). *The Holocaust in American life*. Boston, MA: Houghton Mifflin.

Ofer, D. (1996). "Israel." In D. S. Wyman (Ed.), *The world reacts to the Holocaust* (pp. 839–923). Baltimore, MD: Johns Hopkins University Press.

Ofer, D. (2009). The past that does not pass: Israelis and Holocaust memory. *Israel Studies, 14*, 1–35. doi: 10.1353/is.0.0023

Ofer, D. (2010). Victims, fighters, survivors: Quietism and activism in Israeli historical consciousness. *Common Knowledge, 16*, 493–517. doi: 10.1215/0961754X-2010-008

Oron, Y. (1993). *Ze'hut Ye'hudit-Isra'elit* [Jewish Israeli identity]. Tel Aviv, Israel: Sifriat Poalim.

O'Sullivan, A. (2003). IAF Jets fly over Auschwitz: Commemorate Holocaust victims. Available online http://www.israelnewsagency.com (Downloaded January 6, 2013.)

Porat, D. (2008). *Israeli society, the Holocaust and its survivors*. London, U.K.: Vallentine Mitchell.

Rinkevich-Pave, A. (2008). *Presence of the Holocaust in Jewish Israelis' day-to-day lives*. Unpublished Master's Thesis. Tel Aviv University, Tel Aviv, Israel.

Roccas, S., Klar, Y., & Liviatan, I. (2006). The paradox of group-based guilt: Modes of national identification, conflict vehemence, and reactions to the in-group's moral violations. *Journal of Personality and Social Psychology, 91*, 698–711. doi: 10.1037/0022-3514.91.4.698

Saar, T. (2008). Lo mukhanot la'amod mineged kmo ha-germanim [Unwilling to stand aloof like the Germans]. *Haaretz*. Available online http://www.mouse.co.il/CM.articles_item, 1050,209,22728,.aspx (Downloaded January 6, 2013.)

Schori-Eyal, N. (2011). *The shadows of the past: Effects of historical group trauma on current intergroup conflicts*. Unpublished Doctoral Dissertation. Tel-Aviv University, Tel-Aviv, Israel.

Schori-Eyal, N., Klar, Y., & Roccas, S. (2012). *Perpetual victim or future victimizer: Possible outcomes of group trauma*. Paper submitted for publication.

Schuman, H., Vinitzky-Seroussi, V., & Vinokur, A. D. (2003). Keeping the past alive: Memories of Israeli Jews at the turn of the millennium. *Sociological Forum, 18*, 103–136. doi: 10.1023/A:1022606912871

Segev, T. (2000). *The seventh million: Israelis and the Holocaust*. New York: Holt.

Shapira, A. (1989). *Ha-halikha al kav ha-ofek* [Going toward the horizon]. Tel Aviv, Israel: Am Oved.

Shapira, A. (1998). The Holocaust: Private memories, public memory. *Jewish Social Studies, 4*, 40–58.

Solomon, Z. (1995). From denial to recognition: Attitudes toward Holocaust survivors from World War II to the present. *Journal of Traumatic Stress, 8*, 15–228. doi: 10.1007/BF02109559

Staub, E., & Vollhardt, J. (2008). Altruism born of suffering: The roots of caring and helping after victimization and other trauma. *American Journal of Orthopsychiatry, 78*, 267–280. doi: 10.1037/a0014223

Stauber, R. (2007). *The Holocaust in Israeli public debate in the 1950s: Ideology and memory*. London, U.K.: Vallentine Mitchell.

Spiro, G. (2008). Similar situations [Letter to the Editor]. *Haaretz*. Available online http://www.haaretz.co.il/hasite/spages/1037100.html (Downloaded January 6, 2013.)

Terry, H. (2004). *Golden rules and silver rules of humanity: Universal wisdom of civilization*. Bloomington, IN: Author House.

The Combat Genocide Association (2008). *Sudan Refugees Aid Plan 2008*. The Combat Genocide Association: Tel Aviv, Israel.

van Ijzendoorn, M. H., Bakermans-Kranenburg, M. J., & Sagi-Schwartz, A. (2003). Are children of Holocaust survivors less well-adapted? A meta-analytic investigation of secondary traumatization. *Journal of Traumatic Stress, 16*, 459–469. doi: 10.1023/A:1025706427300

Vardi, D. (1992). *Memorial candles: Children of the Holocaust*. New York: Routledge.

Vollhardt, J. R. (2009). The role of victim beliefs in the Israeli-Palestinian conflict: Risk or potential for peace? *Peace and Conflict: Journal of Peace Psychology, 15,* 135–159. doi: 10.1080/10781919.2011.561185

Vollhardt, J. R. (2013). "Crime against humanity" or "crime against Jews"? Acknowledgment in construals of the Holocaust and its importance for intergroup relations. *Journal of Social Issues, 69,* 144–161.

Wohl, M. J. A., & Branscombe, N. R. (2008). Remembering historical victimization: Collective guilt for current ingroup transgressions. *Journal of Personality and Social Psychology, 94,* 988–1006. doi:10.1037/0022-3514.94.6.988

Wohl, M. J. A., Branscombe, N. R., & Klar, Y. (2006). Collective guilt: Emotional reactions when one's group has done wrong or been wronged. *European Review of Social Psychology, 17,* 1–37. doi: 10.1080/10463280600574815

Yablonka, H. (1999). *Survivors of the Holocaust: Israel after the War.* New York: New York University Press.

Yablonka, H. (2004). *The State of Israel vs. Adolf Eichmann.* Tel-Aviv, Israel: Schocken Publishing House.

Zandberg, E. (2006). Critical laughter: Humor, popular culture and Israeli Holocaust commemoration. *Media, Culture & Society, 28,* 561–579. doi: 10.1177/0163443706065029

Zelikovitz, M. (2010). Me-al me'a elef khotmim: tnu linso'a le-Polin [More than 100 thousand signers: Make it possible to go to Poland]. *Ynet.* Available online http://www.ynet.co.il/ (Downloaded January 6, 2013.)

Zertal, I. (2005). *Israel's Holocaust and the politics of nationhood.* Cambridge, U.K.: Camridge University Press.

Zuckerman, M. (1993). *Shoah ba-kheder ha-a'tum: ha-"shoah" ba-I'tonut ha-israelit be-tkufat milkhemet ha-mifrats* [Shoah in the sealed room: The "Holocaust" in Israeli press during the Gulf War]. Tel Aviv, Israel: Hamechaber.

YECHIEL KLAR is Associate Professor of social psychology in the School of Psychological Sciences at Tel Aviv University. His research on judgment, choice, and decision processes is currently funded by Israel Science Foundation (ISF) and the United States-Israel Binational Science Foundation (SSF). His research on political and moral discourse in societies affected by enduring ethnopolitical conflict and the role of historical memory in this discourse is currently funded by the Germany-Israel Foundation (GIF).

NOA SCHORI-EYAL earned her BA in Psychology (2004), MA in Clinical Psychology (2008), and PhD in Social Psychology (2001) from Tel Aviv University. She is currently a postdoctoral fellow at the Department of Psychology, University of Maryland in College Park. Her main research interest is in the effects of historical group traumas on reactions to current intergroup conflicts. Her most recent research focuses on goal systems.

YONAT KLAR earned her BA from the University of Connecticut and is currently completing her MA in gender studies at Tel Aviv University. She has been involved for many years in Holocaust education in Israel and North America, and is active in women's empowerment groups in the Jewish and Arab communities in Israel.

Journal of Social Issues, Vol. 69, No. 1, 2013, pp. 144–161

"Crime against Humanity" or "Crime against Jews"? Acknowledgment in Construals of the Holocaust and Its Importance for Intergroup Relations

Johanna Ray Vollhardt[*]
Clark University

This article examines the consequences of different representations of the Holocaust for intergroup relations, focusing on the role of acknowledgment of different groups' fate that is inherent in these construals. Holocaust representations have become increasingly universal. Research on recategorization suggests prosocial outcomes of such superordinate representations. However, among minority groups, acknowledging both superordinate and subgroup identities may be crucial in order to prevent backlash. An experimental study among Jewish and non-Jewish participants (N = 163) was conducted to test these ideas. As hypothesized, prosocial responses to outgroup victims of collective violence and acknowledgment of their suffering increased among Jewish participants when both a superordinate categorization of the Holocaust and subgroup (Jewish) fate were presented, compared to when only one of these categorizations were used. Conversely, different categorizations did not affect outcomes among the control group. Practical implications for intergroup relations and memorialization in the aftermath of genocide are discussed.

Over the past few decades, collective memories of genocide and mass killings have increasingly entered the global political discourse. In this discourse, the Holocaust is often considered a prototype of genocide and has become a universal

─────────────

[*]Correspondence concerning this article should be addressed to Johanna Ray Vollhardt, Clark University, Psychology Department, 950 Main Street, Worcester, MA 01610 [e-mail: JVollhardt@clarku.edu].

This research was supported by a SPSSI Grant-in-Aid and was part of the author's dissertation, conducted at the University of Massachusetts Amherst. The author would like to thank Aysha Abraibesh, Caitlin Bourbeau, Franklin Eneh, Callie Ericson, Melissa Huey, Magali Lemahieu, Suyi Liu, and Hillel at the University of Massachusetts at Amherst for their help in data collection, as well as the members of her dissertation committee: Linda Tropp (chair), Ronnie Janoff-Bulman, David Arnold, and Leah Wing. The author is also grateful to Egon Erb for his valuable comments on earlier drafts of this manuscript.

symbol of evil (Alexander, 2009; MacDonald, 2008). Some argue that the Holocaust has been incorporated into a "cosmopolitan memory" (Levy & Sznaider, 2006), providing a framework through which other atrocities can be understood and redressed. However, others have viewed these decontextualized representations of the Holocaust as a denial of distinct Jewish fate (Berenbaum, 1990). This article aims to explore these phenomena through a social psychological lens, examining how (re-)categorization theories (e.g., Gaertner & Dovidio, 2000) and theories of group-based victim beliefs (Vollhardt, 2012) can help us understand the opposite responses that different groups may have to different representations of the Holocaust. In particular, the tension regarding ingroup and outgroup acknowledgment, which is inherent in universal representations of victimization, is explored.

The increasing universality of the Holocaust is evident in its metaphorical use for descriptions of atrocities against ethnic groups worldwide. For example, the term has been invoked in discussions about slavery in the United States, the Rwandan genocide, Aborigines in Australia (see Levy & Sznaider, 2006), as well as in the context of the mass killings of indigenous Maoris in New Zealand, of ethnic groups in Ex-Yugoslavia (MacDonald, 2008), and in many other cases. Several book titles use this term, such as "The Rape of Nanking: The Forgotten Holocaust of World War II" (Chang, 1997), "American Holocaust" (Stannard, 1992), or "The Holocaust of Indian Partition" (Godbole, 2006).

In many cases, the Holocaust terminology is borrowed to gain acknowledgment of the ingroup's suffering, with the hope that if the events can be compared to what is sometimes seen as a universally acknowledged standard of evil, the ingroup's suffering will be acknowledged as well (MacDonald, 2008). The Holocaust imagery has also been used by international actors such as the UN or NGOs acting on behalf of victimized groups, to gain support and draw attention to these groups' fate (Levy & Sznaider, 2006; Power, 1999). Jewish activists have referred to their group's persecution in and prior to the Holocaust as a motivating force to prevent other groups' suffering, such as in the genocide in Darfur (Hoar, 2006).

Despite these positive outcomes, the use of a universal representation of the Holocaust is a double-edged sword, and it has given rise to controversy. On the one hand, some have seen this comparison as a "window of opportunity, giving hope to other groups" (Torpey, 2001, cited in MacDonald, 2008, p. 29) that the inclusive categorization will facilitate acknowledgment of other victimized and historically disadvantaged groups' suffering. On the other hand, this universal representation requires that the Holocaust be ". . . reconfigured as a decontextualized event" (Levy & Sznaider, 2006, p. 5). This detracting from specific features and shifting of Holocaust representations "from Jewish to human experience" (Levy & Sznaider, 2007), however, may be perceived by some as a lack of acknowledgment of distinct group histories in the Holocaust (Berenbaum, 1990; MacDonald,

2008). Therefore, debates about the representation of the Holocaust can result in competitive victimhood (Blumer, in press; Jensen, 2002; see also Noor, Brown, Gonzalez, Manzi, & Lewis, 2008) and are, in part, driven by different groups' need for acknowledgment. Rather than recognizing this shared need, the representation of the Holocaust as either universalistic or particularistic often evolves into a battle for acknowledgment between groups—a zero-sum game in which acknowledgment of commonalities and of distinct groups' fate are seen as mutually exclusive (Rothberg, 2009).

Social psychological theories of (re-)categorization and different responses to superordinate construals among minority and majority group members can shed more light on the underlying psychological dynamics of such debates. These theories also provide ideas how to address these issues and reduce conflict and competitive victimhood while increasing solidarity between members of victimized groups. In the following, I briefly summarize relevant findings and how they apply to group-based victim consciousness (Vollhardt, 2012), integrating these ideas with the broader discussion of group members' need for acknowledgment in the intergroup relations literature, the clinical literature, and in the literature on reconciliation.

Recategorization in the Context of Prosocial Behavior and Mass Violence

From a social psychological perspective, the described differences in representations of the Holocaust can be understood as a matter of the chosen construal level (in the general social cognition literature) or as a matter of social categorization (in the intergroup relations literature).

Construal level theory (e.g., Trope & Liberman, 2010) posits that every object or event can be represented on different levels of abstraction. While low-level construals entail a focus on the subordinate, contextualized, and specific features of the event, high-level construals emphasize the essence of the event and its superordinate, decontextualized features. These differences in construal levels become apparent in the representations of the Holocaust described earlier: the more contextualized and particularistic description of the Holocaust that focuses on specific group histories is a low-level construal, whereas more inclusive and universal as well as decontextualized representations of the Holocaust as a crime against humanity represent a high-level construal of the event. Construal level theory, while developed as a more general theory in the realm of social cognition and not specifically for intergroup relations, provides a theoretical framework for describing these specific representations of mass violence. It also allows one to develop theoretical predictions about when which of these construal levels would be chosen. For example, high-level construals are more likely with spatial, temporal, and other forms of psychological distance (Trope & Liberman, 2010). This might explain why high-level construals of collective victimization events seem to be preferred by members of groups who were not victims of these specific events, and less so by members of groups who were directly affected, and for whom the events have more psychological proximity (see MacDonald, 2008).

These different representations of the Holocaust can also be conceptualized within the recategorization literature in intergroup research. Recategorization strategies take advantage of the fact that people have multiple social identities and group memberships that vary in their level of inclusiveness. When members of different social groups become aware of group memberships they share at a higher level of inclusiveness (e.g., university affiliation instead of major, nationality instead of ethnicity, humanity instead of nationality, etc.), it can result in recategorizing former outgroup members on the less inclusive (subgroup) level into a more inclusive, superordinate category, a so-called common ingroup (Gaertner & Dovidio, 2000).

Most of the research examining the consequences of including previous outgroup members into superordinate categories has focused on the reduction of prejudice towards these groups (e.g., Gaertner & Dovidio, 2000; Hornsey & Hogg, 2000). However, some studies have also examined positive effects of recategorization on prosocial attitudes and behaviors, showing that the salience of a superordinate group membership increases the likelihood of helping (former) outgroup members. This prosocial effect has been shown in laboratory studies with minimal groups (Dovidio, Gaertner, Validzic, & Matoka, 1997), as well as for natural group memberships, including nationality, sports team affiliation, and sexual orientation (Levine, Prosser, Evans, & Reicher, 2005; Levine & Thompson, 2004; Stürmer, Snyder, & Omoto, 2005).

Only very few studies, however, have applied the ideas of recategorization to the realm of intergroup violence and its aftermath. An archival study by Reicher, Cassidy, Wolpert, Hopkins, and Levine (2006) showed that during the Second World War, a superordinate identity based on Bulgarian nationality rather than on religious and ethnic subgroups was invoked to mobilize prosocial actions on behalf of Jews and prevent their deportation. In a study among present-day Canadian Jews, superordinate categorizations of the Holocaust were made salient by describing it as an event in which "humans behaved aggressively toward other humans" (Wohl & Branscombe, 2005, p. 291), as compared to subgroup categorizations in which the distinct group memberships (Germans and Jews) were mentioned. The findings reveal that in the inclusive, superordinate categorization condition, Jewish participants assigned less collective guilt to Germans and were more likely to express willingness to forgive them.

Taken together, these studies provide evidence that inclusive categorizations of a victimized group or of collective violence can give rise to prosocial outcomes toward a victimized group among bystanders, or toward the previous perpetrator group among members of a victimized group. Unexplored to date is whether and under which conditions inclusive categorizations of the ingroup's victimization may also give rise to prosocial outcomes between victim groups, rather than resulting in backlash and competitive victimhood.

Group-Based Victim Consciousness

Superordinate categorizations of ingroup victimization can be referred to as *inclusive victim consciousness*, defined as the subjective interpretation of the ingroup's collective victimization that includes the perception of similarities between the ingroup's and other groups' experiences. In contrast, *exclusive victim consciousness* is defined as the focus on the ingroup's specific victimization and its interpretation as unique and distinct from other groups' experiences (Vollhardt, 2012). While the level of inclusive and exclusive victim consciousness may vary interindividually, Wohl and Bransombe's (2005) studies show that, to some extent, these construals may also be manipulated experimentally by making one construal or the other salient.

Anecdotal evidence shows that inclusive interpretations of "Never Again" have motivated collective action among Jews (and other groups with a history of persecution) on behalf of currently victimized groups. Examples range from activism in the civil rights movement to protests against My Lai, aid missions in Bosnia, in some rare cases actions against the occupation in Palestine, and more commonly in the movement to stop the genocide in Darfur (for reviews see Klar, Schori-Eyal, & Klar, 2013; Vollhardt, 2009, 2012).

Distinctiveness Needs and Need for Acknowledgment in the Context of Recategorization

Importantly, inclusive social categorizations do not always result in positive intergroup outcomes. Especially when inclusive social categorizations are imposed by others—be it through experimental manipulations, or through political speeches and other forms of public discourse—they can give rise to backlash and in fact negatively impact intergroup relations. Building on Brewer's (1991) work on the need for optimal distinctiveness, Hornsey and Hogg (2000) proposed and showed in several experimental studies that superordinate categorizations can pose a distinctiveness threat, and that in response, bias toward outgroups in the superordinate category may actually increase. This is especially true for group members who are highly identified with their subgroup (Crisp, Stone, & Hall, 2006). Minority group members also have a higher need for acknowledgment of distinct subgroup identities than majority group members (Dovidio, Gaertner, & Saguy, 2009; Huo & Molina, 2006). Thus, acknowledgment of the subgroup's distinctiveness within the superordinate, shared category makes the acceptance of this superordinate category more likely, and enables the beneficial intergroup outcomes of recategorization described earlier (Crisp et al., 2006; Hornsey & Hogg, 2000).

These processes can be applied to the aftermath of genocide, and explain some of the tensions that arise in response to overly inclusive representations of the Holocaust. In this context, distinctiveness needs translation to the need for acknowledgment of the ingroup's distinct group history of victimization. While members of groups that were not directly affected by the Holocaust may respond positively to inclusive, superordinate categorizations of the events as a crime against humanity, members of groups who were directly affected may respond with reactance and experience the need for distinct acknowledgment of their group's suffering.

This need for acknowledgment and resistance against too inclusive categories that are not perceived as an adequate representation of the group's history is apparent in the controversies regarding Holocaust memorials, most prominently the one built in 2005 in the center of the capital of Germany, Berlin. Here, a contentious debate evolved about whether or not other victim groups (such as gay and lesbian or Roma and Sinti victims) should be commemorated in the same memorial (Blumer, in press; McGroary, 2008). After much debate, separate memorials were constructed for each group, but even then gay and lesbian interest groups argued about the adequate representation of homosexual victims in the memorial (Jensen, 2002). These debates are an example of competitive victimhood (Noor et al., 2008) between groups that were victimized by the same perpetrators. The discussions also reveal a tension between different levels of acknowledgment that are inherent in the choice of an event's construal: while superordinate categorizations acknowledge multiple groups' histories of victimization, they do not acknowledge the distinctiveness of each of these groups' fate. This is crucial, because several bodies of literature have shown important, positive psychological outcomes of acknowledgment.

Clinical research has shown that societal acknowledgment is associated with reduced trauma symptoms after collective and interpersonal violence. This has been demonstrated, for example, among political prisoners and victims of interpersonal crime (Maercker & Müller, 2004) and Chechen refugees (Maercker, Povilonyte, Lianova, & Pöhlmann, 2009).

In the psychological literature on *reconciliation*, acknowledgment of victimization—for example, through monuments, political speeches, or community members' comments—is considered an important factor in improving intergroup relations after mass violence (Adjukovic & Biruski, 2008; Nadler & Liviatan, 2006; Staub, 2011). In a study among former political prisoners, acknowledgment of their victimization was associated with reduced desire for revenge (David & Choi, 2009). The literature on apologies after mass violence discusses acknowledgment as one of the factors that make apologies effective (Blatz, Schumann, & Ross, 2009). In dialogue groups between Israelis,

Palestinians, and Germans, acknowledgment of the ingroup's victimization in the presence of the adversary in a conflict enabled participants to acknowledge the adversary's victimization as well (Maoz & Bar-On, 2002).

Finally, in the *social psychological intergroup relations literature* on the effects of superordinate categorization and subgroup identities, the term "acknowledgment" is used to talk about the simultaneous consideration of both (e.g., Crisp et al., 2006; Dovidio et al., 2009; Huo, Molina, Sawahata, & Deang, 2005). This distinct acknowledgment of subgroup identities is particularly important to members of minority groups (Dovidio et al., 2009).

Social Psychological Conceptualization of Acknowledgment after Mass Violence

A social psychological conceptualization of mutual acknowledgment in the aftermath of collective violence that will satisfy all groups' needs can be understood as the acknowledgment of each (sub-)group's distinct history of victimization within an inclusive, superordinate category of shared victimhood. By simultaneously acknowledging both, inclusive representations of victimhood should be accepted more readily and give rise to prosocial outcomes toward other victim groups, as well as to increased willingness to acknowledge other groups' suffering. Without the distinct acknowledgment of ingroup victimization and specific group histories, superordinate, inclusive construals of the ingroup's victimization will not have a positive effect, and in fact reduce positive attitudes toward other victimized groups.

Thus, social psychological theories imply a continuum of acknowledgment and denial. While the most extreme form is complete denial of an event or of its characterization as mass killing or genocide (as in the case of the Armenian genocide: see Bilali, 2013), lack of acknowledgment can also entail the minimization of another group's victimization. This may be explicit, through comparisons with the ingroup's suffering that is portrayed as more severe (competitive victimhood: Noor et al., 2008), or implicit, through an overly inclusive (superordinate) categorization that fails to acknowledge the (sub-)group's distinct history. Only when both shared histories of oppression and distinct subgroup fate are explicitly recognized, true acknowledgment is achieved. In the collective memory literature, this dual acknowledgment has been referred to as "multidirectional memory" (Rothberg, 2009).

Hypotheses for the Present Study

The present study is the first attempt to test the effects of inclusive victim consciousness and the role of acknowledgment on relations between victim groups, using an experimental design in the context of the Holocaust and its after-math. Generally, inclusive (superordinate) and exclusive (subgroup) construals of a group's victimization are expected to have different effects on ingroup and out-group members. Specifically, among members of historically victimized groups, (H1) inclusive representations of the ingroup's victimization are only expected to increase prosocial outcomes toward other victim groups when the ingroup's distinct fate is also acknowledged within the inclusive category, whereas a su-perordinate categorization without subgroup recognition is expected to decrease prosocial outcomes (backlash effect). (H2) Dual acknowledgment is also expected to increase the willingness to acknowledge other victim groups, while a superor-dinate categorization will decrease acknowledgment of other victim groups. (H3) Prosocial outcomes and acknowledgment are not expected to increase among those for whom the events are not ingroup victimization events, except when the abstract superordinate categorization includes them in a common ingroup (e.g., "crime against humanity").

Method

Sample

Participants were recruited from two universities in the Northeast of the United States and paid for their participation. Jewish students were recruited through the Jewish student organization Hillel and the Psychology department's subject pool. Non-Jewish, European American students were recruited through the same subject pool and through flyers on campus. Members of ethnic and racial minority groups were not included in the analysis, because their ingroup's history may have also included persecution and affected their responses. Seven participants were omitted from the analysis because they expressed awareness of the hypothesis. The remaining sample consisted of 163 participants ($n = 83$ non-Jewish, $n = 80$ Jewish). The majority of the sample was female (69.9%), and the mean age was 19.32 ($SD = 1.06$).

Design and Materials

The study followed a 2×3, between-subjects design with one quasiexperi-mental factor, group membership (two levels: Jewish and non-Jewish European American), and one experimental factor, the representation of the Holocaust (three levels: superordinate categorization; subgroup categorization; superordinate cate-gorization with subgroup acknowledgment). To manipulate the representation of the Holocaust, participants were presented with seven sentences that described the persecution by Nazis in Europe. The sentences were the same in each condition, with exception of the description of the targets and nature of the persecution. In the superordinate categorization condition, the Holocaust was described abstractly, as a crime against humanity (adapting the manipulation used by Wohl & Branscombe, 2005), without mentioning specific ideologies or groups (e.g.: "The Holocaust is therefore an inconceivable crime against humanity that should never be forgotten and must be met with the decisive response: 'Never again!'"). In the subgroup categorization condition, the Holocaust was described more concretely and exclusively as a crime against Jews (e.g., "The Holocaust is therefore an inconceivable crime against the Jewish people that should never be forgotten and must be met with the decisive response: 'Never again!'"). Finally, in the condition that presented a superordinate categorization with subgroup recognition, the Holocaust was described as a crime against humanity and other victim groups (e.g., Roma and Sinti, political enemies, disabled people) were also mentioned, but in addition the particular Jewish fate in the Holocaust was explicitly acknowledged (e.g., "The Holocaust is therefore an inconceivable crime against humanity in general and Jews in particular that should never be forgotten and must be met with the decisive response: 'Never again!'").

Two manipulation checks were included: First, participants were asked to come up with a title for the text, to check whether their construal of the Holocaust was in line with the condition they had been assigned to. Second, the "Inclusion of the other in the self" measure (Aron, Aron, & Smollan, 1992) was adapted to assess perceived commonality between Jews and other victim groups (see Tropp & Wright, 2001, for the extension to the group level). Specifically, one of the two circles was labeled as the "victimization experienced by Jews" and the other circle as the "victimization experienced by other groups." Participants were asked to indicate which pair of overlapping circles (out of 10, with the two circles within each pair gradually approaching and then increasingly overlapping each other) they believed symbolizes the relationship between the Jewish experience and other groups' experiences.

Three dependent variables were assessed. First, a general measure of *prosocial attitudes toward other victimized groups* was included, using three items on a seven-point scale (from 1, *strongly disagree*, to 7, *strongly agree*): "I feel a personal responsibility to help victims of ethnic violence in other countries," "I would attend rallies to support oppressed groups from other countries," and "I would like to learn more about the victimization of other groups throughout the world." The reliability of these three items was satisfactory (Cronbach's $\alpha = .75$).

A *behavioral measure of prosocial actions* toward a specific victim group was also included. Specifically, participants were given a petition, urging the state's senator to take action to stop the genocide in Darfur. The petition was real, hosted on the website "Save Darfur" at the time of the study. The behavioral measure was whether or not participants signed the petition.

In addition, *acknowledgment of other victim groups' suffering in the Holocaust* and willingness to include these groups in a shared memorial was assessed. Participants read an abbreviated version of a newspaper article describing a debate about a rejected proposal for a Holocaust memorial in the United States in which several victim groups (in addition to Jews) would have been included (Sengupta, 1996). Three positions are described in the article: one arguing that all victim groups should be represented, because "All victims have suffered equally." The second position argues that the inclusion of other victim groups in the memorial "diminishes the enormity of the tragedy that the Jewish people suffered in the Holocaust." The third position argues that "inclusion is not equivalence," and that the distinct fate of all groups would still be preserved. Participants were asked to choose the position they agreed most with. The position that "all victims have suffered" was used to operationalize acknowledgment of other groups' suffering among Jewish participants, and will be the focus of the following analysis.

In addition, several demographic variables were assessed, as well as participants' group identification and involvement in various student organizations. Because these variables did not affect the results, they are not further reported in the following.

Procedure

The study was presented to participants as two separate studies. Participants were told that the ostensible first study was about how people perceive information about ethnopolitical violence, and that they would evaluate a text that had been designed for this purpose. Participants were randomly assigned to one of the three experimental conditions. They first read the sentences describing the Holocaust and were asked to rearrange and write them down in a logical order. Participants were then asked to provide a title for the text and complete the commonality measure as well as several filler items evaluating various aspects of the text (e.g., how informative, educational, interesting it was). They were then told that this was the end of the first study, and given the Save Darfur petition. Participants were told by the research assistant that while waiting for her to return with the materials for the second study, they could read the petition and sign it if they were interested. The research assistant said that she was distributing the petitions as a favor for a friend who was part of a local Darfur activism group. Before leaving, the research assistant pointed to a collection box for the petitions outside of the room. Participants then had a few minutes of privacy to sign the petition or disregard it.

The ostensible second study was presented as a brief pilot study for a new project. Participants read the article about the memorial debate and completed the last dependent measure. After responding to demographic questions participants were debriefed, assured that the petition information would be submitted if they had signed it, thanked, and paid for their participation.

Results

Manipulation Checks

The titles participants chose for the text were in line with the categorization of their condition. In the superordinate categorization condition, 30.2% of the participants wrote a title describing the Holocaust on an abstract level (e.g., "crime against humanity") and 69.8% wrote a neutral title (e.g., "The Holocaust" or "Never Again!"). Nobody in this condition wrote a title describing the Holocaust on a subgroup level (e.g., "crime against Jews"). In the subgroup categorization condition, 20.4% wrote a title describing the Holocaust on a subgroup level, 7.5% described it both in terms of a subgroup- and a superordinate categorization, and 72.1% chose a neutral title. In the condition where both the subgroup and the superordinate group were made salient, 10.7% chose a superordinate construal, 1.8% a subgroup construal, 10.7% a construal reflecting both superordinate and subgroup, and 76.8% chose a neutral title.

A two-way ANOVA revealed a significant interaction between group membership and construal of the Holocaust on perceived commonality between victim groups, $F(2, 155) = 3.10$, $p = .048$, $\eta^2 = .03$, showing that the experimental manipulation had different effects on Jewish and non-Jewish participants. Simple main effects demonstrate that as expected, there were no significant differences between conditions for non-Jewish participants (all $p > .20$). In contrast, there were significant differences in the hypothesized direction between Jewish participants' commonality ratings in the superordinate and the subgroup condition (mean difference $= -1.03$, $p = .04$, Cohen's $d = .60$) and in the subgroup and superordinate plus subgroup recognition condition (mean difference $= .58$, $p = .05$, Cohen's $d = .30$), but, unexpectedly, not between the superordinate only and the superordinate plus subgroup recognition condition (mean difference $= -.42$, $p = .40$). Across conditions, non-Jewish participants reported higher levels of commonality between Jewish and other groups' victimization ($M = 7.67$, $SD = 1.58$) than did Jewish participants ($M = 6.42$, $SD = 1.96$). This difference was most pronounced when the Holocaust was presented as a crime against Jews (see Table 1).

Prosocial Attitudes and Behavior toward Other Victim Groups

Because differences between specific conditions were hypothesized rather than overall differences between all experimental conditions, the following

Table 1. Means, Standard Deviations, and Percentages by Experimental Condition

	Jewish participants			Non-Jewish participants		
	Super-ordinate only	Subgroup only	Superordinate + subgroup	Super-ordinate only	Subgroup only	Superordinate + subgroup
Commonality	6.92	5.89	6.5	7.46	8.07	7.5
	(1.82)	(1.6)	(2.34)	(1.35)	(1.59)	(1.75)
Prosocial attitudes	4.71	5.1	5.26	4.86	4.63	4.93
	(.93)	(1.27)	(1.1)	(1.14)	(.90)	(.95)
Signing petition	64%	64.3%	88%	72%	48.1%	59.3%
Shared memorial	24%	14.8%	39.3%	46.4%	55.6%	46.4%

Note. Mean scores. Standard deviations presented in parentheses.

analysis focuses on those cell differences and reports specific planned contrasts. All means, standard deviations, and percentages for each experimental cell are reported in Table 1.

As hypothesized (H1), Jewish participants indicated significantly higher levels of *general prosocial attitudes toward victimized outgroups* in the condition with simultaneous superordinate and subgroup categorization of the Holocaust, compared to when only the superordinate categorization was presented, $t(51) = -1.97$, $p = .05$, Cohen's $d = .54$. All other conditions were not significantly different from each other (all $p > .21$). In support of the third hypothesis, in the non-Jewish control group these two conditions did not differ significantly from each other, $t(1, 54) = -.25$, $p = .80$, nor did any other conditions (all $p > .24$).

Support for the first and third hypothesis was also obtained for the behavioral measure. Specifically, the likelihood of *signing the petition* urging political leaders to stop the genocide in Darfur significantly increased among Jewish participants when both the superordinate categorization of the Holocaust and subgroup recognition was presented. As Figure 1 shows, there was a 22% greater likelihood of signing the petition when both superordinate and subgroup categorization were acknowledged, compared to when only the superordinate group (humanity) had been presented, $\chi^2(1, 50) = 3.95$, $p = .047$, $\phi = .28$, or only the subgroup (Jewish fate) $\chi^2(1, 53) = 4.01$, $p = .045$, $\phi = .27$. This was not the case for non-Jewish participants, $\chi^2(1, 52) = .93$, $p = .72$ and $\chi^2(1, 55) = .35$, $p = .87$, who were in fact most likely to sign when only the superordinate categorization of the Holocaust as a "crime against humanity" had been presented (Figure 1). The only condition in which the difference between Jewish and non-Jewish participants in signing the petition was statistically reliable was when both the superordinate and

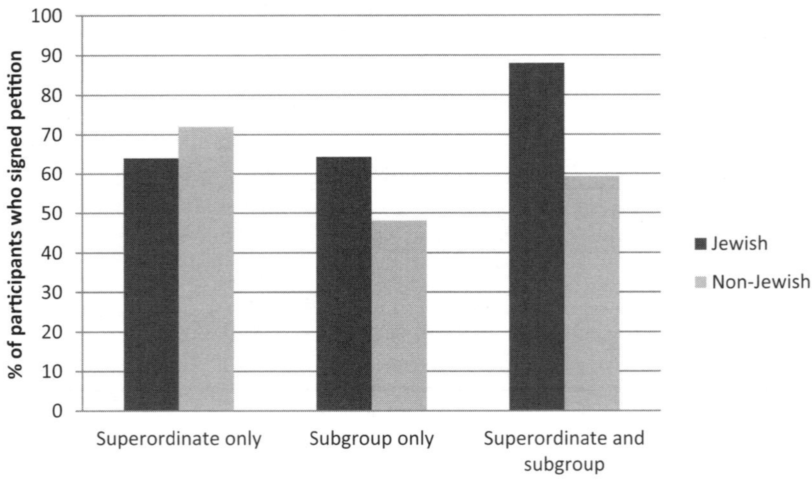

Fig. 1. Percentage of participants (by group membership and experimental condition) who signed the petition urging leaders to act against the genocide in Darfur.

the subgroup categorization were made salient; in this condition over 28% more Jewish participants than non-Jewish participants signed, χ^2 (1, 52) = 5.45, p = .02, ϕ = .32.

Acknowledgment of other Victim Groups in a Shared Memorial

In support of the second hypothesis, Jewish participants were most likely to acknowledge other victim groups' suffering as equal when both their ingroup's and other groups' suffering in the Holocaust had been made salient, compared to when only their group's suffering had been made salient, χ^2 (1, 55) = 3.75, p = .05, ϕ = .26 (see Figure 2). There was a 15% increase of Jewish participants who chose the statement that "all victims [of the Holocaust] have suffered equally" when both the ingroup's and other groups' suffering in the Holocaust were made salient, compared to when only the superordinate categorization was used. However, this difference was not statistically significant, χ^2 (1, 52) = 1.65, p = .20. In regard to group differences, Figure 2 shows that Jewish participants were much less likely than non-Jewish participants to accept the statement that all victims have suffered equally when either the superordinate categorization of the Holocaust was made salient, χ^2 (1, 51) = 3.69, p = .05, ϕ = .27, or the subgroup categorization, χ^2 (1, 53) = 10.59, p = .001, ϕ = .45. When both were represented this difference disappeared, χ^2 (1, 54) = .30, p = .58.

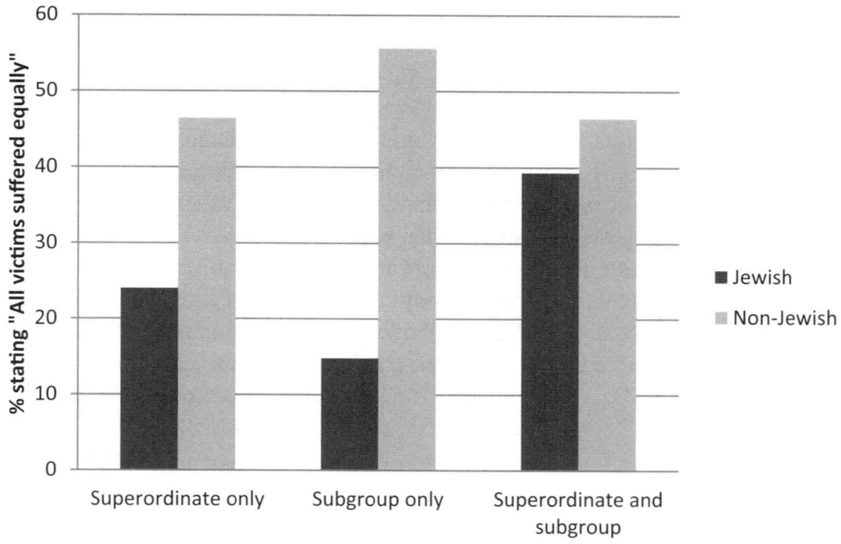

Fig. 2. Percentage of participants (by experimental condition and group membership) agreeing with the statement that "all victims [of the Holocaust] have suffered equally" and that their suffering should be acknowledged in the shared Holocaust memorial.

Discussion

Overall, these findings demonstrate the importance of acknowledging both a shared history of victimization between groups and the distinct history of each group involved in representations of genocide and other mass violence. In line with general findings showing reduced intergroup bias when both superordinate and the subgroup identities are acknowledged (Crisp et al., 2006; Hornsey & Hogg, 2000), among Jewish participants dual acknowledgment resulted in increased levels of prosocial attitudes and behavior toward other victimized groups. Likewise, dual acknowledgment also increased willingness to acknowledge that other victims had suffered equally during the Holocaust. These findings suggest a virtuous circle of positive processes resulting from the acknowledgment of a group's victimization.

For members of groups that were not targeted during the Holocaust (the non-Jewish, European American control group), these different construals generally did not affect the willingness to support victimized groups. However, there was a trend toward favoring the overly inclusive superordinate categorization that did not explicitly acknowledge Jewish suffering, resulting in higher levels of prosocial behavior among non-Jewish participants in this condition than in the condition with dual acknowledgment. This is in line with previous research and not surprising, given that the superordinate category included these participants in a shared ingroup of "humanity" without decreasing the effect by mentioning specific out-groups. Moreover, it corresponds with findings that members of minority groups care more about the dual representation than majority group members do (e.g., Dovidio et al., 2009).

A limitation of this study is the manipulation of the categorization of the Holocaust. Because each categorization requires a different level of detail, the materials were not equal in length, and the superordinate categorization with subgroup recognition required more information that was not mentioned in the other conditions (e.g., other victim groups; the mentioning of antisemitism in the subgroup categorization). These differences in length and detail are common in manipulations of high- and low-level construals of events (e.g., Fujita, Trope, Liberman, & Levin-Sagi, 2006). Nevertheless, future research should tease apart the various elements that are involved in different construals of genocide, focusing separately on the target group(s), ideologies and intentions of the perpetrators, and the construal of the event. This might also clarify the surprising finding of the manipulation check, which did not show the expected differences in perceived commonality between victim groups across experimental conditions—even though the differences were apparent in the assessed dependent measures. Thus, future research will have to replicate these findings and test whether reactance to these construals indeed occurs only in attitudes and behaviors toward other victim groups and not in expressed commonality.

Other limitations include the rather small effects. This may reflect that it is difficult to manipulate peoples' perceptions of their ingroup's history, which is reflected in the large standard deviations of cell means that indicate considerable individual differences in reaction to these construals. Given the personal centrality and importance of these group histories as well as the exposure to collective narratives of the group's history throughout socialization, this can be expected. It also suggests that nonexperimental methods (survey research, interview studies, and other qualitative methods) are crucial for future research on these issues.

Nonetheless, some extensions of experimental research are promising, and this line of future research should (1) replicate these findings with different populations, (2) test individual differences that may moderate these effects, (3) explore the role of different communicators on responses to different construals of ingroup suffering, and (4) test additional outcome variables.

Replications with different populations should include other groups that have been victims of genocide and other mass violence, such as Armenians, Bosnians, Native Americans, and many other groups worldwide. These replications would reveal which processes are more general, and which specific group narratives shape the effects. For example, Jewish tradition includes narratives about social justice (Schwarz & Messinger, 2008), and in recent years Darfur activism has been promoted in many Jewish congregations (Hoar, 2006). These ingroup narratives likely impact participants' responses and should be examined systematically.

In addition to the impact of group-level factors, it is also important to test potentially moderating effects of individual differences, such as ingroup identity strength and political ideology, as well as variables that are related to the events—such as the centrality of ingroup victimization or the exposure to trauma narratives through family members and contact with survivors. Contact with members of other victim groups also seems important, as it might make similarities with other groups' experiences more personally relevant and salient.

Another factor that may affect reactions to inclusive representations of the ingroup's victimization is whether these superordinate categorizations are communicated by ingroup or by outgroup members (Gómez, Dovidio, Huici, Gaertner, & Cuadrado, 2008). Similarly, inclusive representations communicated by a survivor versus someone who is not perceived as having legitimacy to draw comparisons should also be compared. Finally, future research should explore other dependant variables that have practical implications, such as including other victim groups in joint commemorations, or sharing reparations that redress historical victimization.

This kind of research has important policy implications for the design of memorials, the representation of violent histories in textbooks, and generally for public discourse related to the aftermath of mass violence. These studies would also contribute knowledge that is needed to address an important challenge arising from the different reactions people have to representations of collective violence, depending on their group membership. While categorizations that acknowledge both shared fate and ingroup fate resulted in the highest levels of prosocial attitudes and behavior toward outgroup victims among Jewish participants, for non-Jewish participants prosocial behavior tended to be the highest when only the superordinate categorization was used. This suggests that different representations should be chosen when addressing different groups. However, this is not always possible, as audiences are not always separate. Therefore, an important task for future research is to identify conditions under which members of different groups develop an equal preference for representations of mass violence that acknowledge all groups' fate, without resulting in backlash among one group.

This will require perspective-taking and education—among non-victimized as well as victimized groups—about the need for acknowledgment that groups with a history of persecution and mass violence share. Only if all groups and audiences understand these needs will it be possible to achieve representations of historical atrocities that give rise to solidarity and prosocial outcomes between nonvictimized and victimized groups, as well as between members of groups that were targeted in different ways but share a history of suffering.

References

Ajdukovic, D., & Biruski, D. (2008). Caught between the ethnic sides: Children growing up in a divided post-war community. *International Journal of Behavioral Development, 32*, 337–347.
Alexander, J. (2009). *Remembering the Holocaust*. New York, NY: Oxford University Press.

Aron, A., Aron, E., & Smollan, D. (1992). Inclusion of other in the self scale and the structure of interpersonal closeness. *Journal of Personality and Social Psychology, 63*, 596–612.

Berenbaum, M. (1990). *After tragedy and triumph*. Cambridge: Cambridge University Press.

Bilali, R. (2013). National narrative and social psychological influences in Turks' denial of the mass killings of Armenians as genocide. *Journal of Social Issues, 69*, 16–33.

Blatz, C. W., Schumann, K., & Ross, M. (2009). Government apologies for historical injustices. *Political Psychology, 30*, 219–241.

Blumer, N. (in press). From victim hierarchies to memorial networks: Commemorating Sinti and Roma and Jews in Germany's national narrative. In A. Weiss-Wendt (Ed.), *The Nazi genocide of the Gypsies: Reevaluation and commemoration*. New York: Berghahn Books.

Brewer, M. B. (1991). On the social self: On being the same and different at the same time. *Personality and Social Psychology Bulletin, 17*, 475–482.

Chang, I. (1997). *The rape of Nanking: the forgotten Holocaust of World War II*. New York, NY: Basic Books.

Crisp, R. J., Stone, C. H., & Hall, N. R. (2006). Recategorization and subgroup identification: predicting and preventing threats from common ingroups. *Personality and Social Psychology Bulletin, 32*, 230–243.

David, R., & Choi, S. Y. P. (2009). Getting even or getting equal? Retributive desires and transitional justice. *Political Psychology, 30*, 161–192.

Dovidio, J. F., Gaertner, S. L., & Saguy, T. (2009). Commonality and the complexity of 'we': Social attitudes and social change. *Personality and Social Psychology Review, 13*, 3–20.

Dovidio, J. F., Gaertner, S. L., Validzic, A., & Matoka, K. (1997). Extending the benefits of recategorization: Evaluations, self-disclosure, and helping. *Journal of Experimental Social Psychology, 33*, 401–420.

Fujita, K., Trope, Y., Liberman, N., & Levin-Sagi, M. (2006). Construal levels and self-control. *Journal of Personality and Social Psychology, 90*, 351–367.

Gaertner, S. L., & Dovidio, J. F. (2000). *Reducing intergroup bias: The common ingroup identity model*. Philadelphia, PA: Psychology Press.

Godbole, M. (2006). *The Holocaust of Indian partition*. Calcutta: Rupa.

Gómez, A., Dovidio, J. F., Huici, C., Gaertner, S. L., & Cuadrado, I. (2008). The other side of we: When outgroup members express common identity. *Personality and Social Psychology Bulletin, 34*, 1613–1626.

Hoar, J. (2006, May 1). Jews for justice in Darfur. *CBS News online*. Retrieved from: http://www.cbsnews.com/stories/2006/05/01/world/main1567410.shtml

Hornsey, M. J., & Hogg, M. A. (2000). Intergroup similarity and subgroup relations: Some implications for assimilation. *Personality and Social Psychology Bulletin, 26*, 948–958.

Huo, Y., & Molina, L. (2006). Is pluralism a viable model of diversity? The benefits and limits of subgroup respect. *Group Processes and Intergroup Relations, 9*, 359–376.

Huo, Y. J., Molina, L. E., Sawahata, R., & Deang, J. M. (2005). Leadership and the management of conflicts in diverse groups: Why acknowledging versus neglecting subgroup identity matters. *European Journal of Social Psychology, 35*, 237–254.

Jensen, E. N. (2002). The pink triangle and political consciousness: Gays, lesbians, and the memory of Nazi persecution. *Journal of the History of Sexuality, 11*, 319–349.

Klar, Y., Shori-Eyal, N., & Klar, Y. (2013). The "Never Again" state of Israel: The emergence of the Holocaust as a core feature of Israeli identity and its four incongruent voices. *Journal of Social Issues, 69*, 125–143.

Levine, M., Prosser, A., Evans, D., & Reicher, S. (2005). Identity and emergency intervention: How social group membership and inclusiveness of group boundaries shape helping behavior. *Personality and Social Psychology Bulletin, 31*, 443–453.

Levine, M., & Thompson, K. (2004). Identity, place, and bystander intervention: Social categories and helping after natural disasters. *Journal of Social Psychology, 144*, 229–245.

Levy, D., & Sznaider, N. (2006). *The Holocaust and memory in the global age*. Philadelphia, PA: Temple University Press.

Levy, D., & Sznaider, N. (2007). The cosmopolitization of Holocaust memory: From Jewish to human experience. In J. Gerson & D. Wolf (Eds.), *Sociology confronts the Holocaust. Memories and identities in Jewish diasporas* (pp. 313–330). Durham, NC: Duke University Press.

MacDonald, B. (2008). *Identity politics in the age of genocide*. New York, NY: Routledge.

Maercker, A., & Müller, J. (2004). Social acknowledgment as a victim or survivor: A scale to measure a recovery factor of PTSD. *Journal of Traumatic Stress, 17*, 345–351.

Maercker, A., Povilonyte, M., Lianova, R., & Pöhlmann, K. (2009). Is acknowledgment of trauma a protective factor? The sample case of refugees from Chechnya. *European Psychologist, 14*, 249–254.

Maoz, I., & Bar-On, D. (2002). From working through the Holocaust to current ethnic conflicts: Evaluating the TRT group workshop in Hamburg. *Group, 26*, 29–48.

McGroary, P. (2008, January 29). How many more monuments for Berlin? *Spiegel Online International* http://www.spiegel.de/international/germany/0,1518,531865,00.html

Nadler, A., & Liviatan, I. (2006). Intergroup reconciliation: Effects of adversary's expressions of empathy, responsibility, and recipients' trust. *Personality and Social Psychology Bulletin, 32*, 459–470.

Noor, M., Brown, R., Gonzalez, R., Manzi, J., & Lewis, C. A. (2008). On positive psychological outcomes: What helps groups with a history of conflict to forgive and reconcile with each other? *Personality and Social Psychology Bulletin, 34*, 819–832.

Power, S. (1999). To suffer by comparison? *Daedalus, 128*, 31–66.

Reicher, S., Cassidy, C., Wolpert, I., Hopkins, N., & Levine, M. (2006). Saving Bulgaria's Jews: An analysis of social identity and the mobilisation of social solidarity. *European Journal of Social Psychology, 36*, 49–72.

Rothberg, M. (2009). *Multidirectional memory*. Stanford, CA: Stanford University Press.

Schwarz, S., & Messinger, R. (2008). *Judaism and justice: The Jewish passion to repair the world*. Woodstock, VT: Jewish Lights Publishing.

Sengupta, S. (1996, August 18). A rift opens over "other victims' at Holocaust memorial. *New York Times*. Retrieved from http://www.nytimes.com/1996/08/18/nyregion/a-rift-opens-over-other-victims-at-holocaust-memorial.html

Stannard, D. (1992). *American Holocaust: Columbus and the conquest of the New World*. New York, NY: Oxford University Press.

Staub, E. (2011). *Overcoming evil*. New York, NY: Oxford University Press.

Stürmer, S., Snyder, M., & Omoto, A. (2005). Prosocial emotions and helping: The moderating role of group membership. *Journal of Personality and Social Psychology, 88*, 532–546.

Trope, Y., & Liberman, N. (2010). Construal-level theory of psychological distance. *Psychological Review, 117*, 440–463.

Tropp, L., & Wright, S. (2001). Ingroup identification as the inclusion of ingroup in the self. *Personality and Social Psychology Bulletin, 27*, 585–600.

Vollhardt, J. R. (2009). The role of victim beliefs in the Israeli-Palestinian conflict: Risk or potential for peace? *Peace and Conflict: Journal of Peace Psychology, 15*, 135–159.

Vollhardt, J. R. (2012). Collective victimization. In L. Tropp (Ed.), *Oxford handbook of intergroup conflict* (pp. 136–157). New York, NY: Oxford University Press.

Wohl, M., & Branscombe, N. R. (2005). Forgiveness and collective guilt assignment to historical perpetrator groups depend on level of social category inclusiveness. *Journal of Personality and Social Psychology, 88*, 288–303.

JOHANNA RAY VOLLHARDT is an Assistant Professor of Psychology at Clark University, where she is also affiliated with the Strassler Center for Holocaust and Genocide Studies. She received her Ph.D. in Social Psychology from the University of Massachusetts Amherst, with a concentration in the Psychology of Peace and Violence. She has received the Best Dissertation Award of the International Society of Political Psychology in 2010 and the Gert Sommer Award for Peace Psychology in 2009. Her research focuses on inclusive victim consciousness, prosocial behavior, and intergroup relations in the aftermath of collective violence.

Journal of Social Issues, Vol. 69, No. 1, 2013, pp. 162–179

Reconciliation through the Righteous: The Narratives of Heroic Helpers as a Fulfillment of Emotional Needs in Polish–Jewish Intergroup Contact

Michal Bilewicz* **and Manana Jaworska**

University of Warsaw

Postwar Polish–Jewish relations are heavily affected by divergent narratives about the Holocaust. Debates about the role of Poles as passive bystanders or perpetrators during the Holocaust have deeply influenced mutual perceptions of Poles and Jews. Previous research has shown that historical issues raised during Polish–Jewish encounters inhibit positive consequences of intergroup contact, mostly due to frustrated emotional needs related to past genocide. The aim of the present intervention was to reconcile young Poles and Israelis by presenting narratives that could change stereotypical thinking about the past. Our results indicate that the narratives of historical rescuers of Jews during WWII allowed overcoming the negative impact of the past on intergroup contact by fulfilling frustrated needs for acceptance among Polish participants. The article discusses the potential role of the heroic helpers' narrative for reconciliation after mass violence, as it may prevent entitative categorizations of groups as victims, perpetrators, and bystanders.

What will I tell him, I, a Jew of the New Testament,
Waiting two thousand years for the second coming of Jesus?
My broken body will deliver me to his sight
And he will count me among the helpers of death: The uncircumcised.
Czesław Miłosz, "A Poor Christian Looks at the Ghetto"

---

*Correspondence concerning this article should be addressed to Michal Bilewicz, Faculty of Psychology, University of Warsaw, Stawki 5/7, 00-183 Warszawa, Poland [e-mail: bilewicz@psych.uw.edu.pl].

This research was supported from a Ministry of Science and Higher Education IUVENTUS PLUS grant to the first author and BST budgetary funds of Faculty of Psychology, University of Warsaw. We are grateful to Jarosław Ziółkowski, Mateusz Hładki and Andrzej Folwarczny from the Forum for Dialogue among Nations for their efforts in organizing this intervention program and evaluation.

The collective memory of being both a bystander and victim nation became a core of Polish thinking about the Holocaust, shaping present-day Polish–Jewish relations. Regardless of objective Polish suffering during the World War II, Polish–Jewish relations are, to a great extent, influenced by the issue of moral responsibility for the atrocities that occurred on Polish soil during the Holocaust. Polish Nobel Prize-winning poet, Czesław Miłosz, expressed such feelings in his poem "A Poor Christian Looks at the Ghetto" written in 1943—anticipating also future fears of the coming generations of Poles in their contact with Jews (Miłosz, 1988).

The problem of postgenocide reconciliation currently receives much attention among psychologists, social scientists, and lawyers (Byrne, 2004; Staub, 2006; Zorbas, 2004). Most of this research deals with reconciliation between historical victims and perpetrators—as in the case of the Truth and Reconciliation Commission in South Africa (Byrne, 2004; Gibson, 2004), Gacaca trials in Rwanda (Honeyman et al., 2004; Kanyangara, Rimé, Philippot, & Yzerbyt, 2007), or German–Jewish exchange and dialogue programs (Imhoff, 2009; Maoz & Bar-On, 2002). These reconciliation programs very rarely focus on the bystander groups or on two victimized groups. Yet, after eruptions of mass violence there is a need to repair relations not only among the direct victims and perpetrators of the crime, but also among all other sides of genocidal conflict: passive bystanders, heroic helpers, several victim groups struggling for recognition, collaborators, and underground fighters (Vollhardt & Bilewicz, 2013).

A history of genocide threatens basic psychological needs of the descendants of all affected groups—the need for a moral image among perpetrators and bystanders and the need for power and control among the victims (Shnabel, Nadler, Canetti-Nisim, & Ullrich, 2008). At the same time, in the commemoration of genocide, there is a continuous struggle for historical recognition of one's group's innocent victim status. All these processes make reconciliation of the third generation very difficult: it is constrained by social identity threats resulting from potential intergroup encounters. The present article describes an intervention developed to overcome obstacles in postgenocide reconciliation. Aiming to fill a gap in the existing literature, we focus on emotional needs of descendants of a bystander group.

History as a Problem in Polish–Jewish Intergroup Contact

Positive intergroup contact is a clear aim of intergroup reconciliation between descendants of groups involved in and affected by the genocide, as it is known to improve intergroup relations in general (Pettigrew & Tropp, 2006). However, there are not many studies of intergroup contact in postconflict settings (few exceptions include: Cehajic, Brown & Castano, 2008; Hewstone, Cairns, Voci, Hamberger & Niens, 2006; Husnu & Crisp, 2010). The troubled intergroup history might be a serious obstacle in such contact, for several reasons. First, collective emotions about the ingroup's misdeeds (e.g., collective guilt) might decrease the willingness to engage in intergroup contact (Imhoff, Bilewicz, & Erb, 2012). In addition, focusing on such misdeeds might result in intergroup anxiety, an emotion that is known to deteriorate the effectiveness of intergroup encounters (Stephan & Stephan, 1985).

A recent intervention among Polish and Jewish high-school students tested how history might affect Polish—Jewish intergroup contact (Bilewicz, 2007). The program consisted of 2-hour long meetings between Polish high-school students and Jewish high-school students (from Canada, Australia, and the United States) who visited Poland as part of the March of the Living commemorative study tours. Everyday contacts between both groups are virtually nonexistent due to the small size of the Jewish community in Poland (Bilewicz & Wójcik, 2010) and the geographical separation of Poles and Jews in the current world. At the same time, both groups hold strong negative stereotypes of each other. Antisemitic prejudice is still wide-spread in Poland after the systemic transition (e.g., Kofta & Sedek, 2005), and Jews clearly became symbolic scapegoats of Polish economic change (Bilewicz & Krzemiński, 2010), while many Israeli Jews hold anti-Polish resentments, perceiving Poland as a hostile and antisemitic country and Poles as eternal enemies (Feldman, 2008).

The evaluation of this program (Bilewicz, 2007) showed that the effectiveness of Polish—Jewish youth encounters was significantly affected by the content of the conversations, specifically whether students talked about the groups' past or about the present. When the two groups talked about present-day issues, their attitudes toward each other improved: they perceived their counterparts as more similar to the ingroup (an outcome that is typically expected after positive intergroup contact; Bilewicz, 2006) and their level of liking increased. The situation became more complicated when the groups talked about their history. When Polish participants talked with their Jewish counterparts about the past, their attitudes toward Jews did not change: their liking did not increase, nor did perceived similarity to Jews. On the contrary, Jewish participants who talked with their Polish counterparts about the past showed more positive attitudes toward Poles and greater perceived intergroup similarity. However, these effects were still much smaller compared to the group that discussed present-day issues.

The first explanation of these results stressed the role of superordinate categories that are salient among groups discussing present-day issues (Bilewicz, 2007; Gaertner, Dovidio, & Bachman, 1996). After examining the issue more closely, other explanations seem more plausible. It is obvious that historical discussions during Polish—Jewish encounter programs had to touch the issue of Polish behaviors during the Holocaust (Michlic, 2007; Weinbaum, 2007). This is supported by a qualitative study, in which more than 1,000 Polish and Jewish high-school students were asked to name few most troubling questions that they would like to ask each other. Surprisingly, the type of questions that were most frequently asked by Polish students considered potential accusations about Polish passivity or co-perpetratorship during the Holocaust (Bilewicz, 2008; Wójcik, 2008). For example, Polish students in this study asked: "Why do Jews think that we allowed for and helped Germans to build Auschwitz?" or, more explicitly, "Why do you still blame Poles for the Holocaust?" (Bilewicz, 2008).

This fear of being accused for misdeeds or alleged misdeeds of their grandparents' generation was also found in observations and in-depth interviews with Polish students participating in Polish–Jewish encounters (Bilewicz, Ostolski, Wójcik, & Wysocka, 2004). As suggested by the needs-based model of reconciliation (Nadler & Shnabel, 2006), this self-perception creates a threat to one's moral self-image and, in turn, to a heightened need for acceptance during the encounter. If this need for acceptance is not met, the encounters may not be successful in changing attitudes. This provides an explanation for the ineffectiveness of encounter programs focused on history among Polish participants.

Basic Needs among Conflicted Groups

There is a growing consensus among social psychologists and peace researchers that in order to achieve reconciliation between conflicted groups, attention has to be paid to emotional aspects of conflict (Nadler & Shnabel, 2006; Shnabel et al., 2008; Staub & Pearlman, 2006). Moreover, it is now well understood that it is not sufficient to merely punish the perpetrators and address only emotional needs of victims. In order to restore harmonious relations between descendants of all groups affected by genocide, emotional needs of all these groups have to be taken into account (Shnabel et al., 2008; Staub & Pearlman, 2006).

In narratives about historical genocide, groups are usually perceived as homogenous entities, in one of three distinct roles: perpetrators, bystanders, or victims (Hilberg, 1993; Staub, 1985). If entire groups—and not specific individuals that committed the atrocities—are perceived as historical actors, entire groups to which perpetrators belong (or belonged) are perceived as responsible for the genocide (Wohl & Branscombe, 2005). Thus, members of such groups might experience collective guilt and feel responsibility for atrocities they personally did not commit (e.g., Doosje, Branscombe, Spears, & Manstead, 1998). Similar feelings of guilt may arise in members of the bystander group, if they are accused of passivity or of supporting perpetrators' actions. Reports on "witness guilt" or "bystander guilt" can be found in the clinical literature (Herman, 1992; Wilson, Drozdek & Turkovic, 2006). Early research on helping behavior suggests that anticipating future guilt is one of the most important costs of nonhelping in emergencies (Latane & Darley, 1970). Nations occupied by Nazi Germany dealt with passive bystander guilt decades after the end of World War II—and this affected their attitudes toward Jews (Steinlauf, 1997).

According to the needs-based model of reconciliation (Shnabel, Nadler, Ullrich, Dovidio, & Carmi, 2009), members of groups who were either perpetrators or victims of historical crimes suffer from frustration of specific psychological needs. Members of the perpetrator group are afraid of being rejected by other groups because of their group's immoral behavior in the past, assuming that their group will not be accepted as a moral actor (Nadler & Shnabel, 2006). That creates a heightened need for acceptance from other groups, which has to be fulfilled in order to permit members of the perpetrator group to regain a positive social identity. This, in turn, should facilitate reconciliation. Although the authors do not make predictions about bystander groups' needs, it can be assumed that the members of these groups are subject to similar threats and needs, as they can also be perceived as responsible for the victims' fate (Latane & Darley, 1970; Staub, 2006).

In contrast, members of the victimized group suffer from a threat that historical victimization poses to the status and power of their ingroup (Shnabel et al., 2009). Similar to direct victims, members of historically victimized groups may experience feelings of loss of control over their fate (Bar-Tal & Antebi, 1992). Their basic need that has to be fulfilled to enable reconciliation with the perpetrator group is the need for a sense of power and control.

One way of fulfilling needs of groups with a history of intergroup atrocities is when the victim group shows acceptance of the perpetrator group and the perpetrator group empowers the victim group (Shnabel et al., 2009). This can be achieved by political forms of reconciliation, such as official declarations of guilt or forgiveness delivered by politicians in the name of their nations (Blatz, Schumann, & Ross, 2009). However, in this case groups are still treated as entities.

But there is also another way of fulfilling the historically threatened needs of groups engaged in past violence, based on restructuring entitative representations of the past into more individualized representations. By learning about individual life stories, group members should think less of groups as collective actors and come to see that each group consists of distinct individuals who acted in different ways—some of them being passive bystanders, others being perpetrators, victims, or even heroic helpers. Discussing individual life stories provides a unique opportunity for reconciliation between members of historically conflicted groups. It may restore the threatened moral image of descendants of historical bystanders or perpetrators, as well as the threatened sense of control among descendants of victims.

The Potential of Heroic Helpers' Stories for Reconciliation

Kelman (2008) suggests that while confronting history is an important step in reconciliation, it does not require the creation of a joint consensual history—what is needed is rather acknowledgement and acceptance of different historical experiences. Individual life-stories of people remembering the genocide provide a unique opportunity for more concrete representations of history, thereby providing a crucial potential for reconciliation by increasing awareness of different historical experiences (Leone & Mastrovito, 2010).

In the course of genocide, a special group of actors is distinguished by their active opposition to ongoing cruelty: heroic helpers (Oliner & Oliner, 1988; Smolenska & Reykowski, 1992; Staub, 1993). These are people who do not accept the perpetrators' actions and try to prevent them by supporting or even rescuing the victims. The number of heroic helpers during the Holocaust is estimated between 50,000 and 500,000 people who risked their lives by providing shelter or rescuing Jews of Europe (Oliner & Oliner, 1988). They were often connected by a network of friendships and relationships (Paulsson, 2003), being usually highly committed to a set of humanitarian values that distinguished them from the rest of society and those who remained passive (Oliner & Oliner, 1988).

There are numerous historical studies examining the scale and nature of this phenomenon in Nazi-occupied Poland (e.g., Leociak, 2010; Paulsson, 2003; Tec, 1987; Tomaszewski & Werbowski, 2010). Here, helping Jews was penalized by punishment of death, which was often extended to the entire family of a helper. Thus, rescue under these conditions can be considered an extreme act of heroism (Tec, 1987). Neighbors of a helper and sometimes entire villages were repressed because of sheltering Jews (Cherry & Orla-Bukowska, 2007). Although supported by the underground state and its institutions (Tomaszewski & Werbowski, 2010), helping Jews was often met with criticism and even violence from compatriots (Leociak, 2010; Tec, 1987). This is why heroic helpers had to overcome both perpetrators and passive bystanders. The life stories of individual heroic helpers are scarcely used in historical education about genocide and our aim was to present their narratives to young generation of Poles and Jews.

We hypothesized that life-stories of heroic helpers could play an important role in restoring the moral image of current Poles. Showing that not all Poles behaved in the same way during the Holocaust and that at least some of them were engaged in acts of heroism could undermine entitative perceptions of groups during the Holocaust. In turn, the need for acceptance among contemporary Poles could be fulfilled—they might expect that knowing such narratives, contemporary Jews would no longer perceive their whole group as being passive during the Holocaust. This could then enable descendants of the bystander group to restore their moral image and make them feel accepted by descendants of victims.

Contact with Heroic Helpers: A Study of Polish–Jewish Encounters

The present article describes an intervention organized by the Forum for Dialogue among Nations and the Museum of the History of the Polish Jews in 2009 in two Polish cities: Warsaw and Kraków. The intervention included a Polish–Jewish encounter in small groups focusing on history, and a meeting with a heroic helper who rescued Jews during the Nazi occupation of Poland (a recipient of the Yad Vashem Institute honor of "Righteous among the Nations," with which non-Jewish rescuers of Jews are honored).

The aim of the study was to overcome the limitations from previous research on Polish−Jewish relations described earlier (see also Bilewicz, 2007), which found inhibited effects of contact among groups discussing history-related issues, as opposed to groups discussing contemporary issues. Acknowledging that the ineffectiveness of contact involving discussions about the past was the most pronounced in the case of Poles' attitudes toward Jews, we aimed to find an alternative way of discussing historical genocide that could fulfill the deprived need for acceptance among Polish participants.

Method

Participants and Procedure

The sample for this intervention program consisted of 259 students: 122 Israeli high school students (69.1% women, mean age $= 16.84$, $SD = .49$) and 137 Polish high school students (72.9% women, mean age $= 16.96$, $SD = 1.25$).

The intervention effectiveness was assessed in an experimental, posttest only control group design (Cottrell & MacKenzie, 2011). Participants were randomly assigned to one of two conditions: in the control condition, participants completed the questionnaire prior to the intervention, and in the experimental condition they completed the questionnaire after the intervention. This design was employed in order to avoid memory effects that could appear in a pretest−posttest study performed within the same day (especially with such sensitive issues as intergroup attitudes). Participants filled out the questionnaire in their respective native languages (Polish or Hebrew).

Intervention

At the beginning of the intervention, Polish and Israeli students read short descriptions of four people (from Poland, Germany, Italy, and The Netherlands) who had rescued Jews during the war (e.g., "During the occupation, Maria remained in touch with the Jewish friends she had made in her middle school years. When the Krakow ghetto was formed in 1941, she learned that her friend Helena had been taken there with her whole family. Maria spared no effort to help the Jews she knew. On many occasions, she brought food and medicine to the ghetto. In October of 1942, when Jews were being seized from the ghetto and taken to the death camps, Helena's mother's name was on the list of people designated for transport. With the assistance of her friend, Maria organized Helena's escape. (. . .) Helena returned to Poland in 1945 after the war, where she lived until her death in the 1980s. Maria and Helena remained close friends throughout her life").

Students worked in small and mixed Polish–Israeli groups (10 people per group) and discussed possible common characteristics of rescuers during the Holocaust. They listed characteristics on a flip-chart and continued with a plenary discussion. After that, the facilitators introduced a Polish heroic helper to the group (in fact, she was one of the personalities about whom students had just read). Students could freely ask the heroic helper questions and discuss with her the history of the Holocaust. Later on, students continued to discuss with each other without helping and altruism during genocide.

Measures

Perceived similarity to the self. Perceived similarity of the outgroup to the self was measured with a 3-item scale ($\alpha = .81$) developed by Aberson and Howanski (2002). Participants indicated on a 7-point scale (ranging from "not at all" to "very much") their perceived similarity to the outgroup ("Overall, how similar would you rate yourself to young Israelis/Poles?", "How much do you share common interests with young Israelis/Poles?", and "How much do you share common experiences with young Israelis/Poles?").

Needs in reconciliation. Two items measured basic needs from the needs-based model of reconciliation (Nadler & Shnabel, 2006). Participants indicated on 7-point scales (ranging from "not at all" to "very much") to what extent they felt *empowered* and *accepted* in their relations with the respective outgroup members. These two items served as separate indicators of empowerment and acceptance.

Intergroup attitudes. Participants were asked to indicate their feelings toward the outgroup on a graphical thermometer with a scale ranging from $0°$ (very negative) to $100°$ (very positive). The scale captures the explicit affective component of attitudes (Alwin, 1997).

Results

Attitudes before the Intervention (Baseline)

The first analysis compared attitudes and needs of Polish and Israeli participants assigned to the control group (measured before the intervention; see Table 1). Polish participants before the intervention expressed higher perceived similarity to outgroup members than Israeli students did, $t(152) = 4.02, p < .001$, Cohen's $d = .65$. They also expressed significantly more positive attitudes toward Israelis than did Israelis toward Poles, $t(142) = 4.56, p < .001$, Cohen's $d = .76$. Moreover, there were significant differences in both needs: Poles declared that they felt more empowered in relations with Israelis, $t(151) = 2.57, p = .011$,

Table 1. Effects of the Intervention on Positive Affect toward the Outgroup, Perceived Similarity of the Outgroup to the Self, Feeling of Empowerment, and Feeling of Acceptance among Polish and Israeli Participants

Variables	Before intervention (Polish)		After intervention (Polish)		Before intervention (Israeli)		After intervention (Israeli)	
	M	*SD*	*M*	*SD*	*M*	*SD*	*M*	*SD*
1. Positive affect	70.87	21.15	82.41	16.09	48.08	37.21	69.77	26.34
2. Perceived similarity of outgroup to self	4.48	1.24	5.08	1.05	3.59	1.47	4.36	1.73
3. Empowerment	4.13	1.27	4.53	1.36	3.53	1.58	3.83	1.91
4. Acceptance	4.70	1.22	5.40	1.33	3.96	1.73	4.27	1.83

Cohen's $d = .42$, and more accepted in relations with Israelis, $t(148) = 3.02$, $p = .003$, Cohen's $d = .50$, than the Israelis felt in their relations with Poles.

Effectiveness of the Intervention

Due to the differences in the baseline condition, the overall effectiveness of the intervention for Polish and for Israeli students was analyzed independently for Polish and Israeli participants with a series of t-tests (see Table 1). Polish participants in the posttreatment group had more positive attitudes toward Israelis, $t(133) = 3.50, p = .001$, Cohen's $d = .61$, perceived Israelis as more similar to the self, $t(135) = 3.05, p = .003$, Cohen's $d = .52$, and, as hypothesized, perceived greater acceptance from Israelis, $t(132) = 3.15, p = .002$, Cohen's $d = .55$, than Polish participants in the control group. There were no significant differences between these groups on the measure of empowerment, $t(134) = 1.77, p = .078$, Cohen's $d = .30$.

Israeli participants from the posttreatment group perceived Poles as more similar to the self, $t(119) = 2.57, p = .011$, Cohen's $d = .47$, than Israeli participants from the control group and they had more positive attitude toward Poles, $t(110) = 3.33, p = .001$, Cohen's $d = .63$, than Israelis from the control group. There were no significant differences between these groups in regard to acceptance, $t(115) = .90, p = .371$, Cohen's $d = .17$ or empowerment, $t(134) = .92, p = .360$, Cohen's $d = .16$.

Acceptance as a Mechanism of Effectiveness among Polish Participants

In order to test whether satisfying the psychological need for acceptance among Polish participants changes intergroup attitudes after the encounter, and whether this in turn leads to increased perceived similarity of the outgroup to the

Table 2. Zero-Order Correlations between Variables Measured among Participants of the Intervention (Polish Participants below Diagonal, Jewish Israeli Participants above Diagonal)

Variable	1	2	3	4	5
Intervention (pretest–posttest)	–	.08	.08	.23*	.30**
Acceptance	.26**	–	.57**	.51**	.28**
Empowerment	.15	.50**	–	.61**	.46**
Perceived similarity of outgroup to self	.25**	.36**	.39**	–	.57**
Positive affect	.29**	.30**	.12	.40**	–

Note. *p <.05, **p < .01.

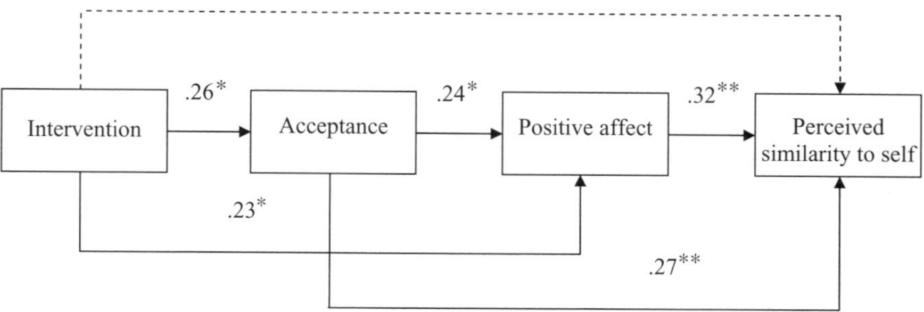

Fig. 1. The path model of the intervention effectiveness among Polish participants (indirect effect of intervention on perceived similarity of the outgroup to the self). Note: **p < .001; *p < .01.

self, a structural equation model was used. The correlation matrix of manipulated and measured variables (for Polish and Israeli participants of the encounter program) is presented in Table 2. As there was no effect of the encounter on any of the psychological needs among Israeli participants, and no effect of the encounter on feelings of empowerment among Polish participants, the mediation model was tested only on Polish participants of the encounter program, with feelings of acceptance and intergroup attitudes as multiple mediators (Baron & Kenny, 1986; Hayes, 2009).

The model was tested as a path model with AMOS 7.0 software without latent variables analysis, due to the relatively small sample size (see Figure 1). The mediational model had a good fit (after rejecting the direct path from the intervention to perception of similarity of outgroup to self): χ^2 (1, $N = 137$) = 1.69, $p = .19$, RMSEA = .07, CFI = .988. This suggests an indirect effect of the intervention on intergroup attitudes and perceptions (Hayes, 2009).

The intervention predicted feelings of being accepted by Jews ($\beta = .26$, $p = .001$), and being accepted by Jews predicted positive attitudes toward Jews after the intervention ($\beta = .24, p = .005$). More positive attitudes, in turn, predicted higher levels of perceived similarity of the outgroup to the self ($\beta = .32, p < .001$). There was also a direct effect of the intervention on positive affect toward Jews

($\beta = .23$, $p = .006$), and of the feeling of being accepted on perceived similarity of the outgroup to the self ($\beta = .27$, $p < .001$).

After including this causal chain into the model, the direct effect of the intervention on perceptions of the outgroup as more similar to the self dropped from $\beta = .25$, $p = .002$ to insignificance, $\beta = .10$, $p = .19$. The indirect effect of the intervention on perceived similarity in the final model was $\beta = .16$, $CI = (.09, .25)$, $p < .001$ (2000 bootstrap samples; as suggested by Hayes, 2009). This means that the change of perceptions of Jews among Polish students after the intervention was caused by fulfillment of the need for acceptance among Poles, in turn giving rise to more positive emotions towards Jews.

Discussion

The contact-based intervention focusing on the personal narrative of a Righteous among the Nations—a heroic helper who rescued Jews during Holocaust—changed the perceptions of Jews among Polish students and, to a certain extent, also the perceptions of Poles among Israeli Jewish students. Intergroup contact in the presence of a heroic helper was found to be entirely effective for the Polish participants of this intervention—improving intergroup affect, changing their intergroup cognitions, and meeting the deprived need for acceptance. In contrast, the intervention did not meet Israelis' needs of empowerment or acceptance; it only affected intergroup cognitions by changing the perception of Poles as more similar to the Jewish ingroup and improving attitudes toward Poles.

These results show that the problem of a genocidal history, which inhibits the effects of intergroup contact between Poles and Jews, may be partially overcome by introducing stories of heroic helpers. Previous research shows that when young Poles and Jews talk about the history of their nations, positive effects of intergroup contact are limited (Bilewicz, 2007).

Based on the needs-based model of reconciliation (Shnabel & Nadler, 2008), we hypothesized that in the case of Poles, contact is not effective because of the frustrated need for acceptance, and in the case of Israeli Jews because of the frustrated need for power and control. To overcome these problems, we decided to switch participants' attention from the group-level representation of history, where whole groups are considered victims, bystanders, or perpetrators, to individual-level stories, where every person has his or her own history, with specific behaviors, problems, and fears. This approach was inspired by a personalization approach to intergroup contact that stresses the role of individuated perceptions of outgroup members during the intergroup encounter (Bilewicz, 2006; Miller, 2002). Because previous research has shown that the inhibition of the effects of Polish–Jewish contact was particularly strong among Polish students, we decided to fulfill the deprived need for acceptance among Polish participants by the presence of a Polish

Righteous among the Nations during contact and by focusing contact on the stories of heroic helpers.

Supporting our predictions, the intervention improved Poles' attitudes toward Jews. After the intervention, Poles had more positive emotions about Jews and felt more similar to them. The mechanism that enabled these expected outcomes of positive intergroup contact to occur was a heightened sense of acceptance by outgroup members. Consistent with the needs-based model, feelings of empowerment (a need associated with victim groups) were unrelated to Poles' attitudes toward Jews.

Before the meeting, Poles could have feared that their Jewish counterparts would think of them as responsible for Jewish suffering (Bilewicz, 2008; Wójcik, 2008). Knowing that Jews met the Polish heroic helper as well, Polish participants could assume that Jewish participants must have recognized the actions of Poles during Holocaust as more positive, or at least as less uniformly passive and negative than commonly believed. This presumably contributed to the heightened feeling of acceptance by Jews among Poles that was revealed in the posttest results. As threats to Polish identity were removed, intergroup contact provided stronger effects and attitudes toward Jews were improved.

Feelings of Jewish youth toward Poles become more positive after the intervention, although the psychological needs of this group were not met during the meeting. The positive effects of such contact among Israeli Jews were smaller than those obtained in other studies of Jews discussing historical issues with Poles—studies that did not focus on the stories of heroic helpers (Bilewicz, 2007). Intergroup contact is less effective among victimized and low-status groups and that it threatens their need for power and status (Dixon, Tropp, Durrheim, & Tredoux, 2010). These two needs seem to be especially threatened when victims' fate is presented as depending on helpers' attitudes and behaviors. Regardless of these obstacles, the intervention was still effective in changing attitudes among young Israeli Jews: after the encounter, Israeli students perceived themselves as more similar to Poles and their attitude toward Poles became significantly more positive. There could be other, unmeasured mechanisms responsible for these effects. One of them could be that personalization occurred in Jewish perceptions of Poles—a mechanism known to improve relations after intergroup encounters (Miller, 2002). Such personalization could obviously occur after participants were presented with an individualized story of a historical heroic helper. Presenting common features of the rescuers of Jews might also highlight the universal character of genocide—which is known to change intergroup attitudes of historical victims (Wohl & Branscombe, 2005). All these explanations could be tested in further studies, focusing on victimized groups.

One possible limitation of this study is that we did not test the long-lasting effects of the intervention. More studies are needed to determine if the effects

of such interventions are short-lived or not. Not addressing victim descendants'
psychological needs is another obvious limitation of this intervention. We focused
on the bystander group's needs because in previous research on Polish–Jewish
encounters, the effects of contact were most limited among Poles (Bilewicz, 2007).
In this previous study, for Jews (victim descendants) intergroup contact proved
effective even when it was focused on history (although this was less effective than
contact that focused on present issues). The findings of the present study demonstrate that it is important in future interventions to take into account the needs of
both groups, victims, and bystanders. For example, the need for power and control
among victims could be fulfilled by the presence of a resistance fighter—a person
who contradicts the stereotype of the victim group's helplessness by demonstrating
heroic behavior of those who were targeted in genocide. Confronting members
of the victimized group with stories of such heroes should meet their need for
empowerment and control, which are consistently threatened by the history of the
Holocaust (Bar-Tal & Antebi, 1992). As loss of control is known to deteriorate
intergroup relations (Frey & Rez, 2002; Fritsche, Jonas, & Fankhanel, 2008), presenting more diverse and individualized histories that also include narratives of
agency and control might help improving intergroup attitudes among descendents
of victim groups.

Nevertheless, it cannot be taken for granted that by presenting atypical historical examples the needs of all groups sharing a history of genocide can be fulfilled
simultaneously. In the present intervention, we focused on relations between bystander and victim groups, but achieving effective intergroup contact between
perpetrator and victim groups could be much more difficult (Bar-On & Kassem,
2004). Members of victim groups typically expect remorse from members of
perpetrator groups, so neglecting perpetrators' wrongdoings and concentrating
on heroic helpers' stories could be perceived by the victim group as an attempt
to avoid responsibility for one's group's actions (Wohl & Branscombe, 2005).
Moreover, for members of victim groups it may be important to be asked for
forgiveness, as well as to receive reparations from the perpetrator group, because
these actions can fulfill the victim's need for empowerment more concretely and
tangibly (Shnabel et al., 2009). In order to engage in apologies and reparations,
members of perpetrator groups must feel collective guilt for past atrocities (Doosje
et al., 1998). Thus, presenting the perpetrators' history in an individualized way
might become an alibi and decrease the emotion of collective guilt. This, in turn,
is conflicted with the satisfaction of victims' need for empowerment. However,
the results of the study by Peetz, Gunn and Wilson (2010, Study 2) give the hope
that stories of heroic helpers may not decrease collective guilt but have rather opposite effects—in this study, German participants engaged less in self-defensive
distancing from the Holocaust when the fact that some Germans rescued Jews was
mentioned.

The practicality of such interventions is limited due to the small number of living eyewitnesses of genocide. With the passage of time, meetings with heroic helpers and resistance fighters become less probable. This makes this type of intervention increasingly difficult, and once all heroic helpers and resistance fighters pass away—impossible. This limitation could be overcome by using the written accounts of the genocide or oral history recordings, instead of face-to-face meetings with people who lived during the genocide (e.g. Bar-On & Kassem, 2004). For example, in the case of Armenian genocide, this could be narratives about the heroic defense of the Musa Dagh mountain (to empower the victims; Werfel, 2002) and about Turks who saved Armenians (to fulfill perpetrator group's need for acceptance; Hovannisian, 1992). In the case of the genocide in Rwanda, these could be narratives about the Rwandan Patriotic Front (Tutsi resistance army; Mamdani, 2001) and the story of the Hutu humanitarian Paul Rusesabagina (Gourevitch, 1998). Such stories could be presented and discussed during Armenian—Turkish or Tutsi—Hutu encounters, facilitating the effectiveness of intergroup contact in attitude change.

To summarize, this intervention showed that by communicating the variety of people's behaviors in the time of violence, it is possible to overcome one of the obstacles that a history of genocide poses to current intergroup relations. Highlighting elements of groups' pasts that contradict their stereotypical positions in historical narratives satisfies frustrated psychological needs, and thereby facilitates positive effects of current intergroup contact. This approach seems very promising, as examples of such behaviors can be found in the history of every conflict or genocide, and they can be applied to various contexts of postgenocidal intergroup animosities.

References

Aberson, C. L., & Howanski, L. M. (2002). Effects of self-esteem, status, and identification on two forms of ingroup bias. *Current Research in Social Psychology, 7,* 225–242. Retrieved from http://www.uiowa.edu/~grpproc/crisp/crisp.html

Alwin, D. F. (1997). Feeling thermometer versus 7-point scales. Which are better? *Sociological Methods and Research, 25,* 318–340.

Bar-On, D., & Kassem, F. (2004). Story telling as a way to work through intractable conflicts: The TRT German—Jewish experience and its relevance to the Palestinian—Israeli context. *Journal of Social Issues, 60,* 404–418.

Baron, R. M., & Kenny, D. A. (1986). The moderator-mediator variable distinction in social psychological research: Conceptual, strategic, and statistical considerations. *Journal of Personality and Social Psychology, 51,* 1173–1182.

Bar-Tal, D., & Antebi, D. (1992). Siege mentality in Israel. *International Journal of Intercultural Relations, 16,* 251–275.

Bilewicz, M. (2006). Polish—Jewish intergroup communication: The mediating role of personalized cognition. *Psychology of Language and Communication, 10,* 95–100.

Bilewicz, M. (2007). History as an obstacle: Impact of temporal-based social categorizations on Polish—Jewish intergroup contact. *Group Processes & Intergroup Relations, 10,* 551–563.

Bilewicz, M. (2008). Społeczna pamięć Holokaustu i Auschwitz wśród licealistów: wokół projektu badawczego "Trudne Pytania" [Collective remembering of Holocaust and Auschwitz among high-school students. Summary of the "Difficult questions" Project]. In P. Trojanski (Ed.), *Auschwitz i Holokaust. Dylematy i wyzwania polskiej edukacji [Auschwitz and the Holocaust. Dilemmas and challenges for Polish education]* (pp. 23–34). Oświęcim: Auschwitz-Birkenau State Museum.

Bilewicz, M., & Krzemiński, I. (2010). Anti-Semitism in Poland and Ukraine: The belief in Jewish control as a mechanism of scapegoating. *International Journal of Conflict and Violence, 4,* 234–243.

Bilewicz, M., Ostolski, A., Wójcik, A., & Wysocka, A. (2004). Pamięć w kontekście międzyetnicznym: "trudne pytania" w kontaktach młodych Polaków i Żydów [Memory in the interethnic context: „Difficult questions" in the contact of Poles and Jews]. *Kultura i Społeczeństwo, 3,* 143–158.

Bilewicz, M., & Wójcik, A. (2010). Does identification predict community involvement? Exploring consequences of social identification among the Jewish minority in Poland. *Journal of Community and Applied Social Psychology, 22,* 72–79.

Blatz, C. W., Schumann, K. & Ross, M. (2009). Government apologies for historical injustices. *Political Psychology, 30,* 219–241.

Byrne, C. (2004). Benefit or burden: Victims' reflections on TRC participation. *Peace and Conflict: Journal of Peace Psychology, 10,* 237–256.

Cehajic, S., Brown, R., & Castano, E. (2008). Forgive and forget? Antecedents and consequences of intergroup forgiveness in Bosnia and Herzegovina. *Political Psychology, 29,* 351–367.

Cherry, R., & Orla-Bukowska, A. M. (2007). *Rethinking Poles and Jews.* Lanham, MD: Rowman & Littlefield.

Cottrell, R. R., & MacKenzie, J. F. (2011). *Health promotion and education research methods.* Sudbery, MA: Jones & Bartlett.

Dixon, J., Tropp, L. R., Durrheim, K., & Tredoux, C. (2010). "Let them eat harmony": Prejudice-reduction strategies and attitudes of historically disadvantaged groups. *Current Directions in Psychological Science, 19,* 76–80.

Doosje, B., Branscombe, N. R., Spears, R., & Manstead, A. S. R. (1998). Guilty by association: When one's group has a negative history. *Journal of Personality and Social Psychology, 75,* 872–886.

Feldman, J. (2008). *Above the death pits, beneath the flag. Youth voyages to Poland and the performance of Israeli national identity.* New York, NY: Berghahn Books.

Frey, D., & Rez, H. (2002). Population and Predators: Preconditions for the Holocaust from a Control-Theoretical Perspective. In L.S. Newman & R. Erber (Eds.), *Understanding Genocide: The Social Psychology of the Holocaust* (pp. 188–221). New York, NY: Oxford University Press.

Fritsche, I., Jonas, E., & Fankhanel, T. (2008). The role of control motivation in mortality salience effects on ingroup support and defense. *Journal of Personality and Social Psychology, 95,* 524–541.

Gaertner, S. L., Dovidio, J. F., & Bachman, B. A. (1996). Revisiting the contact hypothesis: The induction of a common ingroup identity. *International Journal of Intercultural Relations, 20,* 271–290.

Gibson, J. L. (2004). Does truth lead to reconciliation? Testing the causal assumptions of The South African Truth and Reconciliation process. *American Journal of Political Science, 48,* 201–127.

Gourevitch, P. (1998). *We wish to inform you that tomorrow we will be killed with our families.* New York, NY: Picador.

Hayes, A. F. (2009). Beyond Baron and Kenny: Statistical mediation analysis in the new millennium. *Communication Monographs, 76,* 408–420.

Herman, J. L. (1992). *Trauma and recovery.* New York: Basic Books.

Hewstone, M., Cairns, E., Voci, A., Hamberger, J., & Niens, U. (2006). Intergroup Contact, Forgiveness, and Experience of "The Troubles" in Northern Ireland. *Journal of Social Issues, 62,* 99–120.

Hilberg, R. (1993). *Perpetrators, victims, bystanders: The Jewish catastrophe 1933–1945.* New York, NY: Harper.

Honeyman, C., Hudani, S., Tiruneh, A., Hierta, J., Chirayath, L., Iliff, A., & Meierhenrich, J. (2004). Establishing collective norms: potentials for participatory justice in Rwanda. *Peace and Conflict: Journal of Peace Psychology, 10*, 1–24.

Hovannisian, R. G. (1992). The question of altruism during the Armenian Genocide of 1915. In P. M. Oliner, et al. (Eds.), *Embracing the other: Philosophical, psychological, and historical perspectives on altruism* (pp. 282–305). New York, NY: New York University Press.

Husnu, S., & Crisp, R. (2010). Imagined intergroup contact: A new technique for encouraging greater inter-ethnic contact in Cyprus. *Peace & Conflict, 16*, 97–108.

Imhoff, R. (2009). Holocaust at the table – Experiences from seven years of "German-Israeli Exchange". In C. Misselwitz & C. Siebeck (Eds.), *Dissonant memories—Fragmented present. Exchanging young discourses between Israel and Germany* (pp. 35–43). Bielefeld: Transcript.

Imhoff, R., Bilewicz, M., & Erb, H. P. (2012). Collective guilt versus collective regret. Different emotional reactions to ingroup atrocities. *European Journal of Social Psychology, 6*, 729–742.

Kanyangara, P., Rimé, B., Philippot, P., & Yzerbyt, V. (2007). Collective rituals, emotional climate, and intergroup perception: Participation in "Gacaca" tribunals and assimilation of the Rwandan genocide. *Journal of Social Issues, 63*, 387–403.

Kelman, H.C. (2008). Reconciliation from a social-psychological perspective. In A. Nadler, T. Malloy, & J.D. Fisher (Eds.), *Social psychology of intergroup reconciliation* (pp.15–32). Oxford: Oxford University Press.

Kofta, M., & Sedek, M. (2005). Conspiracy stereotypes of Jews during systematic transformation in Poland. *International Journal of Sociology, 35*, 40–64.

Latane, B., & Darley, J. M. (1970). *The unresponsive bystander: Why doesn't he help?* New York, NY: Appleton-Century-Crofts.

Leociak, J. (2010). *Ratowanie. Opowieści Polaków i Żydów [Rescuing. Stories of Poles and Jews].* Kraków: Wydawnictwo Literackie.

Leone, G., & Mastrovito, T. (2010). Learning about our shameful past: A socio-psychological analysis of present-day historical narratives of Italian colonial wars. *International Journal of Conflict and Violence, 4*, 11–27.

Mamdani, M. (2001). *When victims become killers: Colonialism, nativism, and the genocide in Rwanda.* Princeton, NJ: Princeton University Press.

Maoz, I., & Bar-On, D. (2002). From working through the Holocaust to current ethnic conflicts: Evaluating the TRT group workshop in Hamburg. *Group, 26*, 29–48.

Michlic, J. (2007). The Dark Past: Polish—Jewish Relations in the Shadow of the Holocaust. In: D. Glowacka & J. Zylinska (Eds.), *Imaginary Neighbors. Mediating Polish-Jewish Relations after the Holocaust* (pp. 21–29). Lincoln, NE: University of Nebraska Press.

Miller, N. (2002). Personalization and the promise of contact theory. *Journal of Social Issues, 58*, 387–410.

Miłosz, C. (1988). *The collected poems 1931–1987.* New York, NY: The Ecco Press.

Nadler, A., & Shnabel, N. (2006). Instrumental and socio-emotional paths to intergroup reconciliation and the need-based model of socio-emotional reconciliation. In A. Nadler, T. Malloy, & J.D. Fisher (Eds.), *Social psychology of intergroup reconciliation* (pp. 37–56). New York, NY: Oxford University Press.

Oliner, S. P., & Oliner, P. M. (1988). *The altruistic personality: Rescuers of Jews in Nazi Europe.* New York, NY: Free Press.

Paulsson, G. (2003). *Secret city: The hidden Jews of Warsaw, 1940–1945.* New Haven, CT: Yale University Press.

Peetz, J., Gunn, G. R., & Wilson, A. E. (2010). Crimes of the past: Defensive temporal distancing in the face of past in-group wrongdoing. *Personality and Social Psychology Bulletin, 36*, 598–611.

Pettigrew, T. F., & Tropp, L. R. (2006). A meta-analytic test of intergroup contact theory. *Journal of Personality and Social Psychology, 90*, 751–783.

Shnabel, N., & Nadler, A. (2008). A needs-based model of reconciliation: Satisfying the differential needs of victim and perpetrator. *Journal of Personality and Social Psychology, 94*, 116–132.

Shnabel, N., Nadler, A., Canetti-Nisim, D., & Ullrich, J. (2008). The role of acceptance and empowerment in promoting reconciliation from the perspective of needs-based model. *Social Issues and Policy Review, 2*, 159–186.

Shnabel, N., Nadler, A., Ullrich, J., Dovidio, J. F., & Carmi, D. (2009). Promoting reconciliation through the satisfaction of the emotional needs of victimized and perpetrating group members: The needs-based model of reconciliation. *Personality and Social Psychology Bulletin, 4*, 1021–1030.

Smolenska, Z., & Reykowski, J. (1992). Motivations of people who helped Jews survive the Nazi occupation. In P. M. Oliner, M. Z. Smolenska, S.P. Oliner, & L. Baron (Eds.), *Embracing the other: Philosophical, psychological, and historical perspectives on altruism* (pp. 213–225). New York, NY: New York University Press.

Staub, E. (1985). The psychology of perpetrators and bystanders. *Political Psychology, 6*, 61–85.

Staub, E. (1993). The psychology of bystanders, perpetrators, and heroic helpers. *International Journal of Intercultural Relations, 17*, 315–341.

Staub, E. (2006). Reconciliation after genocide, mass killing, or intractable conflict: Understanding the roots of violence, psychological recovery, and steps toward a general theory. *Political Psychology, 27*, 867–894.

Staub, E., & Pearlman, L. A. (2006). Advancing healing and reconciliation. In L. Barbanel & R. J. Sternberg (Eds.), *Psychological interventions in times of crisis* (pp. 213–243). New York: Springer.

Steinlauf, M. (1997). *Bondage to the dead. Poland and the memory of the Holocaust.* Syracuse, NY: Syracuse University Press.

Stephan, W. G., & Stephan, C. W. (1985). Intergroup anxiety. *Journal of Social Issues, 41*, 157–175.

Tec, N. (1987). *When light pierced the darkness: Christian rescue of Jews in Nazi-occupied Poland.* New York, NY: Oxford University Press.

Tomaszewski, I., & Werbowski, T. (2010). *Code Name: Zegota. Rescuing Jews in occupied Poland, 1942–1945: The most dangerous conspiracy in wartime Europe.* Santa Barbara, CA: Praeger.

Vollhardt, J. & Bilewicz, M. (2013). After the genocide: Psychological perspectives on victim, bystander, and perpetrator groups. *Journal of Social Issues, 69*, 1–15.

Weinbaum, L. (2007). Why do Jews accuse Poles of complicity in the Shoah? In M. Kozłowski, A. Folwarczny, & M. Bilewicz (Eds.), *Difficult questions in Polish–Jewish dialogue* (pp.130–135). Warsaw, Poland: Santorski & Co.

Werfel, F. (2002). *The forty days of Musa Dagh.* Cambridge, U.K.: Da Capo.

Wilson, J. P., Drozdek, B., & Turkovic, S. (2006). Posttraumatic shame and guilt. *Trauma, Violence and Abuse, 7*, 122–141.

Wohl, M. J. A., & Branscombe, N. R. (2005). Forgiveness and collective guilt assignment to historical perpetrator groups depends on level of social category inclusiveness. *Journal of Personality and Social Psychology, 88*, 288–303.

Wójcik, A. (2008). Historia stosunków polsko-zydowskich woczach polskiej młodziezy [History of Polish-Jewish relationships in the eyes of Polish youth]. In: J. Zyndul (Ed.), *Różni razem [Diversity in commonness]* (pp. 256–265). Warsaw, Poland: Warsaw University Press.

Zorbas, E. (2004). Reconciliation in post-genocide Rwanda. *African Journal of Legal Studies, 1*, 29–52.

MICHAL BILEWICZ (M.A. 2003, Ph. D. 2007, University of Warsaw) is an Assistant Professor at the Faculty of Psychology, University of Warsaw. He serves as the Director of the Center for Research on Prejudice at the University of Warsaw. He was Fulbright Junior Visiting Researcher at the New School for Social Research in New York and DAAD Post-Doctoral Researcher at Friedrich Schiller University of Jena in Germany. His key research interests are reconciliation processes, linguistic forms of prejudice, anti-Semitism, historyrelated moral emotions, and dehumanization.

MANANA JAWORSKA (M.A. 2010, University of Warsaw) is a doctoral student at the Faculty of Psychology, University of Warsaw. Her research concerns intergroup contact, perspective taking, and other forms of improving intergroup relations. She is a recipient of the Jacek Kuroń Prize for psychological contributions to social justice in Poland.

Journal of Social Issues, Vol. 69, No. 1, 2013, pp. 180–199

A World without Genocide: Prevention, Reconciliation, and the Creation of Peaceful Societies

Ervin Staub[*]

University of Massachusetts, Amherst

This article reviews influences leading to extreme violence between groups. It then describes principles and practices of prevention, especially early prevention, and reconciliation: addressing difficult life conditions in ways that include everyone in society; diplomacy that addresses crises and prevents conflicts from becoming intractable; developing constructive visions and groups which make destructive ideological movements less likely; generating positive orientation to previously devalued others; moderating respect for authority in part by encouraging individual judgment; fostering healing by groups from past victimization and psychological woundedness. The socialization of children for inclusive caring and moral courage, developing societal values of cooperation and community, and active bystandership by citizens, leaders, and the media to resist influences leading to violence and create positive institutions that help fulfill basic psychological needs are all important for a world without genocide. The article also describes interventions promoting reconciliation in Rwanda and neighboring countries and research evaluating their effects.

What can we do to help shape a world without genocide—and more generally, without mass violence? How can we create societies in which intense violence by groups against other groups due to their race, ethnicity, religion, political orientation, conflict over material issues, power relations, or differing world views and ideals becomes highly improbable? Can we envision a path to the development of such societies? The aim of this article is to briefly consider the influences that lead to violence between groups and, in more depth, explore avenues to the prevention of violence and to reconciliation. Reconciliation as a concept and practice usually refers to what people need to do after violence to prevent new violence (Long & Brecke, 2003). But reconciliation can also take place

[*]Correspondence concerning this article should be addressed to Ervin Staub, Psychology Department, University of Massachusetts, 135 Hicks Way, Amherst, MA 01003 [e-mail: estaub@psych.umass.edu].

between intensely hostile groups before significant violence, helping to prevent violence in the first place (Staub, 2006, 2011). As aspects of prevention and reconciliation I will also discuss socialization: the guidance and experiences children need in order to become "inclusively" caring people, who as active bystanders resist the evolution of violence and work to create the institutions of a peaceful society.

A variety of conditions that will be discussed indicate the need for practices of early prevention and reconciliation, which in turn help create peaceful societies. Societal structures or institutions that help people fulfill not only material needs, but also to constructively fulfill psychological needs, make violence unlikely. It should be an aim to develop such structures in all societies. It is not enough, however, to specify what needs to be accomplished, such as members of different groups developing positive attitudes toward each other, or building just institutions. It is essential to identify *how* to bring such outcomes about, in two senses: first, what practices or actions are needed, and second, how to make them happen. Attention to *who* are the appropriate actors is also important. They need to acquire relevant knowledge and skills, and develop a feeling of responsibility that results in action (see Staub, 2011).

The focus in considering the prevention of group violence is usually genocide. However, huge numbers of people can be killed in mass killings, where the boundaries of who is killed are not sharply drawn (Staub, 1989). In addition, genocide is the extreme outcome of an evolution. Early prevention is required, that is, preventive actions when existing conditions indicate the likelihood of group violence, the nature of which cannot yet be known (Staub, 2011). The best prevention is to create societies in which the conditions that lead to violence are minimized.

Brief Overview of the Influences Leading to Extreme Group Violence: Instigating Conditions and their Psychological and Social Effects

What I have called *difficult conditions of life* are one starting point for processes leading to violence between groups (Staub, 1989, 2003, 2011). I combine a number of conditions under this label, because they have a similar impact on groups of people. These conditions include severe and persistent economic problems, especially economic deterioration; political conflict and disorganization; and great and rapid changes in social conditions—in values and human relations, and in technology and the nature of work. War may be thought of as a difficult life condition, or as a separate instigator. It represents an evolution of violence that makes new violence easier and more likely. Genocide often occurs during war, at times against the opponent in the war, at other times against a historically devalued group that ideology had earlier designated an enemy (Staub, 2011; see also Harff, 2003).

Difficult life conditions tend to create societal chaos. They threaten people physically, their material existence. They also threaten people psychologically, as they create uncertainty and unpredictability. They frustrate what I regard (following Maslow, 1971, and others, but with a somewhat different conception) as universal, basic psychological needs. These are needs for security, for a feeling of effectiveness and control over essential matters in one's life, for a positive identity, for positive connections to other people, for autonomy—the ability to make decisions about important matters—as well as for understanding the world and one's place in it. The expressions of these needs will be shaped by culture, such as individualist or collectivist cultures (see Staub, 1989, 2003, 2011).

In response to difficult life conditions and their psychological effects, groups tend to scapegoat other groups. They also tend to create ideologies, visions of social arrangements for the group (or all of humanity) that provide hope in difficult times. Often the ideology is destructive, however, as it identifies enemies who supposedly stand in the way of creating the better future envisioned in the ideology. Extensive case studies indicate that these tendencies are stronger in groups with certain cultural characteristics (see later).

Group processes such as scapegoating and destructive ideological movements help fulfill basic psychological needs. These group processes strengthen identity, create connections, give people a feeling of effectiveness, increase security, and offer a new understanding of reality. However, they rarely address the actual problems. They also tend to fulfill basic needs destructively (see Staub, 2003, 2011), as they lead groups to harm people in other groups. In the end this often brings harm to their own group. In contrast to social identity theory (Tajfel, 1978; Tajfel & Turner, 1986), which has focused on the role of identity, and which has greatly influenced social psychology, this conception suggests that all basic needs are important, and when frustrated they all can motivate destructive group processes. Not only identity, but all basic needs require constructive fulfillment to avoid violence and promote peace (Staub, 2011).

Another important instigating condition for group violence is *persistent conflict* between groups. One form of conflict is material, for example about land or water rights. Another form, in which material and psychological elements are intermixed, is inequality between groups in a society in power, wealth, rights, and access to opportunities and societal processes. Even purely material conflicts usually acquire psychological elements. In the case of inequality, the more powerful group tends to justify its privilege by devaluing the less powerful group, seeing it as less deserving. Legitimizing ideologies (Sidanius & Pratto, 1999) and system justification (Jost, Banaji & Nosek, 2004) tend to be accepted *to some degree* even by the less privileged.

But with changes in the world, especially as difficult life conditions intensify the impact of inequality and relative deprivation becomes more intense (Gurr, 1970), the less powerful group often comes to see the inequality as unjust. Denial of rights and opportunity usually go together with devaluation and are expressed in discrimination. They diminish the experience of effectiveness and control over one's life and create humiliation (Lindner, 2006). As conflict becomes persistent and intractable, violent and resisting resolution, psychological aspects of the conflict, including intense mistrust, make its resolution especially difficult. Each group blames the other for the conflict, and sees itself as right and moral and the other group as responsible and immoral (Bar-Tal, 2000; Kelman & Fisher, 2003; Kriesberg, 1998; Staub, 2011).

Research and theory on genocide and group conflict have been separate, but there are shared principles of their origins, prevention, and reconciliation (Staub, 2011). While occasionally there has been genocide without evident conflict between groups, as in the case of the Holocaust—except conflict in the minds of the perpetrators—more often genocide evolves out of persistent conflict. Sometimes this was low level conflict, as in Turkey, where Armenians wanted more rights and autonomy from the Turks who ruled over them (however, with intense violence against Armenians in 1894–1896; Staub, 1989), at other times conflict was more intense, as in Rwanda between Hutus and Tutsis (des Forges, 1999; Mamdani, 2001; Melvern, 2004; Staub, 1999, 2011). However, group conflict is often intensified by difficult life conditions as it evolves into genocide: in Rwanda, the former Yugoslavia, and Turkey there was both economic deterioration and political disorganization, in Rwanda also a civil war, in Turkey a war, WWI.

Past History and Culture as Influences Contributing to the Evolution of Violence

A *history of devaluation* by one group of another tends to preselect the devalued group as the scapegoat, and usually also the enemy that stands in the way of fulfilling a hope-giving ideology—whether it is nationalism as in Turkey, racial superiority and purity as in Nazi Germany, or a utopian ideology such as "total social equality" as in Cambodia (Staub, 1989, 2011). Another cultural influence is *overly strong respect for authority* in a society, a society with strong hierarchy that limits pluralism, and inhibits questioning of authorities and therefore active bystandership in opposing destructive leadership. In all the countries I just mentioned, as well as in Rwanda (des Forges, 1999), the culture promoted strong respect for authorities through socialization, norms and standards of conduct, and hierarchical institutions.

Another important influence is *past victimization of a group and the psychological wounds* it creates. Apart from trauma symptoms, having been the object of violence creates feelings of vulnerability and a view of the world as dangerous. This can lead to "defensive" violence, unnecessary violent reactions in the case of new conflict or threat. Psychological wounds are often transmitted through the generations. Past trauma can become a "chosen trauma" (Volkan, 2001) if psychological woundedness and a view of the world as threatening becomes part of the culture and the identity of the group. It then shapes the perception of and responses to events (Klar, Schori-Eyal, & Klar, 2013; Staub, 2011; Vollhardt, 2013).

The evolution of violence: learning by doing and the passivity of bystanders. It is the combination of instigating conditions and cultural characteristics that makes violence by a group especially likely. However, intense violence rarely erupts suddenly. Occasionally, after earlier violence between groups, current events and new threat can reopen the chasm that was created by the violence, and lead to the sudden reemergence of violence. But usually there is an evolution of hostility and harmful actions, ranging from discrimination, to lesser violence, to progressively more intense violence. Nazi Germany is a classic example of this.

Individuals and groups learn by doing. They change as a result of their actions. Harmful actions are justified, making more harmful actions possible and likely. Devaluation intensifies, the victims are excluded from the moral realm (Opotow, 1990; Staub, 1989, 2011), societal norms and institutions change. There is not just moral disengagement (Bandura, 1999), but *moral transformation* (Staub, 1989, 2011); in the end many perpetrators seeing killing their victims as morally right, a *reversal of morality*. The evolution is facilitated through just world thinking (the world is just and those who suffer must be deserving of it—see Lerner, 1980), habituation (e.g., adaptation level theory, Helson, 1964), and, very importantly, the passivity of bystanders, people who are neither the perpetrators nor the victims. Passivity, and complicity, a limited form of which is people participating in the system created by the perpetrators, is perceived by the perpetrators as acceptance or even approval of their beliefs and actions (Staub, 1989, 2011).

The passivity of external bystanders, outside groups and nations, which has been the norm, also encourages perpetrators (see Taylor, 1983). Often they are not only passive, as the whole world was in the course of the genocide in Rwanda (Malvern, 2004; Staub, 2011), with the United States even refusing to call it a genocide presumably to avoid the obligation to act inherent in the U.N. genocide convention, but complicit. United States (as well as other countries') corporations were busy doing business in Nazi Germany in the 1930s, in the face of the great brutality of the regime against opponents and the increasing persecution of Jews (Simpson, 1993).

There have been many instances of passivity and complicity by the United States and other countries. Before and during the genocide in Rwanda the French supported the Hutu government in its fight against a Tutsi rebel army in a civil war, never speaking out against the occasional mass killing of Tutsi peasants within Rwanda (des Forges, 1999; Malvern, 2004). In Central and South America the United States supported violent regimes, for example, in El Salvador and Guatemala, while their armies and death squads were killing many civilians (Staub, 2000). But the potential of bystanders to positively influence events is great (Staub, 2011; Thalhammer et al., 2007). To fulfill that potential, to avoid passivity and complicity and create positive bystandership by the international community, requires the training of leaders and actions by citizens.

Prevention and Reconciliation

The focus of this article is on early prevention of extreme violence. While the conditions that make violence probable can be identified (Staub, 2011), where the evolution of violence might lead is difficult to know. Thus, the aim has to be to prevent group violence, not specifically genocide. Late prevention means either prevention in response to a crisis and impending violence or stopping already ongoing substantial violence. While dramatic diplomatic actions can sometimes be helpful, and boycotts and sanctions sometimes help, late prevention often requires some form of military response. To prevent ongoing violence against an often defenseless group is crucial, but ideally prevention will be early, in response to conditions that indicate the probability of violence. Processes of early prevention, as well as reconciliation, can shape values, culture and institutions and contribute to a world without genocide.

Active bystanders are crucial in inhibiting violence and creating institutions that prevent violence and maintain peace. For people to be motivated to become active bystanders requires psychological changes, such as a more positive attitude toward the "other," and changes in values. For conflict to be peacefully resolved and for violence to be prevented, people must resist destructive leadership and generate constructive social processes. Prevention of violence within a society often requires both internal and external actors. The latter can provide material support and psychological support for internal actors. External support can strengthen internal actors and institutions. But such support must be thoughtful. Groups are often suspicious of external influence, and if internal actors appear to be in the service of external parties, others in their society are likely to turn away from them (Staub, 2011).

Constructive Responses to Difficult Life Conditions and Conflict

In difficult times, people require both material and psychological help. The work programs of the Roosevelt administration at the time of the Great Depression helped many people materially, but they also helped people psychologically by making them feel that they are part of the national community. They helped fulfill needs for connection, identity, and effectiveness and also fostered a world view in which people cared about others. Since there was strong political opposition to these policies (Alter, 2006), creating them required "political will"—moral courage and commitment.

Violence between groups under difficult life conditions is more likely in "failed states," poor countries strongly affected by economic problems, and with weak and corrupt state institutions and limited civic institutions. Such countries do not have the capacity to materially help their populations in difficult times, and the civic/community institutions to psychologically support them. Material help by other countries is essential. But it is also essential that outsiders exert influence so that material help will be used equitably and constructively. The unconditional material support of Rwanda that was given by Western countries before the genocide in spite of the increasing hostility and violence against Tutsis (Uvin, 1998) had to suggest that such actions mattered little to outsiders, thereby increasing the likelihood of genocide.

Early efforts to resolve conflict between groups can inhibit their evolution into intractable, violent conflict that resists resolution. One such tool is preventive diplomacy (Hamburg, 2007), such as generating dialogue between the parties, negotiation, mediation and arbitration. For dialogue to take place and be effective it often requires third parties. At times of crises and even before, high level, visible external parties, such as national leaders in other countries and respected international figures, may need to be involved if parties in the conflict are to engage with each other. This happened early in the case of Kenya after the last presidential election there, the results of which were contested and followed by violence (Carson, 2008). However, it often did not happen, such as in Bosnia or the Congo. Unfortunately, leaders, fearing failure, are often reluctant to engage in dialogue. In addition, with the tendency of outsiders to intervene in the service of their own national interest, the parties often resist external help.

Addressing Cultural Characteristics and Responding to Evolving Social Processes

Psychological orientations, culture and social institutions that make violence between groups probable must be changed in order to prevent mass violence and promote peace.

Developing a More Positive Orientation to the "Other"

Efforts to generate a more positive orientation towards people in a devalued group are worthwhile even in the absence of instigating conditions, but gain in importance as instigating conditions arise. These efforts can take a number of different forms. Influential members of a society—leaders, writers, members of the media—can humanize a devalued group in words, stories, pictures. Leaders can engage in symbolic actions such as Arafat and Rabin shaking hands at the White House.

But members of the elite are often in the vanguard of devaluation and discrimination. They hold legitimizing ideologies especially strongly. If devaluation is widespread, they can gain political support by promoting it (Allport, 1954). Keeping a less privileged group down can help them maintain their privilege.

Therefore, members of the elite, who have the most access to the public domain, have to change if they are to humanize the devalued group. Usually, there is a small number of people in most societies that sees the humanity of the less privileged. They can engage in public education, in lectures, workshops, the media, radio and television. When leaders are accessible and willing to participate, trainings and workshops can help them understand the roots of devaluation and discrimination as well as violence, the problems these tend to create over time, and avenues to change—as my associates and I did in trainings in Rwanda (see below). This is an important role for researchers and practitioners, especially psychologists.

When people do humanize a devalued group, it is important to not simply say nice things, but to use substantive information. In Rwanda, such substantive information can be about the actions of Hutus who opposed the genocide or saved lives during the genocide at great danger to themselves (Africa Rights, 2002). Such information can also be about the commonality among people belonging to different groups. An example of this comes from Macedonia, where journalists belonging to different ethnic groups interviewed families belonging to those groups, and wrote articles showing commonalities in their hopes, needs, aspirations and ways of life, which were published in the newspapers of all the groups (Burg, 1997).

Significant, deep contact between members of different groups is another way to help people see the humanity of the other. Social psychologists have provided a great deal of theory and research showing the benefits of positive contact in overcoming prejudice (Allport, 1954; Pettigrew & Tropp, 2006). Significant engagement between people in the course of contact in the service of shared, positive goals is especially valuable (Sherif et al., 1961). The normal environments of people, such as schools, can promote separation and devaluation, as they did in Nazi Germany with Jewish children, and in Rwanda under Hutu rule with Tutsi children (and most likely earlier with Hutu children, under the Belgians who elevated Tutsis to rule in their behalf, see des Forges, 1999; Mamdani, 2001). But schools (Aronson et al., 1978) or the workplace (Varshney, 2002) can be structured so that they provide significant positive contact across group lines. Whether this happens or not depends on the values, norms and initiative of society in general, as well as of administrators, workers, children and their parents.

An important form of contact is dialogue, especially ongoing dialogue. It can humanize the other and promote trust. In the course of the Israeli Palestinian conflict, there has been dialogue between leaders on many occasions, but it has been periodic, not persistent. Moreover, when there is substantial inequality in power and an evolution toward increasing hostility and violence, the dominant party usually has little motivation on its own for contact and dialogue. It requires significant engagement by external bystanders to bring them about.

We need to learn more about the conditions when contact, and other practices, do or do not have lasting effects, and when their effects do or do not spread beyond the participants. The many forms of contact created between Palestinians and

Israelis (Maoz, 2004) have been mostly for limited periods, without significant follow up (Staub, 2011). Still, Israeli and Palestinian children who spent time together in a summer camp maintained positive attitudes they developed for about a year after their return to their communities hostile to each other, which may be considered an impressive outcome, but not beyond (Hammack, 2011). Various approaches may help strengthen the effect of contact, such as having several children/people from the same community participate who can support each other in their new attitudes, and helping participants foresee, and attempting to inoculate them, against opposing influences.

Addressing authority orientation: public education through radio dramas. Violence in a society is less likely to evolve if people have moderate respect for authority. Respecting those in authority is important, but people need to use their own judgment in evaluating the meaning of events, their *critical consciousness*. They need to be ready to challenge those who lead in a destructive direction. This is more likely in a democratic, non-repressive political system (Hamburg, 2007): if schools encourage children and youth to use their judgment and express their views; and if all groups in society can participate in public discourse.

A powerful avenue to promote moderate respect for authority and pluralism is public education. This is one of the aims of our (Ervin Staub, Laurie Pearlman, George Weiss and the organization he leads, La Benevolencija, as well as other associates) educational radio projects in Rwanda, Burundi and the Congo (see Staub, 2011; Staub, Pearlman, & Bilali, 2010).We have created radio dramas that inform about the influences leading to extreme violence by groups against other groups, avenues for the prevention of such violence, as well as for healing and reconciliation.

The radio drama in Rwanda, which has been continuously broadcast since 2004, is a story of two villages in conflict over fertile land between them, which at one point the authorities gave to one of the villages (Staub, 2011; Staub et al., 2010). When there is a draught, people in this village have enough food, people in the other village are hungry. Early in the drama, a leader arises in the poor village who instigates against the better off village. He and his followers attack this village and steal some of the crop. The story shows various personal elements in the leader's motives. For example, according to tradition, as the oldest brother, he would become the head of the family when his father dies. But the father, who also has a wife in the other village, names one of the sons in that village to be head of the family. The story is also about followers, and active bystanders who speak out and attempt to halt the negative actions against the other village. One of them is the leader's sister, who together with a young man from the other village organizes the youth in the two villages to act against hostility and violence. Among the positive findings of a study evaluating the effects of the radio drama after one year was greater independence of authority by listeners than by people in a control group, more willingness to say what they believe, more empathy for survivors, followers, leaders, as well as more participation in reconciliation behaviors (Paluck, 2009; see also Staub, 2011; Staub & Pearlman, 2009).

Open communication in a society and public discourse that all parties can engage in allows and encourages dialogue. The Internet has provided hope that societal dialogue will expand, even in repressive societies. This has been happening, as the Arab Spring has shown, but as events have evolved, for example in Egypt, it has become clear that the ability of people to come together and organize is only a beginning. There have to be further processes to promote a positive evolution. Moreover, the anonymity of the internet also allows devaluation, manipulation and incitement, without responsibility or accountability. Extreme groups shaping people's thinking, promoting hostility, and inciting them to violence abound on the Internet (Sagemen, 2008).

Creating constructive ideologies and groups. At times of difficult life conditions or persistent conflict, people need hope. Hope is often provided by ideologies that are destructive, in that they identify enemies. To prevent violence and promote a peaceful future, people need constructive ideologies, visions of a hopeful future that embraces all groups and motivates all groups to work together for their fulfillment. That is what Nelson Mandela provided in South Africa; and what Abraham Lincoln was in the process of creating after the civil war, by reaching out to the defeated Confederacy before he was killed (Lieberfeld, 2009). Everybody can participate in the creation of positive visions, introducing and discussing ideas in religious and civic groups and with neighbors, writing to newspapers and leaders, supporting constructive ideas and actions. The media, writers, thinkers, leaders, public persons have the greatest potential for influence— both negative and positive.

Destructive ideologies are embodied in movements and groups. Groups are of great importance. They define social reality for people. The connections they generate and the psychological needs they fulfill have great power. It has become a widely accepted view that terrorists act for cause and comrades (McCauley, 2004), but this is also true of others involved in group violence (Staub, 2011). If people have constructive groups to turn to that fulfill their important psychological needs in difficult times, they will be less likely to turn to destructive ones. Such groups can serve a constructive ideology; they can also be in the service of more limited personal goals. Even participation with other people in microcredit projects, especially if they are supported with advice and guidance by others experienced in the business the loan is to be used for, represents a constructive group. Churches, schools, advocates of social change, authorities working to create groups that help people, young and old, fulfill basic needs in difficult times, make it less likely that they will turn to groups that advocate destructive ideologies and foster an evolution leading to extreme violence (Staub, 2011).

Promoting healing-psychological recovery.   Healing from trauma, recovering from the psychological wounds that result from being the object of violence—and also from perpetrating or passively witnessing the violence—enable people to lead better lives and contribute to building and maintaining a peaceful society in the aftermath of mass violence (Pearlman, 2013).

Healing can take place as people in small groups talk about their experiences, providing support to each other. It can take place in larger groups, when people offer testimonials, describing their experiences to others who provide support. It can take place in the course of commemorations. Outsiders joining victims in commemoration provides acknowledgment and emotional support. As the passage of time and healing lessen the pain, even former perpetrators joining in commemoration may be helpful. It is important for commemorations not to focus only on the injuries and pain of the past, and on the continued psychological distress that has resulted from it. Such a singular focus on pain can turn the events of the past into a persisting group trauma, and shape a group identity of woundeness. It is important to include in commemorations, especially after some time, a hopeful vision of the future, ideally a joint peaceful future for all the different subgroups in society (Staub, 2011).

Often people who have been victimized not only carry psychological wounds, but as events activate their experience of threat and danger, they engage in "defensive violence" (Staub, 2011). Their past experience may also lead them to feel hostility and aggression to the world. But some people who have suffered devote themselves to helping others who have suffered, and/or to prevent suffering. It is important to provide people with experiences that help to develop such "altruism born of suffering" (Staub, 2003, 2005; Staub & Vollhardt, 2008). Raising children with love and positive guidance contributes to their resilience. It also may make it more likely that they try to help themselves, or help others, or seek help at a time they are victimized. These experiences and actions are, in turn, likely to contribute to altruism born of suffering. So may bystanders helping people when they are harmed, people supporting them afterwards, and healing experiences. If former victims at some point begin to help others, they learn by doing, and their caring for others develops further (Staub, 2003, 2005; Staub & Vollhardt, 2008).

Many kinds of harmful experiences that may not create trauma can create psychological wounds. While many children are abused, more are harshly treated. People in marriages or in "love relationships" harm each other. Life injuries, such as the death of loved ones, the break up of relationships, or even a favorite friend of a child moving away, can lead to psychological wounds. To diminish vulnerability created by group events or personal experiences, to create harmonious societies, we ought to work on creating 'healing societies.' When communities exist that provide everyone with connection and support in the face of painful experiences (Pearlman, 2013; Staub, 2011), it becomes less likely that people turn to ideas and groups that help them fulfill psychological needs by destructive means.

Understanding the origins of violence, the impact of violence, and avenues to prevention and reconciliation.   Our work in post-genocide Rwanda (in collaboration with Laurie Pearlman; see also Pearlman, 2013) began with a training for 35 people, both Hutu and Tutsi, who worked for eight community organizations. Our aim was to help people understand the origins and impact of genocide and other extreme group violence. We gave lectures about the influences leading to such violence (based on Staub, 1989), its impact on people (Pearlman, 2001; Pearlman & Saakvitne, 1995; Staub, 1998), and the role of basic human needs in both the origins of violence and the resulting trauma or psychological woundedness. We gave examples of what happened in other parts of the world. This seemed important to people, making them feel less alone (If this happened to others, perhaps what happened to us was not God's punishment). In extensive discussion they applied information about the origins and impact of violence to what happened to them in Rwanda.

We did an informal evaluation of the effects of this training on the people we trained and formal research to evaluate it, once removed, on people they then trained. We compared changes in members of newly set up community groups which some of the people in our training facilitated (Staub et al., 2005) with changes in two control groups, from before to two months after the end of training. Hutus and Tutsis in the treatment groups had a more positive orientation to the other group than people in the control groups, fewer trauma symptoms, a more complex understanding of the origins of violence, and expressed more "conditional forgiveness" (I can forgive them if they acknowledge what they did). Our impression was that both our facilitators, and members of the groups they led, gained an *experiential understanding*, as they applied this information to their own experiences in Rwanda. The victims blamed themselves less for what was done to them. Members of the perpetrator group, Hutus, came to understand the influences that led other members of their group to perpetrate the horrible violence in Rwanda. As a result, they seemed to become less defensive, and more open to Tutsis and to reconciliation.

We subsequently conducted similar trainings with many groups, including members of the media and national leaders. In these trainings we included more information about avenues to prevention and reconciliation. It was the approach we developed in these trainings, which I have called the Staub-Pearlman approach (Staub, 2011), that we and our associates subsequently used to create the educational elements of the radio drama and informational radio programs in Rwanda, and then Burundi and the Congo. The educational content was summarized in communication messages. We trained the local producers and writers in each country, and they then used these messages to shape each episode of the radio drama to include educational elements.

After one year the effects of the radio drama were evaluated. People in 6 groups around the country (the treatment group) listened to the programs. People in six other groups (the control group) agreed to listen to an alternative radio show for the year. Those in the treatment group expressed more empathy with varied parties (survivors, bystanders, leaders, even harmdoers), showed changes in a number of relevant beliefs, engaged in more reconciliation behaviors interacting with members of the other group, expressed more willingness to say what they believed—and actually did so, as well as showing more independence of authority in their actions (Paluck, 2009; see also Staub, 2011; Staub & Pearlman, 2009).

In sum, in the aftermath of mass violence, public education about origins, prevention, and reconciliation seems of great importance. Providing people with an experiential understanding, allowing them to apply concepts and processes to their own society and experience, can begin to shift attitudes toward the self and other. It may enable members of different groups to constructively engage with each other.

Awareness of group processes and active bystandership. For the prevention of violence and the creation of peaceful societies, it can be of substantial value to educate people about normal group processes—both about the ways in which individuals are affected and shaped by groups, and how they can influence groups. Social reality, what is right and what is wrong, and beliefs about members of other groups are greatly affected by the views of people around us and our larger group. Historical anti-Semitism and the influence of Nazi propaganda often led people to accept and even to join in the persecution of Jews in German occupied countries during World War II (Fein, 1979; Staub, 1989). In contrast, the capacity to maintain an independent perspective seemed to be a characteristic of one type of rescuers of Jews in Nazi Europe (Tec, 1986). Understanding social influence can increase our ability to use our own judgment.

While independent judgment by citizens is one likely contributor to constructive social processes in a society, individuals need to join with each other if they are to exert influence at the group level. Through conversations, including dialogue with people with opposing views, people can shape each other's views. While people committed to extreme ideological views can rarely be moved, many people can change in such a process, creating a majority committed to a pluralistic, democratic, and harmonious society (Staub, 2007, 2011).

People can join already existing organizations that work for the social good. They can recruit others and together create new organizations. They can influence churches and civic groups they are part of to join with other such organizations. Even single individuals have sometimes exerted powerful influence, especially as they inspired others to join with them (see Staub, 2011). One woman in Liberia attracted the support of other women in her church, women belonging to other religions joined them, and together they had a role in bringing the civil war there to an end (Hebert, 2009). People can write letters to politicians and participate in political parties. In countries with a reasonably free press, writing letters to newspapers, even if they do not publish them, calls their attention to issues and can influence what they report.

Building institutions. Creating institutions that move a society toward greater equality—a justice system that serves equal justice, police that uphold the law equally for different groups, and so on—as well as toward more pluralism and genuine democracy, requires a variety of psychological changes (Staub, 2011). As people begin to change legitimizing ideologies (Sidanius & Pratto, 1999) that justify differences in power, access, and wealth, and as there is lessening of devaluation and discrimination, the motivation to improve institutions can develop in citizens, elites, and leaders.

Wide-ranging change in group psychology represents culture change. It is essential, however, to solidify such changes by creating good institutions. Without this, renewed economic problems or other difficult life conditions are likely to give rise to scapegoating and destructive ideologies, the processes that begin an evolution toward group violence. Institutions that promote just relations, and pluralism with the participation of all groups in public matters, are essential to create a world without genocide. What is also essential is to create high level institutions within governments that have the responsibility to address the potential for violence at home and abroad, and activate responses when violence in other countries begins (Staub, 2011; see also Allbright & Cohen, 2008). Only when this responsibility is focused on high level government officials will active bystandership by nations become a reality.

The evolution of the values of a peaceful society. A source of conflict and hostility between individuals and groups is values, beliefs, and practices that make it difficult to constructively fulfill basic psychological needs. After essential material needs have been fulfilled, the pursuit of material goods, wealth and influence tend to be in the service of fulfilling psychological needs. Given certain societal values and practices, wealth and influence confer a positive identity, show a person's effectiveness, and help gain esteem and positive connections. At the same time, even after essential material needs are fulfilled, in an age of communication when people know how others live, relative poverty can make people feel diminished, ineffective, even humiliated.

Values of cooperation and community, an appreciation of others' humanity and worth that is not based on their material possessions but on their character, capacity for positive relationships, and contribution to their neighbor's lives and community, would make the evolution of violence less likely. Humanizing outsiders, applying such values and developing positive connections to the outside world are also important to avoid violence against other groups. To create such a society requires engagement and active bystandership by every segment of a population. It requires individuals to promote such values in their civic organizations and churches, and to demand that their political representatives and leaders express and model those values in their actions. It requires companies to structure work environments in terms of such values, inspiring people to do well in cooperative rather than competitive environments. It requires authors of books, and members of the media to stress such values. Public education, including media, can also show how different values shape life in a society, their potential consequences in terms of harmony and peace versus disharmony and violence.

Socialization, Caring and Positive Bystandership

An essential source of values is socialization. The learning of positive values, such as caring about other people, including people in other groups or inclusive caring, is to a substantial extent experiential. To care about other people, children have to feel cared about. But they also have to receive positive guidance, which stresses important values, points out to them the consequences of their behavior on other people (Hoffman, 2000), and leads them to actually behave according to rules that are derived from such values (Baumrind, 1975).

Learning by doing also happens in this realm. When children are guided to engage in helpful behavior, they become more helpful. This was found both in experimental research in which children made toys for poor hospitalized children or taught younger children (Staub, 1979, 2005; see also Eisenberg, Fabes, & Spinrad, 2006), and in societies which give children responsibilities that genuinely benefit the family and the group (Whiting & Whiting, 1969). Caring tends to expand, those who help valuing more the welfare of people in general. For example, the Mothers of the Plaza del Mayo in Argentina began to demonstrate after their children disappeared. Over time their concern and engagement expanded to the welfare of others (Thalhammer et al., 2007). Rescuers in the Holocaust who may have intended to help one person for a limited time often become committed over time and did much more (Oliner & Oliner, 1988; Staub, 1989, 1997).

Socialization that leads children to care about other people can limit this caring to members of one's own group, as children learn to draw lines between "us" and "them." But children can also learn to expand their caring beyond the boundaries of their group, as they are guided through words, actions, and positive contact (Oliner & Oliner, 1988). Inclusive caring makes later participation in group violence less likely and increases the likelihood of active bystandership to resist the evolution of violence (Staub, 2005, 2011).

Another important outcome of positive socialization that contributes to a world without genocide is *moral courage*, the capacity and willingness to act according to one's moral and caring values in the face of potential or actual opposition and negative consequences (Staub, 2003, 2005, 2011; Zimbardo, 2007). This requires that children be allowed and encouraged to use their voice, to express what they think. Participation in decision making in the home and in schools can help with this. When children are allowed and encouraged to take risks in expressing their views and in taking positive action, it contributes to the development of moral courage that can lead to active bystandership needed to prevent genocide and other mass violence.

All aspects of positive socialization I described require that parents and teachers develop the values, motivation, and skills that enable them to raise children in these ways. It requires genuine caring on their part, the skills to guide children without harshness to act according to essential values and rules, and enough confidence to allow children to express themselves even if their views are in opposition with their own views. It requires the capacity to create environments, in schools and in the home, that promote caring (Staub, 2003, in press). Many adults require training, both conceptual and experiential, to practice such positive socialization.

Direct training of youth (and adults) in active bystandership is also important. Together with some associates I have developed a training for students in schools, when they witness their peers harassing, intimidating or harming other students. In the course of such training students can develop empathy with victims and even with harmdoers and come to understand what stops people from responding to others' needs. They can learn to use their own judgment and engage others to join them in action, partly by defining the meaning of events and appropriate actions. In an evaluation study the training reduced harmful behavior by 20%, in comparison to control schools (Staub, in press). This training can also be applied to other circumstances.

Conclusions

Creating a world without mass violence requires everyone's participation. It requires psychological changes in individuals and groups, changes in culture, and changes in institutions. These changes are intertwined: as people change psychologically and create new institutions, these in turn further change individual and group psychology and culture. Structural arrangements can limit contact between members of different groups or promote deep contact. Schools with participatory classrooms in which students have a voice help develop a critical consciousness and moral courage (Staub, 2005).

Among the many important forms of engagement in this realm for scholars, researchers and practitioners is public education. Lectures, workshops, seminars, educational television and radio programs, and teaching classes with relevant materials can contribute to societal transformation. Public education can lead to experiential understanding and motivate broad segments of the population to be active bystanders in developing a society in which violence between groups is unlikely; a society which takes action to stop ongoing violence or help prevent violence at home or in other countries when there are indications of the danger of violence.

References

Africa Rights. (2002). *Tribute to courage*. Kigali, Rwanda.

Albright, M., & Cohen, W. (2008). *Preventing genocide: A blueprint for U.S. policy makers*. Washington, DC: U. S. Holocaust Museum.

Alter, J. (2006). *The defining moment: FDR's hundred days and the triumph of hope*. New York, NY: Simon and Schuster.

Allport, G. W. (1954). *The nature of prejudice*. Reading, MA: Addison-Wesley.

Aronson, E., Stephan, C., Sikes, J., Blaney, N., & Snapp, M. (1978). *The jigsaw classroom*. Beverly Hills, CA: Sage.

Bandura, A. (1999). Moral disengagement in the preparation of inhumanities. *Personality and Social Psychology Review, 3*, 193–209. doi: 10.1207/s15327957pspr0303

Bar-Tal, D. (2000). *Shared beliefs in a society: Social psychological analysis*. Thousand Oaks, CA: Sage.

Baumrind, D. (1975). *Early socialization and the discipline controversy*. Morristown, NJ: General Learning Press.

Bilali, R. (2013). National narrative and social psychological influences in the Turkish denial of the Armenian Genocide. *Journal of Social Issues, 69*, 16–33.

Burg, S. L. (1997). Preventing ethnic conflict: Macedonia and the pluralist paradigm. Presentation at the Woodrow Wilson Center, February 19. Retrieved June, 2009, from http://www. wilsoncenter.org/index.cfm?fuseaction=topics.print_pub&doc_id=18947&group_id=7427& topic_id=1422&stoplayout=true

Carson, J. (2008, October 30). *Ambassador Carson speaking on the panel "What went right, what went wrong in Kenya" at the Conference on the Prevention of Genocide, organized by the State Department*, Washington, DC.

Des Forges, A. (1999). *Leave none to tell the story: Genocide in Rwanda*. New York, NY: Human Rights Watch.

Eisenberg, N., Fabes, R. A., & Spinrad, T. L. (2006). Prosocial development. In W. Damon (Ed.), *Handbook of child psychology, Volume 3: Social, emotional, and personality development* (5th ed.), (pp. 646–718). New York, NY: Wiley.

Fein, H. (1979). *Accounting for genocide: Victims and survivors of the Holocaust*. New York: Free Press.

Gurr, T. R. (1970). *Why men rebel*. Princeton, NJ: Princeton University Press.

Hamburg, D. (2007). *Preventing genocide: Practical steps toward early detection and effective action*. Boulder, CO: Paradigm Publishers.

Hammack, P. L. (2011). *Narrative and the politics of identity: The cultural psychology of Israeli and Palestinian youth*. New York: Oxford University Press.

Harff, B. (2003). No lessons learned from the Holocaust? Assessing risks of genocide and political mass murder since 1955. *American Political Science Review, 97*, 57–73. doi: 10.1017/S0003055403000522.

Hebert, B. (2009, January 21). A crazy dream. *The New York Times*, p. 19.

Helson, H. (1964). *Adaptation Level Theory: An experimental and systematic approach to behavior*. New York, NY: Harper & Row.

Hoffman, M. (2000). *Empathy and moral development*. New York: Cambridge University Press.

Jost, J. T., Banaji, M. R., & Nosek, B. A. (2004). A decade of system justification theory: Accumulated evidence of conscious and unconscious bolstering of the status quo. *Political Psychology, 25*, 881–920. doi: 10.1111/j.1467-9221.2004.00402.x

Kelman, H. C., & Fisher, R. J. (2003). Conflict analysis and resolution. In D. Sears, L. Huddy, & R. Jervis (Eds.), *Political psychology*. New York, NY: Oxford University Press.

Klar, Y., Shori-Eyal, N. & Klar, Y. (2013). The "Never Again" State of Israel: The emergence of the Holocaust as a core feature of Israeli identity and its four incongruent voices. *Journal of Social Issues, 69*, 125–143.

Kriesberg, L. (1998). Intractable conflicts. In E. Weiner (Ed.), *The handbook of interethnic coexistence* (pp. 332–342). New York, NY: Continuum.

Lerner, M. (1980). *The belief in a just world: A fundamental delusion*. New York: Plenum Press.

Lieberfeld, D. (2009). Lincoln, Mandela, and qualities of reconciliation-oriented leadership. *Peace and Conflict: Journal of Peace Psychology, 15*, 27–47. doi: 10.1080/10781910802589857.

Lindner, E. G. (2006). *Making enemies: Humiliation and international conflict*. Westport, CT: Greenwood Press and Praeger Publishers.

Long, W. J., & Brecke, P. (2003). *War and reconciliation: Reason and emotion in conflict resolution*. Cambridge, MA: MIT Press.

Maoz, I. (2004). Coexistence is in the eye of the beholder: Evaluating intergroup encounter interventions between Jews and Arabs in Israel. *Journal of Social Issues, 60*, 437–452. doi: 10.1111/j.0022-4537.2004.00119.x.

Mamdani, M. (2001). *When victims become killers: Colonialism, nativism, and the genocide in Rwanda*. Princeton, NJ: Princeton University Press.

Maslow, A. H. (1971). *The farther reaches of human nature*. New York, NY: Viking.

Melvern, L. (2004). *Conspiracy to murder: The Rwanda genocide*. London, U.K.: Verso.

McCauley, C. (2004). Psychological issues in understanding terrorism. In C. E. Stout (Ed.), *Psychology of terrorism* (pp. 33–67). Westport, CT: Praeger Publishers.

Oliner, S. B., & Oliner, P. (1988). *The altruistic personality: Rescuers of Jews in Nazi Europe*. New York, NY: Free Press.

Opotaw, S. (1990). Moral exclusion and injustice. *Journal of Social Issues, 46*, 1–20. doi: 10.1111/j.1540-4560.1990.tb00268.x

Paluck, E. L. (2009). Reducing intergroup prejudice and conflict using the media: A field experiment in Rwanda. *Journal of Personality and Social Psychology, 96*, 574–587. doi: 10.1037/a0011989

Pearlman, L. A. (2001). The treatment of persons with complex PTSD and other trauma-related disruptions of the self. In J. P. Wilson, M. J. Friedman, & J. D. Lindy (Eds.), *Treating psychological trauma & PTSD* (pp. 205–236). New York, NY: Guilford Press.

Pearlman, L. A. (2013). Restoring self in community: Collective approaches to psychological trauma after genocide. *Journal of Social Issues, 69*, 111–124.

Pearlman, L. A., & Saakvitne, K. W. (1995). *Trauma and the therapist: Countertransference and vicarious traumatization in psychotherapy with incest survivors*. New York, NY: W.W. Norton.

Pettigrew, T., & Tropp, L. (2006). A meta-analytic test of intergroup contact theory. *Journal of Personality and Social Psychology, 90*, 751–783. doi: 10.1037/0022-3514.90.5.751

Sageman, M. (2008). *Leaderless jihad: Terror networks in the twenty-first century*. Philadelphia, PA: University of Pennsylvania Press.

Sherif, M., Harvey, D. J., White, B. J., Hood, W. K., & Sherif, C. W. (1961). *Intergroup conflict and cooperation: The Robbers Cave experiment*. Norman, OK: University of Oklahoma Book Exchange.

Sidanius, J., & Pratto, F. (1999). *Social dominance: An intergroup theory of social hierarchy and oppression*. New York, NY: Cambridge University Press.

Simpson, C. (1993). *The splendid blond beast: Money, law and genocide in the 20th century*. New York: Grove Press.

Staub, E. (1979). *Positive social behavior and morality: Vol. 2. Socialization and development*. New York, NY: Academic Press.

Staub, E. (1989). *The roots of evil: The origins of genocide and other group violence*. New York, NY: Cambridge University Press.

Staub, E. (1997). The psychology of rescue: Perpetrators, bystanders and heroic helpers. In J. Michalczyk (Ed.), *Resisters, rescuers and refugees: Historical and ethical issues* (pp. 137–147). Kansas City, MO: Sheed and Ward.

Staub, E. (1999). The origins and prevention of genocide, mass killing and other collective violence. *Peace and Conflict: Journal of Peace Psychology, 5*, 303–337.

Staub, E. (2000). Bystanders to violence. *In the Encyclopedia of Violence in the United States*. New York: Charles Scribner's Sons.

Staub, E. (2003). *The psychology of good and evil: Why children, adults and groups help and harm others*. New York, NY: Cambridge University Press.

Staub, E. (2005). The roots of goodness: The fulfillment of basic human needs and the development of caring, helping and nonaggression, inclusive caring, moral courage, active bystandership, and altruism born of suffering. In G. Carlo & C. Edwards (Eds.), *Moral motivation through the life span: Theory, research, applications* (pp. 33–73). Nebraska Symposium on Motivation. Lincoln, NE: Nebraska University Press.

Staub, E. (2006). Reconciliation after genocide, mass killing or intractable conflict: Understanding the roots of violence, psychological recovery and steps toward a general theory. *Political Psychology, 27*, 865–895. doi: 10.1111/j.1467-9221.2006.00541.x.

Staub, E. (2007). Preventing violence and terrorism and promoting positive relations between Dutch and Muslim communities in Amsterdam. *Peace and Conflict: Journal of Peace Psychology, 13*, 333–361. doi: 10.1080/10781910701471397.

Staub, E. (2011). *Overcoming evil: genocide, violent conflict and terrorism.* New York, NY: Cambridge University Press.

Staub, E. (in press). *The roots of goodness: inclusive caring, altruism born of suffering, moral courage, active bystandership and heroism.* New York: Oxford University Press.

Staub, E., & Pearlman, L. A. (2009). Reducing intergroup prejudice and conflict: A commentary. *Journal of Personality and Social Psychology, 96*, 588–594. doi: 10.1037/a0014045.

Staub, E., Pearlman, L. A., & Bilali, R. (2010). Understanding the roots and impact of violence and psychological recovery as avenues to reconciliation after mass violence and intractable conflict: Applications to national leaders, journalists, community groups, public education through radio, and children. In G. Salomon & E. Cairns (Eds.), *Handbook of peace education* (pp. 269–287). New York, NY: Psychology Press.

Staub, E., Pearlman, L. A., Gubin, A., & Hagengimana, A. (2005). Healing, reconciliation, forgiving and the prevention of violence after genocide or mass killing: An intervention and its experimental evaluation in Rwanda. *Journal of Social and Clinical Psychology, 24*, 297–334. doi: 10.1521/jscp.24.3.297.65617.

Staub, E., & Vollhardt, J. (2008). Altruism born of suffering: The roots of caring and helping after experiences of personal and political victimization. *American Journal of Orthopsychiatry, 78*, 267–280. doi: 10.1037/a0014223.

Tajfel, H. (1978). Social categorization, social identity and social comparison. In H. Tajfel (Ed.), *Differentiation between social groups* (pp. 61–76). London, U.K.: Academic Press.

Tajfel, H., & Turner, J. (1986). The social identity theory of inter-group behavior. In S. Worchel & L. Austin (Eds.), *Psychology of intergroup relations.* Chicago, IL: Nelson-Hall.

Taylor, F. (Translator and editor) (1983). *Goebbels' diaries, 1933–1941.* New York: G.P. Putnam's Sons.

Tec, N. (1986). *When light pierced the darkness: Christian rescuers of Jews in Nazi occupied Poland.* New York, NY: Oxford University Press.

Thalhammer, K. E., O'Loughlin, P. L., Glazer, M. P., Glazer, P. M., McFarland, S., Shepela, S. T., & Stoltzfus, N. (2007). *Courageous resistance: The power of ordinary people.* New York, NY: Palgrave Macmillan.

Uvin, P. (1998). *Aiding violence. The development enterprise in Rwanda.* Sterling, VA: Kumarian Press.

Varshney, A. (2002). *Ethnic conflict and civic life: Hindus and Muslims in India.* New Haven, CT: Yale University Press.

Volkan, V. D. (2001). Transgenerational transmissions and chosen traumas: An aspect of large-group identity. *Group Analysis, 34*, 79–97. doi: 10.1177/05333160122077730.

Vollhardt, J. R. (2013). "Crime against Humanity" or "Crime against Jews"? Acknowledgment in construals of the Holocaust and its importance for intergroup relations. *Journal of Social Issues, 69*, 144–161.

Whiting, B. B., & Whiting, J. W. M. (1969). *Children of six cultures: A psycho cultural analysis.* Cambridge, MA: Harvard University Press.

Zimbardo, P. (2007). *The Lucifer effect: Understanding how good people turn evil.* New York, NY: Random House.

ERVIN STAUB received his Ph.D. from Stanford, and taught at Harvard. He is currently a Professor Emeritus and Founding Director of the doctoral program in the Psychology of Peace and Violence at the University of Massachusetts, Amherst,

USA. His research interests include roots of altruism, the origins of genocide, violent conflict, terrorism, their prevention and reconciliation. He is past president of the International Society for Political Psychology (ISPP) and of the Society for the Study of Peace, Conflict and Violence. His projects in field settings range from promoting altruism in children, to seminars/trainings and educational radio projects in Rwanda, Burundi and the Congo to promote psychological recovery and reconciliation. His awards include life-long contributions to peace psychology and distinguished scientific contributions to political psychology. His latest book, *Overcoming evil: genocide, violent conflict and terrorism* received ISPP's Alexander George award for the best book published in 2011 in political psychology. For other awards and download of articles, see www.ervinstaub.com.

Journal of Social Issues, Vol. 69, No. 1, 2013, pp. 200–208

The Aftermath of Genocide: History as a Proximal Cause

Peter Glick[*]
Lawrence University

Elizabeth Levy Paluck
Princeton University

The current volume represents a crucial first step in examining how past genocidal attacks continue to affect present intergroup relations, and what psychology can offer to help heal the wounds and prevent future violence. Studying the social psychology of genocide's aftermath, in all its messy, real-world complexity, has not been as popular a topic in the intergroup relations literature. This volume begins to correct that neglect, presenting models for how to incorporate both basic theory and historical context into research on the aftermath of intergroup violence. Future work continuing in this tradition should also continue to seek out multidisciplinary collaborations to study genocide's aftermath.

The current volume represents a crucial first step in examining how past genocidal attacks continue to affect present intergroup relations, and what psychology can offer to help heal the wounds and prevent future violence. It is difficult to exaggerate the worth or seriousness of this topic. Yet social psychologists—even those focused on understanding prejudice and intergroup relations—have tended to shy away from studying genocide's aftermath in all its messy, real-world complexity. This volume begins to correct that neglect, presenting models for how to incorporate both basic theory and historical context into research on the aftermath of intergroup violence.

In this commentary, we highlight a common theme that threads through all of the articles: how past relationships between members of victim and perpetrator

*Correspondence concerning this article should be addressed to Peter Glick, Department of Psychology, Lawrence University, 711 E. Boldt Way, Appleton, WI 54911 [e-mail: glickp@lawrence.edu].

groups shape contemporary group identity and intergroup attitudes. For victim groups, conflicting motives lead to ambivalence about remembering versus distancing themselves from the past. By contrast, perpetrator group members tend to seek distance from the past or even to deny that any atrocity occurred. But either response, embracing, or running from the past creates continuing effects. The past continues to cast a shadow on the present. We conclude with a call to arms—or, more accurately, a call to link arms through multidisciplinary collaborations to study genocide's aftermath. We suggest that social psychologists seek out research partners ranging from the clinical psychologists on another floor, to the historians and political scientists across campus, to local scholars and activists situated within nations affected by past genocidal conflicts.

The Past and the Present

Social psychologists' emphasis on proximal situational causes, manipulated within carefully constructed laboratory conditions, is deeply embedded in the field's ethos. This approach has been highly successful as social psychologists have deftly shown the surprising explanatory power of the immediate situation. Iconic research in intergroup relations, such as Sherifs' (Sherif, Harvey, White, Hood, & Sherif, 1961) work on boys in a summer camp and Tajfel's (1970) minimal group experiments, has revealed how intergroup conflict can be created absent any historical hostility or a prior group identity, between groups created on the thinnest of pretexts. Such approaches have not only allowed for tightly controlled tests of causal hypotheses, but the development of broadly applicable theories that show considerable utility for understanding real-world conflicts.

The current volume does not reject these past approaches; indeed, the authors represented here make ample and appropriate use of theories that were developed via controlled studies with experimentally created groups. At the same time, this volume stands as a needed corrective, calling for social psychologists to test and refine theories that were painstakingly developed in the laboratory within real-world contexts with a history of extreme intergroup conflict. Why? Because as social psychologists well know, context matters. In intergroup relationships, context incorporates not only proximal variables, but a past that becomes the lens through which current intergroup identities, emotions, narratives, and relations are perceived (e.g., Brown, Gonzalez, Zagefka, Manzi, & Čehajić, 2008; Wohl, Branscombe, & Klar, 2006).

While we are not calling on psychologists to become historians, a central theme revealed in the current volume is that the *past lives on in the present*. In other words, even the ancient past can represent a proximal cause, because group members' beliefs about the past strongly influence their current intergroup attitudes and behavior. In many cases, this perceived past (i.e., group members' beliefs and narratives about the past) stretches back much further than a recent genocidal attack to centuries and even millennia of intergroup tensions and periodic bouts of violence.

All articles in this volume explore the psychological relationship between past and present, revealing mechanisms by which the past, whether through remembrance or defensive denial, reverberates in the present. Proximal events, some of which outsiders might view as trivial, can initiate extreme reactions because they resonate with narratives about the past. For example, an intergroup incident that symbolically evokes past conflict can reactivate threat and suspicion that elicit intense hostility. Unfortunately, when the past reasserts itself in the present, both perpetrator and victim groups experience threats (though in different forms) that spark defensive reactions, creating obstacles to reconciliation.

Together, the research presented in this volume seems to suggest that members of victim groups experience an ambivalent relationship to the past, arising from conflicting motives. For example, justice motives demand remembrance, as well as that other groups (both perpetrators and bystanders) recognize and acknowledge the victim group's suffering (e.g., Schnabel & Nadler, 2008). But remembrance is also painful, posing threats to positive group identity and perceived control over future outcomes. Thus, victimized group members may often feel the contradictory tugs of approach and avoidance. This ambivalent relationship to the past can create tensions in present-day victim ingroup identity and intergroup attitudes (discussed below). By contrast, perpetrator group members have little incentive to acknowledge the past and strong motivation to create psychological distance from, minimize, reframe, or outright deny past harm-doing by their group. The differences in victim and perpetrator groups' relationship to the past create barriers for reconciliation efforts.

Within victim groups, the past lives on most vividly for individuals who directly experienced the trauma of genocidal attack. Kaplan's (2013) article poignantly describes how survivors relive trauma on a daily basis, through flashbacks and posttraumatic stress, leading to difficulty regulating their affective reactions. Survivors require intensive, individualized clinical treatment to reconstruct their lives. But, as Pearlman (2013) suggests, individual treatment must be accompanied by a community psychology approach. This approach links individual treatment to community-based healing to promote reengagement and reconciliation. Such efforts are necessary when trauma results from group processes, and is especially critical when victimized and perpetrator groups continue to live in close proximity.

But even when the temporal and physical distance from past conflict increases, the centrality of past events to victimized groups' identities may be amplified rather than recede. Klar, Shori-Eyal, and Klar (2013) show the continuing, often contradictory effects the Holocaust has on Israelis' contemporary identity, and they document how the Holocaust's influence has intensified rather than decreased over time. The vast majority of Israelis did not personally experience the traumas of the Holocaust, but this group-based, vicarious victimization experience plays a fundamental role in Israeli identity. Israeli Jews' ambivalent relationship to the past is evident in tensions within contemporary Israeli identity. Holocaust remembrance not only creates solidarity within the group, as well as with other victimized groups, but also strongly motivates Israelis to reject a continuing "victim" identity (e.g., vowing never again to be passive victims). These conflicting responses to past victimization lead to polarized intergroup attitudes and behavior among contemporary Israelis, such as motivating help-giving toward other victimized groups, but also a hard-line stance against groups like the Palestinians, who are perceived as a contemporary threat.

Similarly, Vollhardt (2013) shows how representations of their own group's past victimization influences Jewish students' attitudes and behavior toward other victimized groups in contemporary conflicts (in this case, Darfur). The manner in which reminders of the past are framed can lead to more or less empathy for other victimized groups. Vollhardt finds that victim groups need others to acknowledge their group's particular suffering within more "superordinate," inclusive narratives about genocide as a crime against humanity. The implied denial of the particularity of Jews' victimization in these superordinate narratives about the Holocaust creates defensive reactions among Jews and, in turn, psychological distancing from other victimized groups. By contrast, when others acknowledge the particularity of Jewish suffering in the context of these superordinate narratives, Jewish students show increased desire to help other victimized groups.

Remembering the past can also create tension for current group identity and extreme intergroup attitudes among members of perpetrator groups. However, while victim group members experience conflicting motives to both embrace and avoid the past, perpetrator groups tend simply to distance themselves from the past (Peetz, Gunn, & Wilson, 2010). Just as acknowledging personal past harm-doing represents a threat to a moral and positive self-identity, acknowledging that one's group has caused harm represents a threat to a positive, moral ingroup identity. And just as individuals use a variety of mechanisms to justify harm they personally have caused—by denying or minimizing the damage or by blaming others (e.g., the victim; Tangney, Stuewig, & Mashek, 2007)—research in this volume demonstrates the myriad ways in which members of perpetrator groups minimize or deny harm to protect their group identity.

Indeed, as we write, a new French law criminalizing denial of the Armenian genocide has created a serious rift in relations between France and Turkey (LA Times, 2011). Bilali (2013) shows how Turkish students in the United States (despite their experiences outside their own country) adhere to the Turkish government's official position that vigorously denies that Armenians were victims of a Turkish genocide campaign. She further illuminates psychological mechanisms that contribute to this denial, all related to the goal of maintaining a positive group identity. Importantly, this research illuminates how denial represents not only a way to glorify the ingroup, but also a response to perceived continuing threat from outgroups. Indeed, perceived threat can lead members of perpetrator groups to see themselves as victims rather than as harm-doers. Almost two-thirds of Turkish students in Bilali's sample believed that Armenians and Turks harmed each other equally; more strikingly, a notable minority (10%) believed that the Turks were victims of the Armenians.

It is tempting to view the Turks' denial as a special case, but Leach, Zeineddine, and Čehajić-Clancy (2013) argue otherwise. Their careful review of prior research shows that even when governments officially recognize and apologize for past atrocities toward victim groups, individuals within those nations rarely express strong feelings of shame, guilt, or responsibility, and rarely support reparations. As the past recedes, denial of and distancing from colonialization, mass violence, and genocide increases (e.g., "Why should I feel responsible or pay for atrocities committed by past generations?"). While governments may experience outside pressure to acknowledge past wrong-doing (e.g., as the Turkish government, though still recalcitrant, has been pressured by the European Union), most individuals within these nations or groups may experience little compunction about denying or distancing themselves from the ingroup's past wrongs.

The impulse to deny that one's group has ever caused harm creates a thorny problem for attempts at reconciliation. Put simply, members of perpetrator groups are threatened by reminders that their group has harmed others and, in turn, react defensively. Thus, attempts to raise consciousness about past harm-doing— a crucial first step toward reconciliation and reparation—can backfire. Specifically, Kofta and Sławuta (2013) show that reminders of Polish massacres of Jews during the Holocaust led to increased dehumanization of Jews, unless non-Jewish Poles were first reminded of their cultural similarities with Polish Jews. In the latter case, raising awareness of prior harm-doing led to more positive attitudes and behavioral intentions toward Jews.

Similarly, Imhoff, Wohl, and Erb (2013) demonstrate that Germans readily take advantage of information that allows them to minimize past atrocities. Being told that the victimized group is currently doing well diminishes collective guilt and the perceived need for reparations among perpetrator group members. While this result might suggest that it is crucial to emphasize continued suffering among victim groups, prior research by the first author (Imhoff & Banse, 2009) showed that such reminders can initiate defensive motivations and thereby increase (rather than reduce) prejudice among members of perpetrator groups. Clearly, more research is needed to determine how to short-circuit such defensive reactions. Kofta and Sławuta's (2013) article suggests a moderator variable that could undermine defensiveness: inclusion of the victim group in a shared superordinate category (e.g., they are like us). This suggestion recalls Vollhardt's (2013) cautionary lesson, however, that messages portraying the victim and perpetrator group in one superordinate category without acknowledging their distinct history and suffering might not benefit the victim group.

Bilewicz and Jaworska (2013) nicely encapsulate the ways in which both victim and perpetrator group members are threatened by the past, as well as how each group's desired relationship to the past creates tensions in current intergroup relations. The topic of Polish complicity in the Holocaust elicits incompatible motives among contemporary Jewish and Polish students (despite their lack of direct experience with the Holocaust), which, without careful intervention, can undermine reconciliation. Bilewicz and Jaworska created a way to avoid defensiveness among Poles, for whom the past threatens a moral self-image and who anticipate hostility from members of the victimized group. Specifically, by inviting Israeli and Polish students to discuss narratives about Poles who heroically helped Jews, both groups were able to approach the past with fewer feelings of threat, leading to more positive intergroup outcomes.

In his contribution, Staub (2013) provides a more general framework for such reconciliation interventions, as well as for early prevention of genocide. His account also centers around needs and threat, specifically universal human psychological needs for security, effectiveness and control, a positive identity, positive connections to other people, autonomy, and for understanding the world and one's place in it. Under difficult life conditions when these needs are threatened, violence escalates along a continuum and various forces are needed to halt escalation, including positive community institutions, early educational practices to teach children inclusive caring and moral courage, diplomacy, and the development of constructive and inclusive visions for a superordinate group future.

The authors in this volume have all successfully found ways to apply and develop basic psychological theory while taking account of the particular history of relations between real-world (not laboratory-created) groups. We both applaud this feat and urge others to emulate the examples provided here. Sensitivity to historical context will help to ensure that psychologists who want to make a difference in the world (e.g., by promoting reconciliation in the face of severe intergroup conflict) do not apply basic theory inappropriately. While the current volume clearly illustrates the utility of basic theories developed and tested in controlled conditions with minimal groups, it also provides examples of moderator variables that reveal themselves only when researchers take history and culture into account. For example, many articles in this volume support the basic principle that groups seek positive ingroup identities. But, unlike newly created, artificial groups, the specific threats to positive identity differ for historically victimized versus perpetrator groups. Basic theory provides a general framework that can be applied to interventions, but successful interventions also require sensitivity to particularities of the past.

Careful examination of specific cases in which intergroup relations have a history of severe violence or attempted genocide can not only lead to better intervention, but also to better theories. The needs-based model of reconciliation (Schnabel & Nadler, 2008), for example, represents a general theoretical model derived from careful, historically and culturally informed, analysis of a particular intergroup conflict. Similarly, Glick (2002) developed a general model of scapegoating by analyzing the particular historical circumstances that gave rise to Nazi anti-Semitism, revealing new insights into how scapegoats are chosen.

Social psychologists who are strongly invested in understanding the aftermath or continuation of a particular group conflict may be able to acquire sufficient historical and cultural knowledge on their own to inform new approaches. Alternatively, we encourage collaboration with scholars in other subfields and fields, or with community activists or policymakers grounded in the relevant setting. There are various forms that these collaborations might take, and different yields these collaborations could bear for theory and intervention.

For example, anthropology and sociology are two disciplines that could help psychologists to understand the ways in which particular groups' identities evolved and the current construals of those identities within a culture that has experienced mass violence or genocide. These collaborators may be informative from a distance, such as by providing the literature that psychologists read as they develop their hypotheses, or they might be excellent partners for discussing ways to build historically and politically appropriate complexity into some of the basic models from which psychologists begin. Anthropologists' and sociologists' interviewing skills also represent useful methodological expertise that can be brought to collaborations with psychologists as they test and develop their theories in messy real world contexts.

The complexity uncovered during these collaborations need not translate into theoretical complexity. For example, coming to grips with the historically situated and strategically deployed narratives regarding the conflict's heroes and martyrs (e.g., Bilewicz and Jaworska, 2013) can be commuted into a distilled understanding of different groups' contrasting needs for validation and reassurance. Moreover, collaborating with local activists, historians, and policy makers to construct a timeline of reactions to political, economic, and social developments in the aftermath of a conflict should be thought of as another form of hypothesis development and testing for ideas about the contingencies of trust, threat, or trauma among victim and perpetrator groups.

Collaborations such as these will surely be a two-way street. Scholars from other fields or subfields working on this topic are likely to be interested in social psychologists' research on the social contingency of identity and negative emotions, as well as the non-pathological processes through which identity and negative emotion persist over time. Social psychologists can also offer their unique understanding of the common needs and goals that drive seemingly pathological or self-defeating cycles of violence, and of the narratives, frames, and symbols that change the meaning of communications for different groups. As with any cross-specialty collaboration, the simple act of communicating ideas to nonspecialists can push social psychologists to identify potential boundaries of their theories, spurring further theory development.

The contributions from this current volume are models for the integration of historical, anthropological, political, and other kinds of perspectives with social psychological theory. The integration is methodological as well as theoretical. The authors have constructed an ordered, strong framework on which future research programs can build, serving as a template for a deeper engagement with the aftermath of seemingly incomprehensible acts of mass violence and genocide.

References

Bilali, R. (2013). National narrative and social psychological influences in Turks' denial of the mass killings of Armenians as genocide. *Journal of Social Issues, 69*, 16–33.

Bilewicz, M., & Jaworska, M. (2013). Reconciliation through the righteous: The narratives of heroic helpers as a fulfillment of emotional needs in Polish—Jewish intergroup contact. *Journal of Social Issues, 69*, 162–179.

Brown, R., Gonzalez, R., Zagefka, H., Manzi, J., & Čehajić, S. (2008). Nuestra culpa: Collective guilt and shame as predictors of reparation for historical wrongdoing. *Journal of Personality and Social Psychology, 94*, 75–90.

Glick, P. (2002). Sacrificial lambs dressed in wolves' clothing: Envious prejudice, ideology, and the scapegoating of Jews. In L. S. Newman & R. Erber (Eds.), *Understanding genocide: The social psychology of the Holocaust* (pp. 113–142). Oxford: Oxford University Press.

Imhoff, R., & Banse, R. (2009). Ongoing victim suffering increases prejudice: The case of secondary anti-Semitism. *Psychological Science, 20*, 1443–1447.

Imhoff, R., Wohl, M. J. A., & Erb, H.-P. (2013). When the past is far from dead: How ongoing consequences of genocides committed by the ingroup impact collective guilt. *Journal of Social Issues, 69*, 74–91.

Kaplan, S. (2013). Child survivors of the 1994 Rwandan Genocide and trauma-related affect. *Journal of Social Issues, 69*, 92–110.

Klar, Y., Shori-Eyal, N., & Klar, Y. (2013). The "Never Again" state of Israel: The emergence of the Holocaust as a core feature of Israeli identity and its four incongruent voices. *Journal of Social Issues, 69*, 125–143.

Kofta, M., & Slawuta, P. (2013). Thou shall not kill . . . your brother: Victim-perpetrator cultural closeness and moral disapproval of Polish atrocities against Jews after the Holocaust. *Journal of Social Issues, 69*, 54–73.

LA Times, December 22, 2011. France takes step to criminalize denial of the Armenian genocide (Retrieved December 29, 2011), http://articles.latimes.com/2011/dec/22/world/la-fg-france-armenian-genocide-20111223

Leach, C. W., Bou Zeineddine, F., & Čehajić-Clancy, S. (2013). Moral immemorial: The rarity of self-criticism for previous generation's genocide or mass violence. *Journal of Social Issues, 69*, 34–53.

Pearlman, L. A. (2013). Restoring self in community: Collective approaches to psychological trauma after genocide. *Journal of Social Issues, 69*, 111–124.

Peetz, J., Gunn, G., & Wilson, A. E. (2010). Crimes of the past: Defensive temporal distancing in the face of past in-group wrongdoing. *Personality and Social Psychology Bulletin, 36*, 598–611.

Schnabel, N., & Nadler, A. (2008). A needs-based model of reconciliation: Satisfying the differential needs of victim and perpetrator. *Journal of Personality and Social Psychology, 94*, 116–132.

Sherif, M., Harvey, O., White, B., Hood, W., & Sherif, C. (1961). *Intergroup conflict and cooperation: The Robbers Cave experiment*. Norman, OK: The University Oklahoma Book Exchange.

Staub, E. (2013). A world without genocide: Prevention, reconciliation and the creation of peaceful societies. *Journal of Social Issues, 69,* 180–199.

Tajfel, H. (1970). Experiments in intergroup discrimination. *Scientific American, 223,* 96–102.

Tangney, J., Stuewig, J., & Mashek, D. (2007). Moral emotions and moral behavior. *Annual Review of Psychology, 58,* 345–372.

Vollhardt, J. R. (2013). "Crime against humanity" or "crime against Jews"? Acknowledgment in construals of the Holocaust and its importance for intergroup relations. *Journal of Social Issues, 69,* 144–161.

Wohl, M. J. A., Branscombe, N. R., & Klar, Y. (2006). Collective guilt: Justice-based emotional reactions when one's group has done wrong or been wronged. *European Review of Social Psychology, 17.*

PETER GLICK is Professor of Psychology and the Henry Merritt Wriston Professor in the Social Sciences at Lawrence University in Appleton, Wisconsin. His research on stereotyping and prejudice focuses on ambivalent intergroup attitudes and emotions, especially toward women. In addition to many peer-reviewed journal articles, he has co-edited *The Handbook of Prejudice, Stereotyping, and Discrimination* (Sage) and co-authored *The Social Psychology of Gender: How Power and Intimacy Shape Gender Relations* (Guilford Press).

ELIZABETH LEVY PALUCK is an Assistant Professor in the Department of Psychology and in the Woodrow Wilson School of Public and International Affairs at Princeton University. Her research is concerned with the reduction of prejudice and conflict, including ethnic and political conflict, youth conflict in schools, and gender based violence. She uses large-scale field experiments to test interventions that target individuals' perceptions of social norms about conflict and tolerance, including mass media and peer-to-peer interventions.